Designing with JavaScript

SECOND EDITION

Designing with JavaScript

Creating Dynamic Web Pages

Nick Heinle and Bill Peña

O'REILLY®

Beijing • Cambridge • Farnham • Köln • Paris • Sebastopol • Taipei • Tokyo

Designing with JavaScript, Second Edition

by Nick Heinle and Bill Peña

Published by O'Reilly & Associates, Inc., 1005 Gravenstein Highway North, Sebastopol, CA 95472.

O'Reilly & Associates books may be purchased for educational, business, or sales promotional use. Online editions are also available for most titles (*safari.oreilly.com*). For more information, contact our corporate/institutional sales department by phone at 800-998-9938 or by email at *corporate@oreilly.com*.

Print History:

September 1997:   First edition.

January 2002:   Second edition.

Editor, First Edition:	Richard Koman
Editor, Second Edition:	Paula Ferguson
Production Editor:	Leanne Clarke Soylemez
Cover Designer:	Edie Freedman
Interior Designer:	David Futato

ISBN: 1-56592-360-X

[C]

Contents

Preface

In the beginning there was HTML, and it was good. HTML allowed web authors to create structured pages, with images, text, and hyperlinks. HTML was—and is—a good tool for displaying static information in a comprehensible and often visually appealing manner. But web authors soon realized that HTML was not enough. As the Web grew in popularity, it needed interactivity and instant feedback.

In December 1995, Netscape offered a solution to some of the problems and limitations of static HTML, in the form of JavaScript. JavaScript was designed to be a simple, effective scripting language for the Web, with close ties to HTML. Unlike other programming languages at that time—such as Java, C, C++, and Perl—JavaScript was built directly into the web browser and worked alongside HTML.

Today, JavaScript stands with HTML, Cascading Style Sheets (CSS), and the Document Object Model (DOM) as one of the key standards on which the modern Web is built.

Why JavaScript is important

Throughout this book, you'll become familiar with different facets of JavaScript, and you'll see why JavaScript is important and how it can be used to create more interesting and exciting web sites. The purpose of JavaScript is to add some interactivity to HTML, allowing for user interaction and feedback, multimedia, and animation. Here are some of the reasons why JavaScript is so important to web development:

Event handlers. With event handlers, JavaScript can catch events that occur on a page, such as the clicking of a form button or the mouse moving over a link. JavaScript's event handlers can then execute code in response to these actions, allowing web pages to verify form data when a button is clicked or display animation effects when the mouse moves over a link.

The document object model. With the DOM, JavaScript has the ability to control HTML-defined objects, such as forms, frames, and layers of content. The document object model defines which objects JavaScript can control on a web page and how JavaScript can control them. As you'll discover, the DOM has progressed over several generations of JavaScript-enabled browsers (though this progression has caused some compatibility problems).

With the advent of Dynamic HTML, JavaScript has complete control over every element on the page, allowing JavaScript to be used in the creation of powerful, web-based multimedia applications.

Non-HTML objects. Non-HTML objects give JavaScript access to parts of the browser that are not related to the HTML being displayed in web pages. For example, JavaScript can determine which browser is being used, which platform the browser is running on, and even which plugins are installed in the browser. JavaScript also has access to browser cookies, giving JavaScript the ability to store information, with some limitations, over a long period of time.

As you'll learn throughout this book, you don't need a computer science degree to master JavaScript. Both designers and programmers can use JavaScript to create web sites. That's the main reason JavaScript is important!

Who should read this book

This book is for web authors and designers who want to learn how to use JavaScript to enhance their web pages. It attempts to provide useful, sought-after examples of JavaScript in action, while teaching the concepts and syntax of the language. The examples are designed to be applied immediately in web pages, so explanations focus on the key features and discuss how the scripts can be modified to suit individual needs. This book is written for designers and programmers alike, though it may appeal to designers and non-programmers more than most JavaScript books, because of its practical, real-world applications.

The book assumes a certain level of knowledge about web design and basic HTML. If you are completely new to the Web, you'll want to learn about these topics before you try to learn JavaScript. For this purpose, we recommend *Learning Web Design* by Jennifer Niederst and *HTML and XHTML: The Definitive Guide* by Chuck Musciano and Bill Kennedy, both published by O'Reilly.

What this book covers

This book contains 11 chapters, as follows:

- Chapter 1, *Diving into JavaScript*, presents two simple JavaScript examples, so that you can start enhancing your web pages right away.

NOTE

Be sure to visit the web page for this book at *http://www.oreilly.com/catalog/designjs2/*. You can download all the examples in the book from this site, so that you can start applying them in your web pages today.

- Chapter 2, *Doing Windows*, teaches you how to control, create, and communicate with windows, since everything on a web page takes place in a window.

- Chapter 3, *Controlling Frames*, shows how to build more sophisticated web interfaces by using JavaScript to control frames.

- Chapter 4, *Forms and Validation*, explains how you can use JavaScript to interact with form elements, including using it to validate form data.

- Chapter 5, *Getting in Line with Arrays*, introduces the concept of arrays, which are great for organizing information, and shows how you can use them to advantage in your web pages.

- Chapter 6, *Too Many Browsers? Not Really*, discusses how to use JavaScript to get information about the web browsers that are visiting your site, so that you can make your site look its best on different browsers.

- Chapter 7, *Dynamic Images*, covers JavaScript's ability to change the images displayed on web pages, allowing the creation of various animation effects.

- Chapter 8, *Customizing a Site with Cookies*, talks about how to use JavaScript to create cookies to keep track of visitors to your site.

- Chapter 9, *Dynamic HTML*, introduces the basics of combining JavaScript with the W3C standard DOM and CSS to create a variety of dynamic effects on your web pages.

- Chapter 10, *Interactive DHTML Techniques*, continues the discussion of Dynamic HTML, presenting some more sophisticated, interactive examples.

- Chapter 11, *Advanced Applications*, explores the concepts of object-oriented scripting, which can help make your scripts easier to understand and more efficient.

In addition, the book has four appendixes containing useful reference material for working with JavaScript.

Conventions used in this book

The following typographic conventions are used in this book:

Italic
> Used to indicate URLs, email addresses, filenames, and directory names, as well as for emphasis

Colored roman text
> Used for special terms that are being defined and for cross-references

Constant width
> Used to indicate code examples

Colored constant width
> Used to indicate HTML tags and attributes and JavaScript elements, as well as for emphasis in code examples

Constant width italic
> Used to indicate placeholders for values in HTML attributes and JavaScript expressions

Comments and questions

Please address comments and questions about this book to the publisher:

O'Reilly & Associates, Inc.
1005 Gravenstein Highway North
Sebastopol, CA 95472
(800) 998-9938 (in the United States or Canada)
(707) 829-0515 (international/local)
(707) 829-0104 (fax)

There is a web page for this book, which lists examples, errata, and any additional information. You can access this page at:

http://www.oreilly.com/catalog/designjs2/

To comment or ask technical questions about this book, send email to:

bookquestions@oreilly.com

For more information about books, conferences, Resource Centers, and the O'Reilly Network, see the O'Reilly web site at:

http://www.oreilly.com

Acknowledgments

Second edition

I'd like to dedicate this book to my mother, Delbys Cruz, whose inspiration and love fuels me to this day.

I'd also like to thank the following people:

- My fiancée, Mary Smith, for her love and care through the many long hours I've spent writing this book.

- My editor, Paula Ferguson, for the amazing work she's put into this book, under extreme pressure, to make it a success.

- Rick Scott, for his insightful tech review comments and his willingness to do the review on a crazy schedule.

- Robert Arellano, my former professor and lifetime friend, for convincing me I ever had any writing skill, and for helping me see the beauty of language, El Aleph, through his example.

- The late Frank Willison, Editor-in-Chief of O'Reilly, for giving me this assignment, and for every moment I was lucky enough to spend working with him. We'll miss you, Frank.

—Bill Peña
September 2001

First edition

I'd like to thank the following:

- All the JavaScripting denizens of the Web for visiting my site, reading my material, and giving me original and inspired ideas.

- Andy King and Bob Peyser of webreference.com for giving me their server space and a special place on their site for those eight months JTotW was at its best.

- Richard Koman, my editor, for sending me that fateful email and taking a chance on me.

- My family—my mother, father, brother, and dog—for encouraging my interest in programming and writing and supporting (putting up with) me throughout this whole ordeal.

—Nick Heinle
August 1997

Diving into JavaScript

If you've read other JavaScript books, you may have had to slog through pages and pages about functions, methods, operands, and so on, before ever learning how to write even the simplest script. As you get into JavaScript, you'll need to understand those concepts and more, but you can start spiffing up your web pages just by diving into JavaScript.

That's what this chapter is about. By the time you've finished, you'll know two handy scripts, one to add descriptive comments to the status bar, and the other to use the time to serve custom pages. More importantly, you'll understand why the scripts do what they do, and you'll be ready to wade a little more deeply into JavaScript.

The concepts we'll cover in this chapter include:

- Event handlers

- Variables

- Working with objects

- Writing to a document

- The if statement

IN THIS CHAPTER

Modifying the status bar

Serving custom pages based on the time of day

Using the <script> tag

Understanding the JavaScript tree

Working with the Date object

Adding descriptive links

Do you ever wish links could talk? In other words, wouldn't it be helpful to be able to tell users what to expect if they click on a link? You can do this easily with JavaScript.

Figure 1-1 shows the O'Reilly & Associates web site. Each of the book covers shown on the page takes the user to the book's catalog page, where there is more detailed information about the book. However, a book cover thumbnail doesn't tell users much about where they'll go if they click on the image. To solve this problem, we can display a short description of the link in the browser's status bar when the user moves the mouse over a cover image. If the descriptions are well written, they'll add useful context to the site. Here, putting the mouse over the *Learning Cocoa* cover displays the text "Click here to see the catalog page for this book" in the status bar. This is really quite simple to do, as shown in Example 1-1.

Example 1-1: Code for adding status bar text to a link

```
<a href="http://www.oreilly.com/catalog/learncocoa/"
  onMouseOver="window.status =
    'Click here to see the catalog page for this book'; return true;">
<img width="44" height="100" border="0" src="learning_cocoa.gif"></a>
```

Figure 1-1

Displaying additional information in the status bar

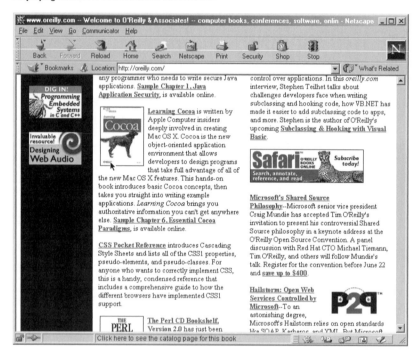

The event

The onMouseOver event handler is invoked when the user moves the mouse over a link.

The link in Example 1-1 looks like a normal link, but it's obviously a little different. Inside the <a> tag, there is a small piece of JavaScript code. The code starts (and the HTML ends) with onMouseOver; this is one of Java-Script's built-in event handlers. An event handler is code that runs when an event occurs. What's an event? It's something that happens, such as the user placing the mouse over a link or a page loading.

In this case, we're dealing with the onMouseOver event, which occurs when the mouse moves over the link. Since this event handler is located in the link that surrounds the image, the event occurs when the mouse is placed over that image, and not anywhere else on the page.

Event handlers can be used in many elements of the page, including links, form buttons, and images. Table 1-1 lists some common event handlers supported by JavaScript, the tags where they can be used, and the events they handle.

Table 1-1: Common event handlers supported by JavaScript

Event name	Where it goes	When it works
onMouseOver	Links (and images within links)	When the mouse moves over a link
onMouseOut	Links (and images within links)	When the mouse moves out of a link
onClick	Links (and images within links), button elements	When the user clicks on a link or button element
onChange	Select menus, text input elements	When an option is selected or the text is changed
onSubmit	Forms	When the form is submitted
onLoad	Body, frameset, images	When the document or image is done loading
onUnload	Body, frameset	When the document is exited

The code that follows onMouseOver runs when the event occurs (in this case, when the mouse moves over the link). Combining the event handler with some useful code gives you a link that does something when the mouse moves over it. In Example 1-1, the code displays the description of the link in the browser's status bar.

It is important to note that onMouseOver is followed by an equal sign (=). The equal sign says, "When onMouseOver occurs, run the following code." The code that follows must be surrounded by double quotes so the handler knows which code to run (all the code in quotes, and nothing else). In programming terms, the equal sign assigns a value to the event handler. Of course, this shouldn't be a foreign concept, as you use the equal sign to assign values to attributes in HTML all the time (e.g., <a href="page.html">).

Applying onMouseOver to your links

Now that you know how to use onMouseOver, it's time to learn about the code that follows it:

```
"window.status =
    'Click here to see the catalog page for this book'; return true;"
```

The code tells the browser's status bar (window.status, as JavaScript knows it) to display the text "Click here to see the catalog page for this book". That's really all there is to it, but there are several things to notice even in this simple code:

- This code is enclosed in double quotes, which are used as a way of indicating where the code starts and where it stops. This, too, should be a familiar construct, since we use double quotes in HTML to indicate the beginning and end of a value (e.g., `<a href="page.html">`).

- `window.status` is JavaScript's way of referring to the status bar. It actually refers to the status property of the window object. We'll discuss what these terms mean later in this chapter.

- The equal sign here is used to assign a value to `window.status`, giving it a string of text to display.

- The text after the equal sign is enclosed in single quotes. Again, we use the quotes to indicate the beginning and end of the value, but here we use single quotes instead of double quotes. That's because the text occurs inside the double-quoted JavaScript string. If we used double quotes for the link description, the JavaScript interpreter would think that the JavaScript code ended with the second double-quote character. Whenever you're nesting a string inside another string, you must alternate between single and double quotes.

- The semicolon after the description text indicates the end of a line of JavaScript. Get used to seeing semicolons; virtually every line of Java-Script ends in a semicolon.

So far so good, but what are the words `return true;` at the end of this code? For now, it's enough to know that it's some magic required to keep the browser from doing its normal job of displaying the URL in the status bar. If those words weren't there, the user would never see our status bar message, because it would be immediately overwritten by the URL. We'll discuss this `return` feature in more detail in a number of scripts later in the book.

To apply this technique to your site, just replace the text between the single quotes (and the URL and content, of course).

If you've tried this script, you've probably noticed that the text in the status bar doesn't go away when you move the mouse out of the link. To solve this problem, we need to add a second event handler, for `onMouseOut` events, to the link, as shown in Example 1-2.

WARNING

Pesky details

If you have an apostrophe inside single quotes, you must place a slash (\) directly before it, as in \'. Again, this is to avoid confusion, since an apostrophe is the same character as a single quote.

The onMouseOut event handler is triggered when the mouse moves out of a link.

Example 1-2: Improved code for adding status bar text to a link

```
<a href="http://www.oreilly.com/catalog/learncocoa/"
   onMouseOver="window.status =
     'Click here to see the catalog page for this book';
     return true;"
   onMouseOut="window.status = '';">
<img width="44" height="100" border="0" src="learning_cocoa.gif"></a>
```

The code for the `onMouseOut` event handler simply sets `window.status` to an empty string (`''`). The `onMouseOut` event handler is triggered when the mouse moves out of the link, so this effectively erases the text in the status bar.

Night and day

Now it's time to make your first real script; this involves learning some new concepts. If you're not familiar with programming (in C, C++, VB, Pascal, or whatever), this script is for you. While the last example did incorporate JavaScript, it was more of an enhanced <a> tag than an actual script. This example is more involved.

Assuming that people's web-surfing interests vary by time of day, your web site might be well served by promoting different content depending on whether it is day or night. For instance, a ski resort could feature skiing information such as trail conditions or snow depth during the day and lodging specials and entertainment at night. Winter Park Ski Resort's home page reflects that variety by rotating different images depending on the time of day. Figure 1-2 and Figure 1-3 show two possible pages.

Figure 1-2

A "day" page

How is this done with JavaScript? In short, a script checks the time and then delivers either the daytime or nighttime HTML. We'll cover a number of concepts in this little script:

- The Date and document objects

- Variables

- Properties and methods

- The if statement

Figure 1-3

A "night" page

Example 1-3 shows the code for a page that displays content that differs, depending on the time of day. We'll explain the code in greater detail in the sections following the example.

Example 1-3: The night and day script

```
<html>
<head>
<title>Night and Day Script</title>
</head>
<body>
<script language="JavaScript">
<!--
var now = new Date( );
var hour = now.getHours( );
if (hour >= 4 && hour <= 16) {
    document.bgColor = "#FFFFFF";
    document.fgColor = "#000000";
    document.write("<img height='150' width='250' src='photo-day.jpg'>");
    document.write("<p>Wouldn't you rather be skiing powder than sitting ");
    document.write("in front of a computer screen?</p>");
}
else {
    document.bgColor = "#000000";
    document.fgColor = "#FFFFFF";
    document.write("<img height='150' width='250' src='photo-night.jpg'>");
    document.write("<p>After a full day of skiing, throw back a few cold ");
    document.write("ones before you settle in for the evening.</p>");
}
//-->
</script>
</body>
</html>
```

The script tag

All scripts start and end with one common element: the script tag. The HTML document in Example 1-3 is basically one big script tag; there's no other content in the body of the document. As you can see, the syntax is:

```
<script language="JavaScript">
```

The browser considers everything within the script tag to be pure JavaScript and nothing else. This is where most of your scripts will reside. script tags can be placed anywhere inside an HTML document, in the head or in the body. In this case, the script tag is placed where the script does its work of printing out a page—in the body. In other documents, you'll see functions defined in a script tag in the head of the document and then called from other script tags placed elsewhere on the page.

You may be asking yourself, "Why is there a language attribute in the script tag?" That's because JavaScript is not the only web scripting language. VBScript, a scripting language based on the Visual Basic programming language, can also be used. But VBScript is supported only in Internet Explorer, which limits its practical use.

There are also different versions of JavaScript, each supported by different browsers. JavaScript 1.0 appeared in Netscape Navigator 2.0. Since then, JavaScript has evolved to Version 1.5, currently supported by Netscape 6 and Internet Explorer 5.5 and later. JavaScript has also been standardized under the name ECMAScript (ECMA-262).

So, are these different versions something you need to worry about? Usually, no. Most of the scripts in this book use features supported by all the browsers released in the last four years. When they don't, we'll let you know. If a script uses a feature in the latest version of JavaScript, you need to make only a slight modification to your script tag:

```
<script language="JavaScript 1.5">
```

The Date object and variables

The first part of the night and day script detects the time of day, using the system clock on the user's computer. It does this with the Date object, which is built right into JavaScript:

```
var now = new Date();
var hour = now.getHours();
```

The first line simply creates a new Date object and gives it the name now. In programming parlance, now is called a variable, which is just a fancy way of saying that it's a name associated with a piece of information. Thus, from this point on, the current date and time can be referred to as now. Next the script says, "Take now (the current date and time), ask it for the current hour (getHours()), and call the answer hour." As you'll understand shortly, getHours() is a method of the Date object. Now we can also refer to the current hour by name, using the variable hour.

Separate JavaScript files

Later, when you've become a JavaScript whiz, you may want to keep your longer scripts in separate files, distinct from your HTML. The script tag's src attribute lets you include an entire file of JavaScript. If you stored your script in the file *my_script.js*, you can include that code with the following script tag:

```
<script src="my_script.js"
language="JavaScript">
</script>
```

For now, all of our scripts will be short enough that keeping them in the HTML makes sense. But by the later chapters of this book, we'll be ready to start using this technique.

NOTE
What's in a name?

A variable name must start with a letter or an underscore character. Subsequent characters can be letters, underscores, or digits. Thus, these are valid variable names: myCan, Can1, and _Can1. These are not: 1Can, $Can, and !Can.

Hiding JavaScript from really old browsers

The only problem with putting a script in a web page is that really old browsers don't understand the script tag and will display the code in the web page as normal text. But there is a simple way to get around this using HTML comments:

```
<script language="JavaScript">
<!-- hide me from antiquated technology
JavaScript code
// stop hiding me -->
</script>
```

Older browsers will ignore the <script> tags and everything between the <!-- and the -->. These types of comments can only be used at the beginning and the end of a script, and it is important to put these comments on their own lines. If you put them on the same line as some code, that code will be commented out and your script won't work. For more details on how these comments work, see the "A few comments" sidebar, later in this chapter.

We've used the script hiding technique in Example 1-2, so that you can be familiar with what it looks like. But we won't be using it in any of the other examples throughout the book, since virtually all browsers understand the script tag nowadays.

NOTE

Case matters

In JavaScript, variable names (and function names) are case-sensitive. For instance, now and Now refer to two different variables. After you create a variable, be sure that you always use the same case to refer to that variable.

As you can see in the night and day script, we create a variable with var followed by the name of the variable. Once we've created a variable, we can assign a value to it with the equal sign followed by the initial value for the variable, as we've done here with now and hour.

Displaying the page

Now that we have the current hour, we need to do something with it. This script's whole purpose is to use that information to display (or "print," in programmer-speak) the appropriate content.

This brings us to one of the most useful applications of JavaScript: the ability to "print" HTML directly onto a web page. This is done with a method called document.write( ):

```
document.write("<img height='150' width='250' src='photo-day.jpg'>");
```

Everything between the double quotes in the call to document.write( ) is printed onto the page. This example prints the HTML to display the image, but you can print any text or HTML this way, including tables, forms, or whatever.

As you'll see as we progress through this book, much of what you do in JavaScript involves functions and methods. In JavaScript, a function is simply a name for a set of instructions to the web browser. Methods are similar, but there's a subtle difference; see the sidebar "Objects, properties, and methods" later in this chapter for the details. Some methods, like document.write( ), are built into JavaScript; we'll be using lots of

A few comments

Code comments allow you to place descriptions of your code within the code itself. Comments are useful both as a reminder to yourself about what the code does and as an aid to other scripters who may be looking at your code. In large scripts or scripts that are used and modified by lots of other people, comments are essential. Code comments are also useful for temporarily taking a line or two of code "out of commission" when you are testing a script. We will use comments throughout this book to describe and discuss code.

There are two types of JavaScript comments: one-liners and block comments. One-liners comment out a single line:

```
// This is a one-line comment
```

The two forward slashes (//) are what indicate the comment here. Everything after the // is ignored. One-liners can also be used on the same line as some actual code:

```
var now = new Date()      // Create a Date object
```

Block comments can span multiple lines, so they have both an opening indicator, /*, and a closing indicator, */. For example:

```
/* This comment
        spans a number
            of lines */
```

Everything between the /* and the */ is ignored.

Outside of the script tag, we can also use HTML comments:

```
<!-- This is an HTML comment -->
```

Now you can see that our technique for hiding JavaScript from really old browsers takes advantage of both HTML and JavaScript comments. The comment that starts the hiding process is a plain HTML comment. The ending comment, however, combines a JavaScript comment with an HTML comment, //-->. As the closing HTML comment (-->) is not valid JavaScript code in itself, we need to add an additional JavaScript comment (//) in front of it to prevent any potential JavaScript error from being generated.

built-in methods in this book. JavaScript also allows you to define your own functions, as we'll discuss in Chapter 2.

Putting it all together

You now have two pieces of knowledge: how to get the current time in hours and how to print out the page. But how do you combine the two so you can print appropriate content based on the hour? You use something called an if statement. if statements use a very simple concept: "If this condition is true, then do that." In JavaScript, the simplest form of an if statement looks like this:

```
if ( this is true ) {
    run this code
}
```

It looks like fractured English, and there's a reason—after all, JavaScript is a language. Every if statement consists of the word if followed by a

The document.write() method allows you to print HTML directly onto a web page.

statement in parentheses and then a block of code in braces. The parentheses contain the condition that is being checked. The braces contain the code that is run if the condition is met. Consider the following code:

```
if (hour > 22) {
    document.write("My, it's getting late!");
}
```

If the variable hour is greater than 22, meaning it is later than 10 P.M. (hours are specified with a 24-hour clock), the code prints a message about how late it is.

An if statement runs some code if a condition is true, and optionally some other code if it is not.

An if statement can also have an else portion that contains code that is run if the condition isn't met:

```
if ( this is the case ) {
    then run this code
}
else {
    otherwise run this code
}
```

This is the format we're using in the night and day script, where we're checking the hour and displaying the time-appropriate graphic and promotional text. If the hour is between 4 A.M. and 4 P.M., we'll serve the daytime photo; if it's between 4 P.M. and 4 A.M., we'll serve the nighttime photo. Here is a simplified version of the code from Example 1-3:

```
if (hour >= 4 && hour <= 16) {
    document.write("<image src='photo-day.jpg'>");
}
else {
    document.write ("<image src='photo-night.jpg'>");
}
```

The first line says, "If the value of the variable hour is greater than or equal to 4 and less than or equal to 16, run the code in braces." You probably remember the greater-than or equal (>=) and less-than or equal (<=) signs from math class; the double ampersands (&&) mean "and".

What happens if it's 7 P.M? Since we weren't testing for this time, the else statement applies. With else, we're saying, "If the condition isn't true, then do this instead." If it's 7 P.M., it's not between 4 A.M. and 4 P.M., so the script runs the code following the word else. In this case, the code prints out the nighttime image and text.

Document properties

Now that we've conquered the logic of if and else, let's look at the actual code for these pages. Notice that not only the graphics and text are different, but the background color and the text color as well.

If the hour is between 4 and 16, the script changes the background color to white and the text color to black, displays the graphic *photo-day.jpg*, and writes the text about skiing powder. If the hour is not between 4 and 16, the else statement tells the script to change the background color to black and the text color to white, display the graphic *photo-night.jpg*, and write the text about having a drink.

Changing the colors involves setting two properties of the current web page, or, as JavaScript knows it, the document object. The properties of the document object describe different characteristics of the object. Assigning a hexadecimal value to the document.bgColor property changes the background color; document.fgColor changes the text color. You can change the background color on the fly, at any time during the document's existence, but in some browsers, the property for the text color can only be changed when the document is initially displayed, so it is best not to change this after the document has been displayed. We'll learn how to change the color and appearance of text on the fly in Chapter 9.

The JavaScript tree

The document object and its bgColor property are separated by a period. Thus, document.bgColor refers to the background color property of the document. That seems simple enough, but what do you make of this?

```
document.mailform.address.value
```

It refers to the value of the address element of a form called mailform, which is in the document. Clear as mud? It makes a little more sense if you think of it as a tree.

In general, JavaScript organizes all parts of the browser window and all elements on a page (e.g., forms and images) like a tree. First, there's a main object (the trunk), then there are objects off the main object (branches), and finally there are methods and properties off those objects (leaves). As you'll see in later chapters, this is referred to technically as the document object model, but the tree metaphor is an easier way to think about it for now.

The main object, the trunk, is always the current browser window, referred to as window. There are many branches off the browser window: the page currently displayed in the window, called document, the current location of the window, called location, the history of all the visited pages of the window, called history, and the value of the status

bar, status. Inside each of these branches, you'll find more objects. For example, the document object contains all the elements on a given page: forms, images, and links are all reflected as objects. To illustrate this concept, the figure shows a small "slice" of the JavaScript tree.

As you can see, the tree begins with the browser window and branches off from there. (This is by no means the complete JavaScript tree, which would take up about 20 pages.) Whenever you want to access something in the JavaScript tree, you have to "climb" up to it. To better understand this, let's create our own example of "climbing the tree" using a simple HTML document:

```
<html>
<body>
<form name="mailform">
<input type="text" name="address">
</form>
</body>
</html>
```

The names of the form and the text input field specified in their HTML tags correspond to the names used by JavaScript. Here we have a form named mailform that contains a text input field named address. To get the text entered by the user, you need to ask for the value of address. That's the value of address in form mailform in the document in the window:

```
window.document.mailform.address.value
```

Because it is very common to access elements in the current page, JavaScript lets you take a shortcut and start climbing the tree at document. Thus, you can also access the text of the address field as:

```
document.mailform.address.value
```

What else can you do with the date?

In the night and day script, we worked with the time in hours. Of course, JavaScript lets you access all parts of the date and time, but the syntax isn't exactly plain English. Table 1-2 shows how to get the various parts of the date and the form in which they're returned.

Table 1-2: Getting the time from JavaScript

Unit of time	How to get it	How to use it
Second	second = now.getSeconds( );	The time in seconds is returned as a number 0 through 59.
Minute	minute = now.getMinutes( );	The time in minutes is returned as a number 0 through 59.
Hour	hour = now.getHours( );	The time in hours is returned as a number 0 (midnight) through 23 (11 P.M.).
Day	day = now.getDay( );	The day of the week is returned as a number 0 (Sunday) through 6 (Saturday).
Month	month = now.getMonth( );	The month of the year is returned as a number 0 (January) through 11 (December).
Year	year = now.getFullYear( );	The year as a full four digit year (e.g., 1998, 2001).

Keep in mind that when you get times and dates from JavaScript, they are returned as numbers, not words. This means that if you ask a Date object for the day of the week, using getDay( ), you get a number 0 through 6, not the name of a day, like Sunday or Monday. Though numbers are useful for database applications and the like, you may want to put them into a more digestible form. For example, you can create a script that uses getDay( ) in combination with if statements to translate the numeric values to their actual names, as shown in Example 1-4.

Example 1-4: Connecting number values to day names

```
<script language="JavaScript">
var now = new Date( );
var day = now.getDay( );
var dayname;
if (day == 0) {
    dayname = "Sunday";
}
if (day == 1) {
    dayname = "Monday";
}
if (day == 2) {
    dayname = "Tuesday";
}
if (day == 3) {
    dayname = "Wednesday";
}
if (day == 4) {
    dayname = "Thursday";
}
```

Example 1-4: Connecting number values to day names (continued)

```
if (day == 5) {
    dayname = "Friday";
}
if (day == 6) {
    dayname = "Saturday";
}
document.write("Today is " + dayname + ". <br>");
</script>
```

So how does this work? First, a new Date object named now is created, and the day of the week, which is in number form, is given to a variable named day. Then a series of if statements matches up the number of the day with the day's full name and stores the name in the variable dayname. For example, if day is 0, it must be Sunday; if day is 1, it must be Monday, etc. Finally, the day's full name, in variable dayname, is displayed on the page using document.write(). Note that this script creates the variable dayname without giving it a value at the same time; the value is assigned later when we actually figure out what day it is.

You can use this technique for various parts of the date to create a script that displays the fully formatted date on the page (e.g., Monday, July 30, 2001). The best way to do this involves arrays, something you'll learn more about later in this book. If you're curious, see "Doing the date right," in Chapter 5.

Time shifts

The Date object is not limited to the current time; you can also create a Date object for a specific date in the past or future. For example, to create a new Date object for October 31, 2001, any of the following is acceptable:

```
var then = new Date("October 31, 2001");
var then = new Date("October 31, 2001 00:00:00");
var then = new Date("Oct 31, 2001");
var then = new Date(2001, 9, 31);
```

Notice that you are passing a specific date to the new Date object. In JavaScript terminology, the information you pass to an object, whether it is a string of characters, a number, or even another object, is called an argument. When an object (or function) receives an argument, the object uses the data to perform its job. In this case, the Date object uses the argument to create a Date object for the specified date.

This feature of the Date object is commonly used to create countdowns to specific times or dates, such as anniversaries, product launches, etc. So, if you need a script to display the number of days between now and Halloween, create a Date object for the current date, a Date object for Halloween, and subtract to find the difference. The script in Example 1-5 shows you how to do this.

== versus =

Notice that Example 1-4 uses == to check the value of day and then = to assign the appropriate value to dayname:

```
if (day == 2) {
    dayname = "Tuesday";
}
```

The difference is a subtle one, but you need to understand it to avoid errors in your JavaScript code.

In the condition portion of an if statement, we often want to check whether two values are equal. The equality operator in JavaScript is ==; any time you want to test two values for equality, you must use ==. In the first line of our if statement, we are saying: "If day is equal to 2…" Anytime you see ==, you should read it as "is equal to". You can also test for inequality with != (read as "not equal to").

In the second line of the if statement, we are assigning the value "Tuesday" to the variable dayname using =. While you could read this code as "dayname is equal to Tuesday," you will be better off if you learn to read it as "dayname is assigned the value Tuesday." In JavaScript (as in most programming languages), = is called the assignment operator and is used to assign a value to a variable. Assignment is a different operation than testing for equality, which is why there are two different operators.

Using = instead of == to test for equality is a common beginner's mistake, so be sure to keep an eye out for this when you are first learning JavaScript.

Objects, properties, and methods

There are millions of "objects" in the real world: trees, telephones, people... almost everything we deal with is an object. You could even say that we live in an object-oriented world. Because of this, some programming languages, such as Java and C++, are object-oriented as well. JavaScript is also an object-oriented language, although it does things a little differently than Java or C++, so some programmers don't consider it a true object-oriented language. Regardless, you should treat JavaScript as an object-oriented language.

In JavaScript, there are a large number of objects, the majority of which will be discussed in this book. For example, the page is an object: document. The (browser) window is an object as well: window. Another one we encountered in this chapter is Date, which refers to the date and time showing on the user's computer.

In JavaScript, we can do things not only to objects but also to their properties. For instance, in our first script, the status bar is a property of the window object, referred to as window.status.

To understand how this works, it's helpful to relate it to real life. Let's be a little abstract and think of your car in terms of JavaScript. First of all, let's create a new Car object, which we'll call myCar:

```
var myCar = new Car();
```

You saw this syntax in the night and day script, when we created a new Date object. Now we can begin to manipulate the myCar object, and in the process learn a few things about object-oriented programming.

The property concept

Your car has many different properties: color, brand, horsepower, and price, to name a few. What if you want to paint your car red? In JavaScript terms, you would change the color property of your car to red, like so:

```
myCar.color = "red";
```

Your car object, myCar, is separated from its property, color, by a dot. This is the equivalent of saying, "the color of myCar." After you have referred to your car's color property in this way, you can then do something with that property.

In this example, the color property of myCar is set to "red" using =. This is like finishing the sentence, "I want the color of myCar... to be red."

To apply this to JavaScript, let's introduce another property of the window object: location. Simply put, the location property controls the location of the window (i.e., the file that is currently being displayed). The following code, for example, takes the (browser) window to a document located at *http://www.yahoo.com*:

```
window.location = "http://www.yahoo.com";
```

Just as color is a property of your car, location is a property of the browser window. To change the location of the window, use the same syntax you used before, separating the window object from its location property with a dot and setting the combination to a value.

Methods to the madness

With properties, we can change certain attributes of our objects, but to do more with JavaScript, we have to use methods. A method, like a function, is simply a name for a set of instructions to the browser. The difference is that a method is directly associated with an object and operates on that object exclusively.

Think about it again in terms of your car: myCar. In addition to having properties, your car has actions that you can do to it, such as accelerate, brake, and honk. These actions, when associated with the car object, are referred to as methods. To accelerate your car object, you might run its accelerate( ) method:

```
myCar.accelerate();
```

This looks like a property, but it has one important difference: those parentheses indicate that this is a method. A more useful accelerate( ) method would allow you to tell the car object by how much you want to accelerate. Perhaps you could pass it the speed in miles per hour:

```
myCar.accelerate(15);
```

This would accelerate the car by 15 miles per hour.

In the night and day script, we used the getHours() method of the Date object to get the current hour and the document.write( ) method to display some HTML on the page. You always pass the document.write( ) method a value, as you did with myCar.accelerate( ). The value that you pass to document.write( ), most likely some text or HTML, is displayed on the page:

```
document.write("My, it's getting late!");
```

There are a multitude of objects in JavaScript, and therefore a multitude of properties and methods as well. Learning to use JavaScript is largely a matter of learning how to manipulate the properties and methods of built-in objects to achieve the effects you want.

Example 1-5: How long until Halloween?

```
<script language="JavaScript">
var now = new Date( );
var then = new Date("October 31, 2001");
var gap = then.getTime() - now.getTime( );
gap = Math.floor(gap / (1000 * 60 * 60 * 24));
document.write ("Only " + gap + " days  \'til Halloween");
</script>
```

First, the script creates a new Date object named now for the current date and another named then for Halloween. The current date, now.getTime( ), is then subtracted from Halloween's date, then.getTime( ), and the resulting value (the remaining time between the two dates) is stored in the variable gap. So we have the difference in time between now and Halloween in the variable gap, but there's a problem: it's in milliseconds. We need to convert milliseconds to days. We do this by dividing gap by the number of milliseconds in a day (1000 milliseconds × 60 seconds × 60 minutes × 24 hours):

```
gap / (1000 * 60 * 60 * 24)
```

The difference in time, which is now in days, is then rounded down to the nearest full day with Math.floor( ). Finally, the number of days is displayed on the page with document.write( ).

TIP

View source

One of the best ways to learn JavaScript is to examine and experiment with existing code. Fortunately, it is easy to look at other people's code, using the View → Source feature that is built into every web browser.

Chapter 2

Doing Windows

Everything that happens on a web page takes place in a window. This chapter will teach you how to control, create, and communicate with windows. You can control their location and history, as well as create new windows with precise control of their size and appearance. And, most powerfully, your windows can talk to one another. Remote controls, which you'll learn in this chapter, are just the beginning.

Window basics

Let's start with some simple window controls. Back in Chapter 1, we used the status property of the window object to add descriptive content to the status bar. In this section, we'll use some other window properties and methods to change the URL the window displays and to create links for moving backward and forward in the user's browsing history.

Changing the window's location

The simplest example of manipulating a window with JavaScript is to load a new page in the current window. Example 2-1 shows the code for this.

Example 2-1: Loading a new page in the current window

```
<script language="JavaScript">
window.location = "http://www.yahoo.com/";
</script>
```

Web surfers usually think in terms of going to a different page or moving from site to site. Of course this is metaphorical. The browser isn't going anywhere; rather, a different page is being loaded into the browser. Thus, in JavaScript, you can change the current URL by changing the location property of the current window. Just as color is a property of a car, location is a property of a window.

The location of the page displayed in a web browser window is one of the window's properties.

The current window—the one where the script resides—goes by the name window. (Actually, it doesn't need to be known as window; you can also refer to it as `self`.) When you say `window.location`, you are referring to the `location` property of the current window. This property determines which file the current window displays. In Example 2-1, the window displays Yahoo!'s home page.

Loading an arbitrary page into the current window isn't something you're likely to do very often, but it can still be useful. Say the URL for a document has changed, for example, from *http://www.example.com/oldpage.html* to *http://www.example.com/newpage.html*. You can set `window.location` in the old page to point to the new page, and users won't know that the URL has changed (note that you could use a Redirect header for the same effect). The real power of `window.location` lies in being able to change the page that is displayed in another window, as we'll see later in this chapter.

Changing locations with a button

Let's make `location` a little more useful. How about creating a form button that loads a new page when the user clicks on it? We haven't yet dealt with forms and JavaScript, but, assuming you know the basics of creating forms in HTML, this should be a breeze.

First let's create a simple form that contains a single button, as shown in Example 2-2.

Example 2-2: Creating a button in an HTML form

```
<form>
<input type="button" value="Go to Page">
</form>
```

Now we have a simple form button, but how do we connect it to the script? In Chapter 1, you learned about event handlers, little statements that "catch" an event and then "handle" it. As you'll see, event handlers come into play whenever you want to make your page interactive.

An onClick event handler goes into action when the user clicks on the object to which the handler is attached.

In this scenario, we want to load a different page when the form button is clicked. Do we use `onMouseOver`, as we did in Chapter 1? Not here. The event we want to handle is the clicking of the button. JavaScript's handler for that event is `onClick`. If you add the `onClick` event handler to the form button, the specified code is executed when the user clicks on the button.

Example 2-3 shows a form that loads a file called *page.html* when the button is clicked. (When referring to a location, you can use either a relative or absolute URL; in this case, we are using a relative one.)

Example 2-3: Loading a new page when the form button is clicked

```
<form>
<input type="button" value="Go to Page"
       onClick="window.location = 'page.html';">
</form>
```

Again, having a button that loads an arbitrary new page isn't terribly useful. But it is easy to imagine combining a button with a select menu to allow the user to choose from a number of different pages.

Manipulating a window's history

You can make a window travel backward and forward in its history—the sequence of documents the user has visited during the current browser session—with minimal code by accessing the window's history object. The history object provides a go( ) method for moving the window backward and forward in time.

The number that you pass to history.go( ) determines how far and in which direction the window will travel in the browser's history. To move backward in the history, use a negative number; to move forward, use a positive number. Here are some examples of using the go( ) method:

A window's history is the sequence of documents it has visited.

```
// Move back one page
window.history.go(-1);
// Move forward one page
window.history.go(1);
// Move back three pages
window.history.go(-3);
// Move forward three pages
window.history.go(3);
```

Suppose you want to create two links that achieve the same effect as the browser's Forward and Back buttons. Example 2-4 shows the code for these two buttons.

Example 2-4: Creating back and forward buttons

```
<a href="#" onClick="window.history.go(-1); return false;">Previous</a>
<a href="#" onClick="window.history.go(1); return false;">Next</a>
```

Note that we have altered the default action of each link in Example 2-4 by specifying a hash mark (#) as the href attribute. This symbol refers to the top of the current document. But since we are overriding the default behavior of the link using the onClick event handler, we can use # as a convenient placeholder for the href attribute. Note also that we are saying return false; at the end of each onClick event handler. This is to override the default action of the link, which would be to go to the location specified by href.

Launching new windows

JavaScript is not limited to controlling and working with only one browser window. It can create and manipulate multiple windows just as easily. New windows are useful when you want to present related content: you can control their dimensions and appearance, and the user can get back to your page easily by just closing the new window. (Of course, some web sites abuse new windows, using them for advertisements, but you would never do that, right?!)

Figure 2-1 shows a typical use of a new window. On this REI catalog page, if the user clicks on the "Sizing Chart" image, sizing information is presented in a new window.

Figure 2-1

Clicking on the "Sizing Chart" link to open a new window

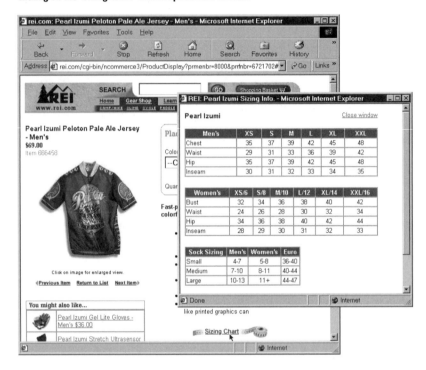

Open those windows

How do you open a new window? It's not terribly hard, but to make much use of it, there are a few things you have to learn. First, let's look at the code for the image that launches the popup window. Example 2-5 shows the `<a>` tag used for that image.

The window object's open() method lets you open a new window with specified characteristics.

Example 2-5: Opening a new window

```
<a href="#" onClick="window.open('size.html', 'sizechart',
  'width=500,height=400,scrollbars=yes,resizable=yes,status=yes');">
<img src="sizechart.gif" width="163" height="26" border="0"></a>
```

As you can see, the only thing that's unusual about this link is the presence of the `onClick` event handler, which calls the `window.open()` method. As you might guess, this method opens a new browser window. Note that we are using the same trick we used in Example 2-4, specifying a # for the `href` attribute. Since we are again using `onClick` to override the default behavior of the link, we can safely use # as a placeholder.

The open( ) method of the window object provides a standard way to open a new window. It also lets you specify a bunch of characteristics for the new window, such as height, width, and whether or not the window has a status bar or scrollbar, as shown in Example 2-5. window.open( ) takes the following arguments, and they must appear in the following order:

- A URL for the file to be displayed in the new window

- A name for the new window

- A string of window characteristics

Each of these values is enclosed in quotes, and the values are separated by commas.

The first two values are simple enough: a URL and a name for the window. The URL specifies the file to be shown in the new window; in Example 2-5, this is the file *size.html*. The window's name (in this case, we've specified sizechart) can be used to control the contents of the new window from within the original window, using the target attribute. This is more commonly done with frames, but it also works with windows.

What about the third value? This value is a single string that contains window features and their values. A comma separates each name/value pair, and the name is separated from the value by an equal sign (=), but the values themselves are not enclosed in quotes. These name/value pairs control the size of the window and various other characteristics, such as whether there is a toolbar, status bar, scrollbars, and so on. In this example, the window width is 163 pixels, the height is 26 pixels, the window is resizable (that is, the user can change the size of the window), and it has a status bar and a scrollbar.

Table 2-1 shows the key characteristics that can be specified for a new window.

Table 2-1: Characteristics controlled with window.open( )

Name	Value	What it controls
width	*number*	The width of the window in pixels
height	*number*	The height of the window in pixels
toolbar	yes/no	Whether the window has the standard browser toolbar
menubar	yes/no	Whether the window has the application menus at the top of the window
status	yes/no	Whether the window includes the small status bar, which often contains useful information, at the bottom of the window
scrollbars	yes/no	Whether the window displays scrollbars
resizable	yes/no	Whether the user can resize the window

The first two features, height and width, are self-explanatory. Just specify the desired height and width of the window in pixels. The rest of the characteristics shown in Table 2-1 can be set to either yes or no (or to 1 or 0,

> **WARNING**
>
> ## Pesky details
>
> There cannot be any spaces or carriage returns (the thing that happens when you press Enter or Return) in the window features string. In other words, the third argument to window.open( ) must be on one uninterrupted line. If it is not, your new window may not appear or you may get some very strange error messages.

Doing Windows

where 1 is equivalent to yes and 0 is equivalent to no). You can also specify a feature just by including its name without a yes value. In the words, the following are equivalent and both include scrollbars:

```
window.open("page.html", "thewindow",
    "height=200,width=200,scrollbars");
window.open("page.html", "thewindow",
    "height=200,width=200,scrollbars=yes");
```

If you don't include a particular feature name in the window-opener code, that feature is set to no automatically. For instance, the following code creates a window 200 pixels in height and width, with no other features:

```
window.open("page.html", "thewindow", "height=200,width=200");
```

No toolbar, no status bar, no scrollbars, no menu bar, just a plain window with *page.html* displayed inside it. If you take this one step further, however, and remove the height and width properties, you get the default browser window, toolbars and all.

Closing down

If you look back at Figure 2-1, you'll notice that the new window has a "Close window" link. This is a nice feature to add to any browser windows you create. Best of all, it's quite easy to do. Example 2-6 shows the code for this link.

Example 2-6: A link that closes a window

```
<a href="javascript:window.close();">Close window</a>
```

This link introduces a new technique for incorporating JavaScript into a web page. The value of the href attribute is not a standard URL. Instead, it contains JavaScript code. The value starts with javascript:, which specifies that the link contains a JavaScript pseudo-protocol URL. ("Pseudo" because it's not actually a protocol, like http: or ftp:, but it works the same way.) In essence, the javascript: in the link tells the browser that the link contains JavaScript code; the browser then runs any code that follows javascript: in the link. In this case, the JavaScript code is simply a call to the window.close() method, which, as you might expect, closes the current window.

Opening on demand

A JavaScript function is a set of instructions to the web browser.

Now that you understand how to open a window, it's time to get more control. The first step is to put the window-opening code inside a function, so that we can launch windows at will, without rewriting all the window-opening code in each event handler.

As we discussed in Chapter 1, in JavaScript, a function is just a name for a set of instructions to the web browser. Example 2-7 displays the openWindow() function, which simply calls the window.open() method to create a window that displays *page.html*. (Don't worry about the details of creating a function right now; we'll cover them in the "Writing functions" sidebar later in this chapter.)

Example 2-7: Defining a function to open a window

```
<html>
<head>
<title>Open Sesame</title>
<script language="JavaScript">
function openWindow( ) {
    window.open("page.html", "newwindow",
        "width=500,height=400,scrollbars=yes,resizable=yes,status=yes");
}
</script>
</head>
```

Earlier in the chapter, we learned how to change a window's location with a form button. Now let's use that same technique to open a new window. Just include the onClick event handler for the button and use it to run the function, as shown in Example 2-8.

Example 2-8: A form button that opens a new window when clicked

```
<body>
<form>
<input type="button" value="Open Window" onClick="openWindow( );">
</form>
</body>
</html>
```

Instead of using a button, you can set up a page so that the user clicks on a link to launch a new window, similar to what we saw in the REI example; just create a link that runs the openWindow( ) function when it is clicked. One option is to create a normal link (using # as a placeholder) and include an onClick event handler inside it, as shown in Example 2-9.

Example 2-9: Adding an onClick event handler to a link

```
<body>
<a href="#" onClick="openWindow( ); return false;">
<img height="100" width="100" src="image.gif"></a>
</body>
</html>
```

Note that the onClick event handler contains return false; at the end. As with the status bar example back in Chapter 1, we use this bit of code to cancel the default action of the link. By default, when the user clicks on a link, the browser loads the URL specified by the href attribute. In this case, we are using # for the href attribute, so the browser displays the top of the current document by default. In this example, this default behavior isn't a problem, because we don't have very much content on the page (in other words, displaying the top of the document displays the whole document). If this link were at the bottom of a long page of content, however, the default action would force the browser to scroll to the top of the page, causing the user to lose his place in the document. Including return false; at the end of the onClick event handler prevents the browser from performing the default action.

There's one final way to create a link that uses openWindow() to launch a new window, and in fact we've saved the best for last. The best way to open a new window is to use the JavaScript pseudo-protocol, as shown in Example 2-10. This technique is completely different from using an event handler, so don't get the two confused.

Example 2-10: Using openWindow() with the JavaScript pseudo-protocol

```
<body>
<a href="javascript:openWindow( );">
<img height=100 width=100 src="image.gif"></a>
</body>
</html>
```

When the user clicks on this link, the browser runs the code that follows javascript: in the link. That code simply runs the openWindow() function, which launches the window. Since the link encompasses a graphic, we have created a window-launching graphical button. And unlike using the onClick event handler, you don't have to worry about canceling the default action of the link, because the link itself runs the code.

Being even more demanding

Our openWindow() function (Example 2-7) always opens the same document. This is useful if you have multiple links (or buttons, etc.) that all need to open the same document in a new window, but what if you need links that open different pages?

One solution is to create a separate window-opening function for each document, but that would get tedious if you needed to open lots of different pages. Fortunately, there's a better technique.

Arguments are bits of information that must be given to a function when it is called. The function uses this information to perform its task.

Instead of including the name of the document in the window-opening function, we can pass the URL for the page to the function as an argument. Arguments are bits of information that are given to a function when it is called; the function uses this information to perform its task.

Example 2-11 shows a new version of the openWindow() function that takes one argument, called url. The function uses url as the first argument to the window.open() method, so the new window displays the page at the location passed into openWindow().

Example 2-11: Defining a function to open a window to a specific location

```
<html>
<head>
<title>Open That Window</title>
<script language="JavaScript">
```

Example 2-11: Defining a function to open a window to a specific location (continued)

```
function openWindow(url) {
    window.open(url, "newwindow",
        "width=500,height=400,scrollbars=yes,resizable=yes,status=yes");
}
</script>
</head>
```

Now, when you want to open a specific page using the window-opening code, you can simply pass openWindow( ) the URL of the page, as shown in Example 2-12.

Example 2-12: Specifying the page when opening a new window

```
<body>
<a href="javascript:openWindow('page.html');">
<img height="100" width="100" src="image.gif"></a>
</body>
</html>
```

This is a good example of how to use functions, a fundamental part of any programming language, to make your scripts more efficient.

Remote control

Creating windows that interact intelligently can result in a number of valuable interfaces. For example, a "remote control" window created with JavaScript can be used to manipulate content in the main browser window. Your audience can use it to jump around your site, run a search, and perform a variety of other tasks. The advantage is that your visitors see a familiar metaphor (the remote control), and you save space on all your pages (no need for navigation bars). Even if you keep your on-the-page navigation devices, the remote complements them nicely.

Figure 2-2 shows Camworld, the weblog of Cameron Barrett. Clicking on the icon next to "Sites I Visit Often" launches a new remote control window that can be used to access a number of other sites. If the user selects a site in the remote control window, the content for that site is loaded in the main browser window. This technique makes it easy for the viewer to check out a number of different sites.

Creating the remote window

Let's look at how to create a remote like the one used on Camworld. To begin, we'll create code to open the remote window. This code should be in the form of a function, as shown in Example 2-13.

What's in a name?

As you experiment with these different techniques for launching a window with openWindow( ), you might expect that you'd quickly have lots of new browser windows open on your screen, all displaying *page.html*. But, in fact, you'll have just one such window. That's because the browser lets you create only one window with a given name, in this case newwindow, as specified in the second argument to window.open( ). This name assigns the window a unique identity, and there cannot be two windows with the same name.

The first time window.open( ) is called with a particular window name, the method opens a new window. The next time it is called with that window name, however, the method reuses the existing window. If the document to be displayed in the window is the same, the browser simply refreshes the window. But if the URL is different, the new document is displayed in the existing window. This can be useful if you want to create one new window and then update the contents based on user actions. If you want to create multiple new windows, however, you need to give them different names.

Figure 2-2

A remote control for accessing other sites

Example 2-13: Creating a remote window

```
<html>
<head>
<title>Remote Control</title>
<script language="JavaScript">
function openRemote(url){
    var remote = window.open(url, "weblogWindow",
        "width=180,height=490,scrollbars=yes,resizable=yes");

    if (remote.opener == null) {
        remote.opener = window;
    }
}
</script>
</head>
```

First, we declare the function openRemote( ). The function takes one argument, the URL of the document to be opened in the remote window.

Writing functions

Functions, like the one we just used to open a window, are a core aspect of JavaScript, one we'll use throughout the rest of the book. Every function has this basic form:

```
function function-name (arguments) {
    code to be run
}
```

There are four steps to writing a function:

- Declare a function using the word function.
- Name the function. Whenever you want to use the function later on, you will refer to it by this name.
- List the arguments to the function in parentheses. An argument (or parameter) is information that is passed directly to the function when it is called. Inside the function, arguments can be used just like variables.
- Finally, within curly braces ({}), write the code that the function will run every time it is called.

Functions are usually defined in the head of an HTML document and then called from within the body, as in the window-opening examples.

Your first function

Here's a very simple function:

```
function sayHello() {
    alert("Hello");
}
```

This function, named sayHello( ), pops up a JavaScript alert box that says "Hello".

To run the function, just call it by name:

```
sayHello( );
```

Notice the use of parentheses after the function's name; they are always included with the function's name when you run it. When you pass arguments to a function, which you will learn to do in a moment, they are placed inside these parentheses.

Using arguments

Let's make this a little more versatile and add the user's name after the word "Hello". To do this, we need to add an argument to the function:

```
function sayHello(yourName) {
    alert("Hello " + yourName);
}
```

This creates a function named sayHello( ) that takes one argument, yourName. To run this function, we have to pass it a name inside the parentheses:

```
sayHello("Susan");
```

The function takes the data we pass to it—in this example, "Susan"—and stores it in the variable yourName for use inside the function. Then the function appends the value of yourName to "Hello" and pops up an alert box with the text "Hello Susan".

In the next line, we use the window.open( ) method to create a new window named weblogWindow that is 490 pixels in height and 180 in width. The only thing that's new about this line is that we have created a variable named remote and assigned the result of window.open( ) to it. The open( ) method returns an object that represents the window we have just created. In previous examples, we haven't needed to do anything with the window, so we haven't kept track of this object. For our remote control, however, we need to be able to manipulate the new window, so we assign the object to the variable remote.

Finally comes an `if` statement. This line is very important. If a browser window creates (or opens) a new window through JavaScript, the original browser window is referred to as the new window's `opener`. This relationship is reflected in the `opener` property of the new window, which should be set to the original `window` object. However, some versions of Navigator don't do this automatically, so the `if` statement makes sure that `opener` is set properly. In other words, the statement sets `remote.opener` to `window`, which is the main browser window. From now on, when the remote window communicates with the original browser window, it always refers to the original window as `opener`.

This check for the `opener` property sees if `opener` is equal to `null`. `null` is a special value in JavaScript that means "no value." In other words, if `opener` is equal to `null`, it means that `opener` does not have a value, so we need to set the value.

To launch the remote, all we need is a link somewhere in the page, as shown in Example 2-14.

Example 2-14: A link that opens the remote window

```
<body>
<a href="javascript:openRemote('weblogs.html');">
<img src="popup_icon.gif" width="9" height="9" border="0"></a>
</body>
</html>
```

Or we can simply call the `openRemote( )` function from the `onLoad` event handler of the `body` tag:

```
<body onLoad="openRemote('weblogs.html');">
```

The onLoad event handler is triggered when the HTML document has finished loading.

The `onLoad` event handler is triggered when the HTML document has finished loading; it is a good place to run JavaScript code that needs to be executed before the user starts interacting with the page.

Inside the remote

So now we have loaded a page called *weblogs.html* in the new window. This page contains the actual remote code. For the most part, this document contains regular HTML links, with a few exceptions. The most important difference is that we need to redirect links to display in the main browser window (`opener`), not the remote window. The function for doing this is simple, as shown in Example 2-15.

Example 2-15: Redirecting links to the opener window

```
<html>
<head>
<title>Weblogs</title>
<script language="JavaScript">
```

Example 2-15: Redirecting links to the opener window (continued)

```
function go(url) {
    opener.location = url;
}
</script>
</head>
```

The go( ) function takes the URL that you pass to it and tells the main browser window, opener, to go to that URL. Example 2-16 shows how the links in *weblogs.html* should look.

Example 2-16: Links that open in the main browser window

```
<body>
<a href="javascript:go('http://10.am/')">10.am</a><br>
<a href="javascript:go('http://a.jaundicedeye.com/weblog/')">
    A Jaundiced Eye</a><br>
</body>
</html>
```

These links use the JavaScript pseudo-protocol to run go( ) and redirect the link when it is clicked. Include a URL of your choice and the remote will work accordingly.

With the opener property, you have direct access to the original browser window. This means that you can treat the opener as you would any other window. Changing its location (URL) is just one possibility; accessing its document object is another. With this understanding, it's obvious that you can make your remote do a lot more than redirect links.

The opener property gives you direct access to the original browser window.

Remote searching

Wouldn't it be nice to offer search capabilities in a remote control, so that your users can type search terms into the remote, with the results appearing in the main browser window? With just a few modifications to our existing remote control code, it is easy to enable it to support search functionality. Note, however, that we're just going to talk about how to set this up in the remote control, not how to actually implement a search engine for your site (that's beyond the scope of this book). Figure 2-3 shows how such a remote searching feature might be implemented on the O'Reilly site.

It is easy to implement the form elements for the search functionality in the remote window. The trick is in displaying the search results in the main browser window. As before, the first step is to create a function that opens the remote. Example 2-17 shows a modified version of the openRemote( ) function that we can use for opening our remote search window.

Figure 2-3

Search result redirected to the main browser window

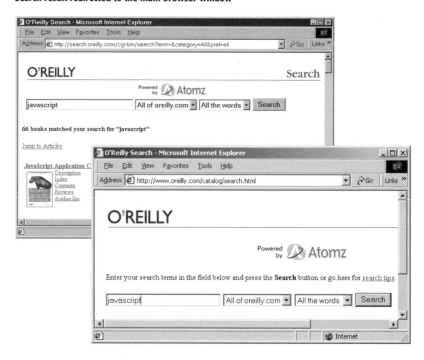

Example 2-17: Creating a remote search window

```html
<html>
<head>
<title>Remote Searching</title>
<script language="JavaScript">
function openRemote(){
    var remote = window.open("search.html", "searchWindow",
        "width=350,height=400,scrollbars=yes,resizable=yes");

    if (remote.opener == null) {
        remote.opener = window;
    }
    remote.opener.name = "openerWindow"
}
</script>
</head>
```

The main change in Example 2-17 is the addition of a line that sets the name property of the opener window. The name property corresponds to the window name that is set by the second argument to window.open( ). But we didn't create the opener window (because it is the main browser window), so we don't know its name. Fortunately, we can still set the name as shown in the example.

The name property is like the name attribute you use with frames, but we are setting it with JavaScript instead of HTML. As with frames, where the target attribute is used to redirect links and forms to a particular frame,

Wait a second . . . isn't this redundant?

You may be wondering why we didn't we use this target technique with the links in the first remote example. The reason is simple: using this method alone eliminates almost all the control that JavaScript has over the main browser window. Since JavaScript can do more than redirect links, you should first learn how to control the opener through JavaScript rather than through simple, limited HTML. The remote can morph into many different things: a dialog box, a control panel, etc., all of which need JavaScript to work. By combining these two techniques, you get the best of both worlds.

we can use `target` to redirect links and forms from the remote window to the main window, as long as we know the `name` for that window. For example, a link in the remote can be redirected to the main browser window simply by putting `target="openerWindow"` inside the link. This is just an HTML naming technique; don't confuse it with the JavaScript `opener` property. The `opener` property is totally different, as we discussed earlier, and is only accessible through JavaScript.

Now that we have our `openRemote()` function, all we need to do is create the search form in the remote, as we would in any other scenario. There is only one thing that needs to be changed: the form's `target` attribute. Since the opener is now named `openerWindow`, we can set `target` to this value, as shown in Example 2-18.

Example 2-18: Targeting form actions to the main browser window

```
<form target="openerWindow" action="search.cgi">
...
</form>
```

The form works in the remote as it does in any other page. The difference is that the results of the form (e.g., the search results) are displayed in the main browser window, not in the remote. What's great about this technique is it can be used with a wide range of forms, not just for searches.

A note on debugging

Now that you're getting a little more accustomed to JavaScript, I want to give you a word of warning. Just like in any sort of web design work, you will have moments of frustration when working with JavaScript. I'm sure you've had times when you couldn't figure out why a layout didn't work or why fonts weren't displaying properly. Similarly, there is frustration involved in any sort of programming. The topics covered in this book straddle the line between designing and programming. While you may be familiar with the pitfalls of design, you might not know how to deal with problems when your JavaScript goes awry.

Code errors are called bugs, and the process of finding and fixing them is called debugging. When you start learning a programming language, you'll find yourself doing a lot of debugging. Don't panic; it's natural. It's just like learning a spoken language: with practice, you'll become more fluent, and in time, you'll be conversing with ease. If you do get stuck, here are a few useful techniques for getting yourself back on track:

Read any error messages carefully. Error messages usually tell you exactly where the web browser is hitting an error; they give you the line number and character where the browser stopped, so you can focus your attention on that code and save time. To help with tracking down bugs, Netscape 6 provides a handy

tool called the JavaScript console, which is a separate window that lets you step through error messages produced by your page and run individual lines of code to check them for errors. To bring up the JavaScript console, go to Tasks → Tools → JavaScript Console.

Mind your p's and q's. I once spent two and half days trying to figure out why a script I was working on was freezing, only to discover that I had mistyped a "1" where there should have been an "i," thereby breaking everything after it. Unfortunately, though JavaScript is designed to be relatively easy to use, it's also very picky about syntax. Unlike HTML, which can be badly formatted yet still display on the screen (ever close a `<p>` tag?), JavaScript doesn't give you that luxury. So, before you get frustrated, make sure you've checked for any typos or syntax errors, and you'll save yourself a lot of stress down the road.

Take a walk. If you are really stuck and can't seem to pinpoint what's going wrong, get up and walk away. After you've been staring at code for a while, it can all begin to look the same, and you'll be prone to miss even easy mistakes. Taking a breather from your code will let you see it with a fresh perspective once you start again, and it may even give you a few new ideas.

Chapter 3

Controlling Frames

As I'm sure you already know, frames allow you to carve the browser window into several sections, each of which is a window in its own right. With JavaScript, you gain a great deal of control over frames, so you can manipulate them in a variety of ways. This chapter shows you how to build a more sophisticated interface to your site by using JavaScript to control frames.

The toolbar design

Frames are often used as navigational devices, with a side frame that provides a consistent navigational toolbar and a main frame that displays the content. This classic use of frames is illustrated in Figure 3-1, which shows the home page for Safari, Tech Books Online. The narrow frame on the left contains links to the topic areas on the site. Clicking on one of these links loads the corresponding document in the large frame on the right. If you clicked on the "Web Development" link, for example, a list of the books in that category is loaded in the main frame, as shown in Figure 3-2.

Controlling links in HTML

It's relatively simple to create this navigational toolbar effect in HTML. Example 3-1 shows example code for the frameset that describes the layout of this site; the frameset specifies the document that is displayed by each frame. The `frameset` tag divides this page into two columns: the first (lefthand) column is 140 pixels wide, and the second column takes up the remainder of the browser window. The `frame` tags specify the document source and the name for each frame. Here the first frame is named `toolbar` and the second is named `main`.

Figure 3-1

The Safari site's small navigational frame and big content frame

Figure 3-2

Clicking on the "Web Development" link in the navigational frame

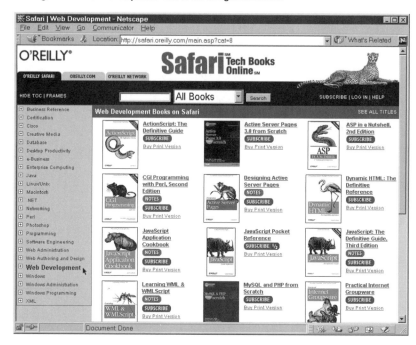

Example 3-1: The frameset for the Safari home page

```
<html>
<head>
<title>Safari | O'Reilly Books Online</title>
</head>

<frameset cols="140,*">
<frame src="frame/toc.html" name="toolbar">
<frame src="frame/main.html" name="main">
</frameset>
</html>
```

Inside the toolbar document, *toc.html*, you use the target attribute to tell the links where to load their documents. Example 3-2 shows the fragment of HTML used to load *web_development.html* in the main frame when the user clicks on the "Web Development" link in the navigation frame.

Example 3-2: Opening a document in the main frame

```
<html>
<head>
</head>
<body>
...
<a href="web_development.html" target="main">Web Development</a>
...
</body>
</html>
```

Controlling links in JavaScript

To target frames in JavaScript, you need to do things a bit differently, though the idea is the same:

```
parent.main.location = "web_development.html";
```

The key here is main.location: it tells JavaScript to access the location property of the frame named main, not that of the current window (which would be window.location). You may be puzzled by the use of parent here. Whenever you create frames, like main and toolbar, they become properties of the frameset (the document that defines the frames). Therefore, when you want to access main from toolbar, you have to climb up to the frameset that defined toolbar (which, by default, is named parent) and then access main from there—in other words, parent.main.location, as depicted in Figure 3-3.

When you create a frame, it becomes a property of the frameset that contains it.

Frames and remotes

Now that we have the syntax down, we can use JavaScript to control frames in ways that HTML cannot. Think back to the remote we created in Chapter 2. If you were to allow the user to launch a remote from toolbar, all the links in the remote would be targeted back to toolbar, not

Figure 3-3

Changing the document in main from toolbar

to the frameset. This is because the remote document contains the following function (see Example 2-15):

```
function go(url) {
    opener.location = url;
}
```

This function is used to target every link in the remote window to the opener window. Since toolbar is the window that opened the remote (frames are considered windows in their own right), all the links would be targeted there. But you want the links to be targeted to main, of course. A simple modification to the code will do the trick:

```
function go(url) {
    opener.parent.main.location = url;
}
```

The concept here is simple: since toolbar is the opener, you can access main by climbing up from toolbar (opener) to the frameset (parent) and then down to main. To change the whole frameset, thereby removing all the frames and displaying the linked document in the full browser window, the same idea holds true:

```
function go(url) {
    opener.parent.location = url;
}
```

Now you're targeting toolbar's frameset (parent) directly.

Expanding and collapsing

Another good reason to use JavaScript is that it lets you expand and collapse your frames. For example, you might want to let users get rid of the `toolbar` frame in order to save space. Just create a link in `toolbar` that changes the location of the frameset, `parent`, to the location of `main`, as shown in Figure 3-4. The result is that the document in `main` suddenly takes up the full window:

```
<a href="javascript:parent.location = parent.main.location;">Hide TOC</a>
```

This takes care of the expanding effect. The collapsing part is much easier: instruct your visitors to click the Back button on the browser (or provide them with one, as described in the sidebar "Backing up and moving forward") to return to the framed setup.

Figure 3-4

Expanding main into the full browser window

Controlling Frames

Don't get framed

Here's an important warning: don't get framed. Getting framed happens when another site that is using frames links to yours, opening your site in one of their frames. The result is that readers see your site through their (smaller) peephole. Figure 3-5 shows a mock-up of the O'Reilly web site, where one page is framed inside another (of course, O'Reilly would never *really* make such a mistake!). Getting framed is ugly, and it can confuse and annoy even the most weathered web surfers, so it is best to try to avoid this problem.

Figure 3-5

Framed!

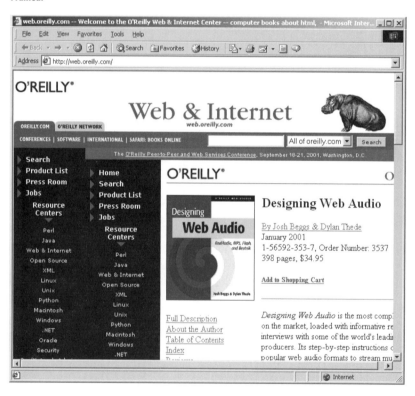

Although getting framed may not happen often, it's just one of many issues that can come up when sites rely heavily on frames. JavaScript offers a solution, however. Inside every frameset on your site, include these lines of code:

```
if (parent != window) {
    parent.location = window.location;
}
```

This code makes sure that the current frameset is the one and only frameset in the browser window, by ensuring that our document's window (or frameset) is "on top" (i.e., that there is no frame enveloping it). The `if` statement determines whether the document is "on top" by comparing the `window` object and the `parent` object. The `parent` object always equals the `window` object if there is no frameset containing the document, which is why testing for the inequality (`!=`) of `parent` and `window` does the trick. If the document is not "on top," the code makes it so by assigning the location of `parent` (the parent of the given window or frame, if it exists) to the current document's location. Example 3-3 shows how to use this code in a frameset.

Example 3-3: Code for a frameset that can't be framed

```html
<html>
<head>
<title>No you don't!</title>
<script language="JavaScript">
if (parent != window) {
    parent.location = window.location;
}
</script>
</head>

<frameset cols="30%, 70%" frameborder="no" border="0" framespacing="0">
<frame name="toolbar" src="toolbar_document.html">
<frame name="main" src="main_document.html">
</frameset>
</html>
```

One click, many links

If you're using the toolbar/main frame scenario we've been discussing, you may find that you want to change two, frames with one click. Wouldn't it be nice if clicking on one of the links in the navigation frame not only displayed the appropriate file in the `main` frame but also changed the display in the `toolbar` frame?

That's what Safari does, reloading the table of contents (the left frame) to synchronize with the page shown in the main document frame, as you can see in Figure 3-6. As you click through the site, the table of contents displays the appropriate listing in context, the same way a file manager like Windows Explorer lists folders on the left and the files within the selected folder on the right.

Not surprisingly, there is a little JavaScript code involved in changing the locations of multiple frames. Example 3-4 shows a function, called `changePages( )`, that changes two frames with one click.

Figure 3-6

Updating the navigation frame based on the contents of the main content frame

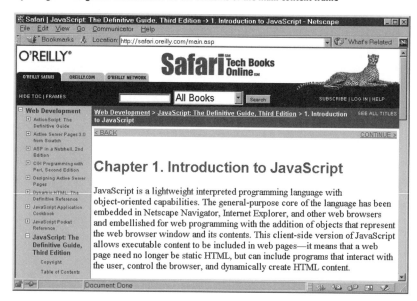

Example 3-4: Function to change the contents of two frames with one click

```
function changePages(toolbarURL, mainURL) {
    parent.toolbar.location = toolbarURL;
    parent.main.location = mainURL;
}
```

Use the JavaScript pseudo-protocol to run the function and change the contents of several frames with one click.

The changePages() function changes the locations of both the main frame and the toolbar frame when you pass it the appropriate URLs. For example, to change the location of the toolbar frame to *toolbar_document2.html* and the location of the main frame to *main_document2.html*, create a link with the JavaScript pseudo-protocol that runs the changePages() function:

```
<a href="javascript:changePages('toolbar_document2.html',
    'main_document2.html');">Make that a double</a>
```

To change additional frames when the user clicks, just add references to those frames in the function, as shown in Example 3-5.

Example 3-5: Function for changing three frames with one click

```
function changePages(toolbarURL, mainURL, anotherURL) {
    parent.toolbar.location = toolbarURL;
    parent.main.location = mainURL;
    parent.another.location = anotherURL;
}
```

Rotating pages

Frames offer a great way to rotate content. For example, Macromedia's frames-based advertisement system, shown in Figure 3-7, displays all of its ads in a small frame on the lower righthand corner of the screen.

Figure 3-7

Macromedia displays ads in the lower-right frame

The Macromedia page displays a new ad each time a new frameset is loaded. Let's take this one step further and rotate the ads every five seconds, so that if a user is viewing the page for a while, she'll see several different ads instead of just one. (Yes, this is annoying, but we must keep those advertisers happy!) Having the ads in a frame allows us to use Java-Script to keep them fresh. Example 3-6 shows the stripped-down frameset we'll work with to create our own rotating ads.

Example 3-6: Frameset for a page with rotating ads

```
<frameset onLoad="rotate();" cols="30%, 70%" frameborder="no"
          border="0" framespacing="0">
  <frameset rows="*, 200" frameborder="no" border="0" framespacing="0">
    <frame name="little" src="little.html">
    <frame name="rotateFrame" src="rotate1.html">
  </frameset>
  <frame name="big" src="big.html">
</frameset>
```

This setup consists of three frames: big, little, and rotateFrame. The rotateFrame frame is where the rotated HTML documents are displayed. When the frameset is loaded, a function called rotate() is run. We'll also need to define a few variables that control various aspects of the rotation. These variables are shown in Example 3-7.

Example 3-7: Variables for the rotation system

```
var prefix = 'rotate';
var currentPage = 0;
var totalPages = 3;
var lullTime = 5000;
```

There is a special naming scheme for the pages (ads) we'll be rotating. All the HTML documents need to have the same prefix in their filenames, as defined by the variable prefix. After the prefix, the name of the document should contain a number (starting at one and going up). In this example, we've made the prefix rotate; thus, to rotate three documents, they need to be named *rotate1.html*, *rotate2.html*, and *rotate3.html*.

The variable currentPage keeps track of which page is being displayed, and totalPages specifies how many pages are being rotated. It's set to 3 here. Finally, lullTime specifies the delay between rotations (in milliseconds). We've set a 5-second delay (5,000 milliseconds).

After we've defined all these variables, we need to create a function to rotate the pages sequentially. Example 3-8 shows this function, called rotate().

Example 3-8: The rotate() function

```
function rotate() {
    if (currentPage < totalPages) {
        currentPage++;
    }
    else {
        currentPage = 1;
    }
    parent.rotateFrame.location = prefix + currentPage + '.html';
    setTimeout('rotate()', lullTime);
}
```

This function, which is run as soon as the frames are initially displayed (note the onLoad event handler in Example 3-6), begins by determining if the current page, currentPage, is less then the total number of pages, totalPages. If it is, the function increases currentPage by 1; if not, the function sets currentPage back to 1.

The next part of the function sets the location of rotateFrame to the document that corresponds to the value of currentPage. That is, if currentPage is 2, the location of rotateFrame frame is set to *rotate2.html* ("rotate" + 2 + ".html"). Finally, the setTimeout() method runs the rotate() function again after waiting the amount of time specified in lullTime.

Example 3-9 shows the full source for the rotation system.

Timing the rotation

The setTimeout() method is JavaScript's way of timing the execution of different events. It is a built-in JavaScript method that lets you create a counter that waits a given amount of time (in milliseconds) before executing a function. In this example, we use it to control the timing for the rotation of pages in a frame. This method is a staple for any JavaScript programmer who wishes to add timed events (such as a countdown clock in a game) to her creations. Here's a quick overview of how to use it:

```
setTimeout("code to run",
    time to wait);
```

The first argument is the code you want to run after the timeout is over; this must be inside quotes and is usually a function. The second argument specifies how long setTimeout() should wait before running the code that you gave it; this is always specified in milliseconds.

Example 3-9: The full content rotation system

```html
<html>
<head><title>A Little Rotation</title>
<script language = "JavaScript">
var prefix = 'rotate';        // Prefix for all rotated pages
var currentPage = 0;
var totalPages = 3;           // Total number of rotated pages
var lullTime = 5000;          // Lull time for display of each page

function rotate() {
    if (currentPage < totalPages) {
        currentPage++;
    }
    else {
        currentPage = 1;
    }
    parent.rotateFrame.location = prefix + currentPage + '.html';
    setTimeout('rotate()', lullTime);
}
</script>
</head>
<frameset onLoad="rotate();" cols="30%, 70%" frameborder="no"
        border="0" framespacing="0">
  <frameset rows="*, 200" frameborder="no" border="0" framespacing="0">
    <frame name="little" src="little.html">
    <frame name="rotateFrame" src="rotate1.html">
  </frameset>
  <frame name="big" src="big.html">
</frameset>
</html>
```

QuickTime VR on a budget

Because a web browser can—at least in theory—view any page on the Web, web users have taken to exploring the world through their PCs. One technology that has flourished in travel, real estate, and scientific web sites is QuickTime VR (*http://www.apple.com/quicktime/qtvr/*). QuickTime VR offers 360° panoramic views, giving users the feeling of being able to see all around a space, not just what's captured within the 3 x 5-inch frame of most snapshots. Though QuickTime VR has a variety of more advanced effects, like zooming and dragging, we can create a basic panoramic photo viewer with frames and a little JavaScript.

Ski Zermatt is a skiing resource site for people travelling to Switzerland. It features stunning 360° photographs of the Swiss Alps, taken in different seasons and locations, that are sure to pique the interest of any snow-lover. Figure 3-8 shows the index page for Ski Zermatt's panoramas, a catalog of thumbnail images with links to the full-size images.

Though the photographs themselves are great, a little bit of JavaScript can take these basic panoramic images and make them interactive. In this section, we'll create an auto-scrolling viewer for panoramic images.

Figure 3-8

Ski Zermatt's panoramic photos

The frameset

The first step is to create a simple frameset with two rows, as shown in Example 3-10.

Example 3-10: Frameset for auto-scrolling viewer

```
<html>
<head>
<title>JavaScript Frame AutoScroll</title>
</head>
<frameset rows="308,*" cols="*">
  <frame name="pictureFrame" src="picture.html" noresize="noresize"
         marginwidth="0" marginheight="0">
  <frame name="controlFrame" src="control.html">
</frameset>
</html>
```

The file *picture.html* contains a panoramic mountain photo, while the file *control.html* contains the control buttons for scrolling the frame, as shown in Figure 3-9. The top frame is trivial; it just displays an image with no margins. The bottom frame is where all the power is: it includes buttons to scroll the image to the left and right, to stop scrolling, and to reset the image. Big deal, you're thinking—I can already do that with the scrollbar. What's exciting about the Left and Right buttons is that they pan through the image automatically. The user can just click once and watch the entire image scroll by slowly, giving the effect of movement. Figure 3-10 shows our mountain photo a little while after the Right button has been pressed.

Figure 3-9

The auto-scrolling viewer as it first appears

Photo courtesy www.ski-zermatt.com

Figure 3-10

The view a short while after the Right button is clicked

Photo courtesy www.ski-zermatt.com

Control buttons

The body of the control document consists of four form buttons, each of which calls some JavaScript functions that affect the upper frame. Example 3-11 shows these buttons. Note the use of the `onClick` event handler to call the `scrollToLeft()`, `scrollToRight()`, `stopScroll()`, and `resetScroll()` functions.

Example 3-11: Control buttons

```
<body>
<div align="center">
  <form>
    <input type="button" value="Left"
           onClick="stopScroll(); scrollToLeft();">
    <input type="button" value="Stop" onClick="stopScroll();">
    <input type="button" value="Reset" onClick="resetScroll();">
    <input type="button" value="Right"
           onClick="stopScroll(); scrollToRight();">
</form>
</div>
</body>
```

Scrolling

Moving the page a step at a time, everu few milliseconds, creates the illusion of motion.

To scroll the image, we want to move it from a beginning position to an end position slowly enough that the user can see everything that is going by. If we were to change the image's position in one step, the viewer would see only a sudden change from left to right, without having a chance to appreciate the content in between. Therefore, we need to move the page a step at a time, every few milliseconds, to create the illusion of motion. Example 3-12 shows some variables for our scrolling functions, and it also lists the scrollToRight( ) function.

Example 3-12: Variables and scrollToRight( ) function

```
var position = 0;
var imageWidth = 3024;
var step = 2;
var timeout;

function scrollToRight( ) {
    if (position < 0) {
        position = 0;
    }
    if (position <= (imageWidth - window.document.width)) {
        position = position + step;
        window.parent.pictureFrame.scrollTo(position, 0);
        timeout = setTimeout("scrollToRight( )", 50);
    }
}
```

The variable position is the starting horizontal position of the top frame; the scrolling functions all use this variable to keep track of the frame's current position. imageWidth specifies the width of the image being displayed in the upper frame; we need this information to know when to stop scrolling to the right. The variable step sets the pixel increment used to scroll the frame each time scrollToRight( ) or scrollToLeft( ) is called.

As you might guess, the scrollToRight( ) function scrolls the upper frame to the right. After checking the value of position to make sure we aren't at the left or right edge of the image, scrollToRight( ) increments position by `step` and then calls the `scrollTo()` method of `pictureFrame`. Note that we use `window.document.width` to get the width of the browser window; this property is only supported by Netscape Navigator, so this example doesn't work with Internet Explorer.*

`scrollTo()` is a `window` method that takes two integers specifying the (x,y) location of the top left corner of the viewable document area. When a page is first loaded, its scroll position is automatically (0,0), or the top left corner of the document. To scroll the document 2 pixels to the right, we simply add 2 to the x coordinate to get (2,0). That's how this method, used within our `scrollToRight()` and `scrollToLeft()` functions, controls what the user sees in the upper frame. Notice how we've climbed the Java-Script tree from the current frame (`window`) to the frameset (`parent`) and then back down to `pictureFrame` to call the `scrollTo()` method for the upper frame.

The scrollTo() method scrolls the top left corner of the viewable document area to the (x, y) coordinates passed to it.

`scrollToRight()` also uses the `setTimeout()` method, which we saw in our earlier content rotation example. In this case, we are using `setTimeout()` to call `scrolltoRight()` repeatedly, where each call moves the upper frame a few pixels to the right. `setTimeout()` is what lets us create the illusion of motion. The second argument to `setTimeout()` controls how often `scrollToRight()` is called. We're using a value of 50, which corresponds to 50 milliseconds; this causes the image to move 20 times per second. Note that the value returned by `setTimeout()` is assigned to the variable `timeout`; we'll use this variable elsewhere to stop the repetition.

The `scrollToLeft()` function is almost identical to `scrollToRight()`, except the motion—and therefore some of the math—is reversed, as shown in Example 3-13.

Example 3-13: The scrollToLeft() function

```
function scrollToLeft() {
    if (position > (imageWidth - window.document.width)) {
        position = imageWidth - window.document.width;
    }
    if (position >= 0) {
        position = position - step;
        window.parent.pictureFrame.scrollTo(position, 0);
        timeout = setTimeout("scrollToLeft()", 50);
    }
}
```

Our final two functions, `stopScroll()` and `resetScroll()`, provide additional control. These functions are shown in Example 3-14.

---

* This is one of those times where the incompatibilities between Navigator and IE can cause problems. In Chapter 6, we'll discuss how to detect the browser being used, so that you can provide alternate implementations on different browsers. In this case, we could have used a Dynamic HTML technique (covered in Chapter 9) to get the browser window width in IE.

Controlling Frames

Example 3-14: The stopScroll() and resetScroll() functions

```
function stopScroll( ) {
    clearTimeout(timeout);
}

function resetScroll( ) {
    stopScroll( );
    position = 0;
    window.parent.pictureFrame.scrollTo(position, 0);
}
```

The stopScroll( ) function uses clearTimeout()—setTimeout()'s complementary function—to stop the timeout that repeats the scrollToLeft( ) and scrollToRight( ) functions. Finally, the resetScroll( ) function brings the top frame back to its original position, by setting position to 0 and calling scrollTo( ).

The clearTimeout() function stops a timeout set by setTimeout().

As you can see, none of these functions are terribly complicated, but used in combination and tied to buttons, they create an interesting new way to let readers leap into your corner of the world.

Example 3-15 shows the complete script. In order to customize this script for yourself, simply change the filenames, set imageWidth to the appropriate value for your image, and, if you like, adjust the step variable to change the speed, and you're all set!

Example 3-15: The complete auto-scrolling panoramic viewer

```
<html>
<head>
<script language="JavaScript">
var position = 0;
var imageWidth = 3024;
var step = 2;
var timeout;

function scrollToRight( ) {
    if (position < 0) {
        position = 0;
    }
    if (position <= (imageWidth - window.document.width)) {
        position = position + step;
        window.parent.pictureFrame.scrollTo(position, 0);
        timeout = setTimeout("scrollToRight( )", 50);
    }
}

function scrollToLeft( ) {
    if (position > (imageWidth - window.document.width)) {
        position = imageWidth - window.document.width;
    }
    if (position >= 0) {
        position = position - step;
        window.parent.pictureFrame.scrollTo(position, 0);
        timeout = setTimeout("scrollToLeft( )", 50);
    }
}
```

Example 3-15: The complete auto-scrolling panoramic viewer (continued)

```
function stopScroll() {
    clearTimeout(timeout);
}

function resetScroll() {
    stopScroll();
    position = 0;
    window.parent.pictureFrame.scrollTo(position, 0);
}
</script>
</head>

<body>
<div align="center">
  <form>
    <input type="button" value="Left"
           onClick="stopScroll(); scrollToLeft();">
    <input type="button" value="Stop" onClick="stopScroll();">
    <input type="button" value="Reset" onClick="resetScroll();">
    <input type="button" value="Right"
           onClick="stopScroll(); scrollToRight();">
  </form>
</div>
</body>
</html>
```

Chapter 4

Forms and Validation

In this chapter, we'll deal with the forms interface—select menus, radio buttons, text input fields, and so on. We'll create a fun JavaScript twist on the classic Madlibs game, demonstrating how forms and JavaScript work together. Then, in a more practical mode, we'll learn how to use JavaScript to validate forms.

Getting to know that form

Before we get into our examples, let's take a moment to understand how JavaScript accesses forms. If you know how to create a form in HTML, you're halfway there. Let's begin by creating a basic form, shown in Figure 4-1, and showing you how to use JavaScript to access the information inside that form. Example 4-1 shows the HTML for our simple form.

Example 4-1: A simple form containing a text input field and a submit button

```
<html>
<head>
<title>A Simple Form</title>
</head>
<body>
<form name="simple">
<input type="text" name="stuff">
<input type="button" value="Okay">
</form>
</body>
</html>
```

Whenever you refer to anything in JavaScript, you refer to it by name. In most cases, the name of an HTML object (such as a form) is determined by the name attribute of its tag. For example, this form's name is simple. Inside this form, there is a text input field and a button. The text input field is named stuff, and the button doesn't have a name.

So, how do we access the text that the user types into stuff? We have to climb the JavaScript tree that we learned about in Chapter 1. As you know, everything on the page is part of an object called document. When

Figure 4-1

A simple form

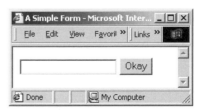

Try this

When you refer to a specific form object, such as `document.simple.stuff.value`, it takes a lot of typing to access that last little element. Fortunately, JavaScript offers a shortcut that uses a single word to save you all of this typing: `this`. In JavaScript, the word `this` plays a special role, allowing an object (or element) to refer to itself. In real life, for example, you refer to yourself as "I," not by your full name. Similarly, a form (or any object) can refer to itself using `this`. When you refer to the form in Example 4-1 using its full name, it looks like this:

```
document.simple
```

But if you are working inside the form (say if you are writing an event handler in the `form` tag), you can refer to it as:

```
this
```

In the event handler, we can get at the value of the text input field with a bit less typing using `this`:

```
alert(this.stuff.value);
```

you refer to something in the document, such as a form, it's always a property of the `document` object. Since we know the form's name, `simple`, accessing it through JavaScript is easy: `document.simple`. To get to the text input field, we have to climb a little higher. Just as the form is a property of the document, the form's elements (e.g., the text input field and the button) are properties of the form. Therefore, to refer to the value of text input field named `stuff`, we have to say, "Give me the `value` of the text input field named `stuff` inside the form named `simple` inside the document." In JavaScript, that looks like this:

```
document.simple.stuff.value
```

Note that from now on, when we refer to the current document, we'll use `document`, not `window.document`.

To display this information, treat it as you would a variable. For instance, you can have it displayed inside a dialog box:

```
alert(document.simple.stuff.value);
```

Once you understand this syntax, you can write many interesting scripts, such as the Madlibs script in the next section.

Madlibs

Madlibs: America's favorite party game...20 years ago. A bit passé today, perhaps, but it's still a great way to learn how to combine forms with JavaScript. If you're not familiar with the game, here's how it works: the player enters various verbs, nouns, adjectives, and other parts of speech into a form. The provided words are then inserted into appropriate spots in a prefabricated story, such as a poem, an advertisement, or the Gettysburg address, pretty much anything that fits into a few pages. The resulting story is often humorous and always unpredictable.

Filling out the form

We begin by creating a form to gather words from the user. The words entered into this form will eventually be plugged into a story and displayed in a separate window through JavaScript.

Our input form, named `madlibs`, specifies six parts of speech and provides text input fields for the user to enter these words, as shown in Figure 4-2. In the HTML for the form, each input field has a unique name; we'll need these to assemble the final story. Example 4-2 shows the code for this form.

Example 4-2: HTML for the Madlibs form

```
<html>
<head>
<title>Madlibs Form</title>
</head>
```

Example 4-2: HTML for the Madlibs form (continued)

```html
<body>
  <form name="madlibs">
    <table>
      <tr>
        <td>Plural Noun:</td>
        <td><input type="text" name="input1"></td>
      </tr>
      <tr>
        <td>Part of Body:</td>
        <td><input type="text" name="input2"></td>
      </tr>
      <tr>
        <td>Verb:</td>
        <td><input type="text" name="input3"></td>
      </tr>
      <tr>
        <td>Plural Noun:</td>
        <td><input type="text" name="input4"></td>
      </tr>
      <tr>
        <td>Politician:</td>
        <td><input type="text" name="input5"></td>
      </tr>
      <tr>
        <td>Adjective:</td>
        <td><input type="text" name="input6"></td>
      </tr>
    </table>
    <input type="button" value="Create Story" onClick="makeMadlibs();">
  </form>
</body>
</html>
```

At the bottom of our input form, there is a button labeled "Create Story", which contains an event handler to run a function called makeMadlibs(). After the user fills out all the text input fields, he can click on this button to create the Madlibs story. The function combines the entered values with the story and then displays the result in a separate window.

Alternatively, you can use a link to run the function:

```html
<a href="javascript:makeMadlibs();">Create Story</a>
```

Creating the story

Figure 4-3 shows the story that results when the user's responses to the form are combined with the makeMadlibs() JavaScript function shown in Example 4-3.

Example 4-3: The makeMadlibs() function

```html
<script language="JavaScript">
function makeMadlibs() {
    var story = "<html><head><title>Julius Caesar</title></head>" +
        "<body><h1>Julius Caesar 'Libs</h1><p>" +
        "Friends, Romans, " +
        document.madlibs.input1.value + ", lend me your " +
        document.madlibs.input2.value + ";<br>I come to " +
```

Figure 4-2

The Madlibs form asking users to provide various words

Example 4-3: The makeMadlibs( ) function (continued)

```
            document.madlibs.input3.value + " Caesar, not to praise
                him.<br>" +
            "The evil that men do lives after them;<br>" +
            "The good is oft interred with their " +
            document.madlibs.input4.value + ";<br>So let it be with " +
            document.madlibs.input5.value + ". " +
            "The noble Brutus<br> Hath told you Caesar was " +
            document.madlibs.input6.value + ":<br>" +
            "If it were so, it was a grievous fault,<br>" +
            "And grievously hath Caesar answer'd it.</p></body></html>";
        libsWin = window.open("", "madlibs",
            "width=400,height=250,scrollbars=yes");
        libsWin.document.write(story);
        libsWin.document.close( );
    }
</script>
```

Figure 4-3

The Madlibs story window

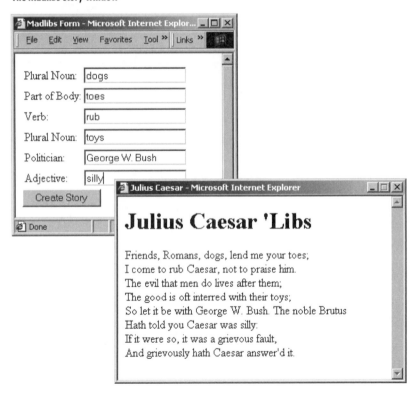

The function makeMadLibs( ) is where all the action occurs. It inserts the user's word choices into the story and displays the complete version in a new window.

First, the function creates a new variable named story. This variable is assigned a combination of prefabricated story material and text input values from the form. Combining this information in the correct order results in the final product: a Madlibs story. Let's take a look at a few of the lines added to story to understand how this works:

```
"Friends, Romans, " +
document.madlibs.input1.value + ", lend me your " +
```

These lines combine the static story text with a value entered in the form. This phrase begins, "Friends, Romans," and continues by adding the entered value from the first text input field: document.madlibs.input1.value (the value of the text input field named input1 inside the form named madlibs inside the document). Next, the function adds the phrase ", lend me your ".

Let's say, for example, that the user entered the word "dogs" into input1. The resulting string of text would say "Friends, Romans, dogs, lend me your..." This same procedure is applied to create the rest of the story.

After the story is pulled together and placed in the variable story, it needs to be displayed. The last three lines of the function accomplish this. First, the function creates a new window (400 by 250 pixels) and names it libsWin. Next, document.write() prints the information in story into the new window. Notice that the function says libsWin.document.write(story). If instead we used document.write(story), we would display the story in the current window's document, not the new window's document. By climbing the tree to the new window, libsWin, we display the information there.

The last line of the script, libsWin.document.close(), is a minor but important detail: it tells the window that you've finished writing to it and that it should display what you sent. This is often referred to as closing the stream. Although this line is not usually needed when using document.write(), it is required if you are writing to any window but the current one.

This lighthearted Madlibs example (shown in its entirety in Example 4-4) demonstrates how JavaScript can take static information and automate it, often without a great deal of work. I hope you'll be able to use this script as a starting point for more useful ideas. (Or maybe Madlibs were just what you were looking for!)

Example 4-4: The complete Madlibs script

```
<html>
<head>
<title>Madlibs Form</title>
<script language="JavaScript">
function makeMadlibs() {
    var story = "<html><head><title>Julius Caesar</title></head>" +
        "<body><h1>Julius Caesar 'Libs</h1><p>" +
        "Friends, Romans, " +
        document.madlibs.input1.value + ", lend me your " +
        document.madlibs.input2.value + ";<br>I come to " +
        document.madlibs.input3.value + " Caesar, not to praise
            him.<br>" +
        "The evil that men do lives after them;<br>" +
        "The good is oft interred with their " +
```

Example 4-4: The complete Madlibs script (continued)

```
            document.madlibs.input4.value + ";<br>So let it be with " +
            document.madlibs.input5.value + ". " +
            "The noble Brutus<br> Hath told you Caesar was " +
            document.madlibs.input6.value + ":<br>" +
            "If it were so, it was a grievous fault,<br>" +
            "And grievously hath Caesar answer'd it.</p></body></html>";
        libsWin = window.open("", "madlibs",
            "width=400,height=250,scrollbars=yes");
        libsWin.document.write(story);
        libsWin.document.close();
    }
</script>
</head>

<body>
  <form name="madlibs">
    <table>
      <tr>
        <td>Plural Noun:</td>
        <td><input type="text" name="input1"></td>
      </tr>
      <tr>
        <td>Part of Body:</td>
        <td><input type="text" name="input2"></td>
      </tr>
      <tr>
        <td>Verb:</td>
        <td><input type="text" name="input3"></td>
      </tr>
      <tr>
        <td>Plural Noun:</td>
        <td><input type="text" name="input4"></td>
      </tr>
      <tr>
        <td>Politician:</td>
        <td><input type="text" name="input5"></td>
      </tr>
      <tr>
        <td>Adjective:</td>
        <td><input type="text" name="input6"></td>
      </tr>
    </table>
    <input type="button" value="Create Story" onClick="makeMadlibs();">
  </form>
</body>
</html>
```

Stop that form!

When you ask users to provide information in a form, you never know what you're going to get. The general tactic for dealing with this problem is to validate the data before you do anything with it. In the early days of the Web, before JavaScript, the only way to validate form data was to send it to the web server, have a separate program (a CGI script, typically) check it for accuracy, and send back a response indicating any problems. With JavaScript, some of the work of form validation can be done in the web browser, before the data is sent to the server. (Not all

More about this

In the Madlibs script, we accessed the value of each text input field with its full name (e.g., `document.madlibs.input1.value`). You may be wondering why we didn't use `this` to shorten the name. The problem is that you must be inside an object to use `this` to refer to it. In the `makeMadlibs()` function, we aren't inside any object, so `this` doesn't have any meaning.

However, with a little bit of thought, we can use shorter names to access the input values. The `makeMadlibs()` function is called from the `onClick` event handler of our form button. In that event handler, we can use `this` to refer to the button, and, more importantly, we can use `this.form` to refer to the form that contains the button. This is because every form element has a `form` property that refers to the form that contains the element. Thus, from within the `<input>` tag that creates the button, `this.form` is equivalent to `document.madlibs`.

To take advantage of this, we need to rewrite `makeMadlibs()` to take a single argument: the containing form. Here's a fragment of the revised function:

```
function makeMadlibs(form) {
    var story = "<html><head><title>Julius Caesar</title></head>" +
        "<body><h1>Julius Caesar 'Libs</h1><p>" +
        "Friends, Romans, " +
        form.input1.value + ", lend me your " +
        ...
}
```

We've passed the containing form to `makeMadlibs()`, where it is stored in the variable `form`. Now we can access the first input value with just `form.input1.value`, which is equivalent to `document.madlibs.input1.value`.

Of course, to make this work, we also need to modify the way we call `makeMadlibs()`. Here's the revised button for our Madlibs form:

```
<input type="button" value="Create Story"
       onClick="makeMadlibs(this.form);">
```

Besides reducing the amount of typing you need to do, this technique has the added advantage that it works regardless of the actual name of the form. In other words, for the code in Example 4-4 to work, the form has to be called `madlibs` because that's the form name that `makeMadlibs()` expects. With these revisions, however, we never refer specifically to the name of the form, so even if we change it, the example still works.

The main reason you need to understand this technique is that almost all scripts on the Web use this method with their forms. If you plan to learn to script by studying examples, as most people do, it helps to understand how `this` works.

validation can be done in the browser: sometimes you need to validate against data that is available only to the server, such as customer IDs in a server-side database.)

There are some significant advantages to using JavaScript to validate your forms. First, it improves the user's experience with your web site, because you can catch many problems right away, without forcing the user to wait for the data to go to the server to be validated. It also saves your server from having to do quite so much work.

Using JavaScript to validate your forms will make users happy, because they won't have to wait for the server to validate the data.

Forms and Validation

Figure 4-4

The "Send Us a Message" form

The form validation process involves catching the form data before it's sent to the server, checking what has been entered, and then deciding whether to continue sending the data. With JavaScript, this can all be done with just a few basic functions.

Catching the form

To catch a form before it is submitted, you need to incorporate an onSubmit event handler. This special event handler is designed specifically to catch a form for validation. Figure 4-4 shows a simple form that asks users to send in a comment, and Example 4-5 shows the code for this form.

Example 4-5: The HTML for the message form

```
<html>
<head>
<title>Feedback</title>
</head>
<body>
<h1>Send Us A Message</h1>
<form name="feedbackForm" onSubmit="return isReady(this);" method="post"
      action="/cgi-bin/messageform.cgi">
<p><textarea name="message" rows="6" cols="20" wrap="wrap"></textarea></p>
<p><input type="submit" value="Submit">
<input type="reset" value="Reset"></p>
</form>
</body>
</html>
```

The onSubmit event handler is triggered when the user submits a form by clicking the Submit button or pressing the Enter key.

Notice the placement of the onSubmit event handler—right in the form tag. This is the only place you can use onSubmit. When the user submits this form, either by clicking the Submit button or by pressing the Enter key, the code inside the onSubmit handler is run. In this case, the form passes itself to the isReady() function using this. In other words, since we are inside the form itself, we can use this to refer to the form.

Here's the important part: if the code that onSubmit runs returns a true value, the form gets submitted, but if the code returns a false value, the form submission is stopped. Notice that the call to isReady() is preceded by the word return; this is required syntax with the onSubmit handler. To better understand what this means, let's take a look at the function that validates the form.

Validation is the name of the game

In our example form, the isReady() function, shown in Example 4-6, is run whenever a user attempts to submit the form. The function takes a form as its single argument. In the form in Example 4-5, this was passed to the function, indicating the current form.

Example 4-6: The isReady( ) function

```
function isReady(form) {
    if (form.message.value != "") {
        return true;
    }
    else {
        alert("Please include a message.");
        form.message.focus();
        return false;
    }
}
```

The function first checks the value of the text area named message using an if statement. The if condition says, "If the value of the form element named message is not empty, allow the submission to continue." (Empty is denoted by empty quotes.) This is where true and false come into play. If message is not blank, the function returns true, which tells the form that it can continue its submission. If message is blank (that is, if the user attempted to submit the form with no message), the else condition applies and the next three lines of code are run.

If the user tried to submit a blank message, our code uses the alert( ) function to pop up an alert box, shown in Figure 4-5, that asks the user to include a message. After the user clicks OK in the alert box, the script shifts focus to the text area (message) in the main browser window, which causes the browser to bring up the part of the page with the text area and place the cursor there so the user can type. The focus( ) method is built into most form elements and makes it much easier for visitors to fix any errors made when filling out the form. Finally, the function returns false to cancel the form submission.

Example 4-7 shows the entire script. Of course, this is very rudimentary form validation. Determining whether a form element is blank is just the beginning, as you'll see in the rest of this chapter.

The focus() method, built into most form elements, shifts browser focus to the element on which it is called.

Example 4-7: The entire Send Us a Message script

```
<html>
<head>
<title>Feedback</title>
<script>
function isReady(form) {
    if (form.message.value != "") {
        return true;
    }
    else {
        alert("Please include a message.");
        form.message.focus();
        return false;
    }
}
</script>
</head>

<body>
<h1>Send Us A Message</h1>
```

Figure 4-5

The alert box that pops up if the user fails to include a message

Forms and Validation

Example 4-7: The entire Send Us a Message script (continued)

```
<form name="feedbackForm" onSubmit="return isReady(this);" method="post"
    action="/cgi-bin/messageform.cgi">
<p><textarea name="message" rows="6" cols="20" wrap="wrap"></textarea></p>
<p><input type="submit" value="Submit">
<input type="reset" value="Reset"></p>
</form>
</body>
</html>
```

Is that really your email?

One of the most commonly used forms on the Web is the email form. An email form typically asks the user to enter a name, an email address, and a message. Often, users submit these forms without an email address or with an improper address. If this becomes a recurring problem, it can become an annoyance, and that's when it's time to call on JavaScript.

The generic email form

Figure 4-6 shows a run-of-the-mill email form. The user enters a name, email address, and comments, and clicks the Send button. As you can see from the code in Example 4-8, this form uses a CGI script to process the form submission. But before the form gets submitted to the CGI script, we'll use JavaScript to validate what the user has entered.

Figure 4-6

A simple email form for collecting user comments

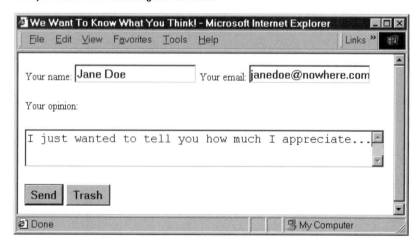

Example 4-8: The HTML for the simple email form

```
<html>
<head>
<title>We Want To Know What You Think!</title>
</head>
<body>
```

Example 4-8: The HTML for the simple email form (continued)

```
<form name="mailForm" action="/cgi-bin/mailform.cgi" method="post"
      onSubmit = "return isReady(this);">
<p>Your name: <input name="fullname" type="text">
Your email: <input name="address" type="text"></p>
<p>Your opinion:</p>
<p><textarea name="opinion" rows="6" cols="50" wrap="wrap"></textarea></p>
<p><input type="submit" value="Send">
<input type="reset" value="Trash"></p>
</form>
</body>
</html>
```

As in our earlier example, the onSubmit event handler runs isReady() when the form is submitted, but this time isReady() does a lot more than just validate a single form element. It sends the individual form elements to functions that determine whether the elements have been filled out correctly. We'll be focusing on three different form elements: address, which contains the user's email address; fullname, which contains the visitor's name; and opinion, which contains the content of the message.

Validation

The isReady() function, shown in Example 4-9, depends on two other functions to validate specific form elements: isEmail() detects a valid email address, and isFilled() makes sure a form element has not been left blank. Assuming that the other functions have been defined, you can write a master function, like isReady(), to run them.

Example 4-9: The isReady() master function

```
function isReady(form) {
    if (isEmail(form.address) == false) {        // A real email address?
        alert("Please enter a valid email address.");
        form.address.focus();
        return false;
    }

    if (isFilled(form.fullname) == false) {      // A full name?
        alert("Please enter your name.");
        form.fullname.focus();
        return false;
    }

    if (isFilled(form.opinion) == false) {       // A message/opinion?
        alert("Please enter your opinion.");
        form.opinion.focus();
        return false;
    }

    return true;
}
```

As in our earlier validation function (Example 4-6), the isReady() function in Example 4-9 starts by declaring the function with an argument called form. The rest of the function is divided into three if statements, each of which runs another function.

Let's talk Booleans

In programming, the words true and false are called Booleans. One useful aspect of Booleans is that they can be shortened when used to determine if something is true or false in an if statement. For instance, isEmail() returns a Boolean after determining whether or not address is a valid email address. Here is the if statement used to handle this:

```
    if (isEmail(form.address)
    == false)
```

This if statement is actually the same as this shorter version:

```
    if (!isEmail(form.address))
```

The exclamation point (!) in front of the function is just a short way of saying, "If this is false . . ."

A similar shorthand can be used when testing whether something is true. Here's the long version:

```
    if (isEmail(form.address)
    == true)
```

And here's the shorthand:

```
    if (isEmail(form.address))
```

Including nothing other than a value as the if condition tells the if statement to test if the value is true.

It's not that you can't live without knowing this shorthand, but you'll see it used a lot in scripts that are out on the Web, so it's good to know what it means.

The first if statement runs a function called isEmail( ), which determines whether a form element contains a proper email address. For isEmail( ) to do anything, it needs to look over a form element. In this script, we've passed the form's address element to isEmail( ). This is the element in which the user enters an email address.

isEmail( ) tries to determine whether address contains a valid email address, where a valid email address has both an @ symbol and at least one period. If address is valid, isEmail( ) returns true and the validation continues. If the user has not entered a valid email address in this field, however, the next three lines of code in the if statement are run. This code pops up an alert box telling the user to enter a valid email address, brings the user to the address element using focus( ), and then stops the submission by returning false.

Similarly, the two other if statements run a function called isFilled( ), which checks to see whether the fullname and opinion elements have been filled out. If either check fails, an alert is raised, the form is focused, and form submission is halted. If both checks pass, however, that means that the entire validation has succeeded. In this case, the script returns true and the form submission continues.

That's not an email address!

So far so good, but how do the validation functions verify that the user has entered valid data? To answer that, let's look at isEmail( ), shown in Example 4-10.

Example 4-10: The isEmail( ) function

```
function isEmail(elm) {
    if (elm.value.indexOf("@") != "-1" &&
        elm.value.indexOf(".") != "-1") {
        return true;
    }
    else {
        return false;
    }
}
```

When you look closely at this function, you may wonder where the variable elm comes from. Remember that for isEmail( ) to do anything, you need to pass it a form element to examine. In the isReady( ) function (Example 4-9), the address element is passed to isEmail( ).

When the form element arrives at the isEmail( ) function, it is given a new, shorter name—elm (for element). Instead of saying the address element's full name—document.mailform.address—we can now refer to it simply as elm. The same goes for any form element that you pass to isEmail( ). There's a good reason for all this passing of variables and form elements: you can use isEmail( ) over and over to check different form elements in different forms.

isEmail() takes the form element you pass to it and checks the element for a valid email address by first searching for an @ sign and a period and then making sure the form element is not blank. If there is an @ sign and a period, the element contains some sort of email address, so the function returns true. If the element has no @ sign or no period, isEmail() returns false to the if statement that ran it, thereby stopping the submission.

A valid email address can be anything from *billg@microsoft.com* to *nobody@nowhere.com*. The point is, isEmail() makes sure that some sort of email address is in the form element that you pass to it. You'd be surprised how many people who would otherwise ignore the email field include their legitimate addresses when this type of validation is used. (Keep in mind, though, that a bogus "email address" like *x@y.z* would also pass this validation check, so this is a very weak test for whether an email address is valid.)

This isEmail() function uses a common JavaScript string method called indexOf() to search through the value of the form element. Here's an example of how it works. Say we have a variable called question that contains the sentence "Will you find me?"

```
var question = "Will you find me?";
```

We can now use indexOf() to search through the sentence. To look for the word "me", we run the indexOf() method with a search for "me" on the variable question:

```
var location = question.indexOf("me");
```

What does this give you? The number 14. indexOf() returns the placement of the word (by its first character) in the string of text.

But wait—you just counted the characters, and the "m" in "me" is the fifteenth character in the string! So why does indexOf() return 14? One of the peculiarities of JavaScript (and most other programming languages, in fact) is that it starts counting with zero (0). In other words, the first character, "W", is character 0 in the string. If you start counting with 0, you'll see that "m" is, in fact, the fourteenth character in the sentence.

Using indexOf(), you can find the placement of any character inside a string of text. But what if indexOf() doesn't find "me" in question? In this case, the function returns a value of –1.

The if statement in isEmail() uses this behavior to do its work. If there is an @ sign in the email address entered by the user, a search for "@" will not return a –1. In other words, if the returned value is not –1, there must be an @ sign somewhere in the email address. Similarly, the next line of the if statement uses indexOf() to search for a period.

If the value entered by the user passes both these tests, isEmail() returns true (remember that && means "and"). If not, the function returns false.

indexOf() is a string method that returns the position of the first occurrence of the string that is passed to it. (It returns –1 if the string is not found.)

Forms and Validation

Fill in the blanks

After making sure the address field contains a valid email address, isReady( ) (Example 4-9) checks the form's remaining elements, fullname and opinion. It does this using the function isFilled( ), which simply determines whether a form element is empty, as shown in Example 4-11.

Example 4-11: The isFilled( ) function

```
function isFilled(elm) {
    if (elm.value == "" || elm.value == null) {
        return false;
    }
    else {
        return true;
    }
}
```

Because isFilled( ) is just checking for any content at all, it's a simple function. When a form element, such as fullname, is passed to isFilled( ), the element is given a shorter name, elm, just as in isEmail( ). Next, isFilled( ) looks at the element and determines whether it is blank (empty quotes). If the element has nothing in it, isFilled( ) returns false; otherwise, it returns true.

The big picture

Now that you understand how individual elements are validated, we can go back and look at the big picture. Example 4-12 shows the entire script for our email form. As you can see, isEmail( ), isFilled( ), and isReady( ) are all defined in the head of the document.

Example 4-12: The complete form validation script

```
<html>
<head>
<title>We Want To Know What You Think!</title>
<script>
// Check for valid email address: look for @ and .
function isEmail(elm) {
    if (elm.value.indexOf("@") != "-1" &&
        elm.value.indexOf(".") != "-1") {
        return true;
    }
    else {
        return false;
    }
}

// Check for blank fields
function isFilled(elm) {
    if (elm.value == "" || elm.value == null) {
        return false;
    }
    else {
        return true;
    }
}
```

Example 4-12: The complete form validation script (continued)

```
// Check entire form
function isReady(form) {
    if (isEmail(form.address) == false) {        // A real email address?
        alert("Please enter a valid email address.");
        form.address.focus();
        return false;
    }

    if (isFilled(form.fullname) == false) {      // A full name?
        alert("Please enter your name.");
        form.fullname.focus();
        return false;
    }

    if (isFilled(form.opinion) == false) {       // A message/opinion?
        alert("Please enter your opinion.");
        form.opinion.focus();
        return false;
    }

    return true;
}
</script>
</head>

<body>
<form name="mailForm" action="/cgi-bin/mailform.cgi" method="post"
    onSubmit = "return isReady(this);">
<p>Your name: <input name="fullname" type="text">
Your email: <input name="address" type="text"></p>
<p>Your opinion:</p>
<p><textarea name="opinion" rows="6" cols="50" wrap="wrap"></textarea></p>
<p><input type="submit" value="Send">
<input type="reset" value="Trash"></p>
</form>
</body>
</html>
```

To recap:

1. When the user hits Send, the form is passed to isReady() for validation.

2. isReady() uses a series of if statements to validate the individual elements in the form. Each of these if statements passes a particular form element (e.g., address) to a particular validation function (e.g., isEmail()). If the form element survives inspection, validation proceeds with the next element. If it fails, however, isReady() pops up an alert box, brings the user to the problematic element, and returns false to cancel the form submission. (Figure 4-7 shows the different alert boxes that can be displayed by this script.)

3. If all of the elements pass inspection, isReady() returns true, and the form is submitted to the CGI script on the server.

When it comes time to validate your own forms, isReady() is the only thing you need to modify; the validation functions are designed to play along. You'll need to change the names of the form elements to match the

Figure 4-7

Validation errors

names used in your form. You should also change the messages passed to the various alert( ) functions, to match your application. Of course, you can add more if statements to validate additional form elements. You may also want to use some of the additional validation functions that are presented in the next section.

Validate this!

For your experimenting pleasure, here are a few other functions that you may find useful in validating your forms. All of these can be plugged right in, just like isEmail( ) and isFilled( ).

Is it an integer?

The isInt( ) function, shown in Example 4-13, can be used to check the value of a form element and determine if it is an unsigned integer. If it's not an integer, the function returns false.

Example 4-13: The isInt( ) function

```
function isInt(elm) {
    if (elm.value == "") {
        return false;
    }
    for (var i = 0; i < elm.value.length; i++) {
        if (elm.value.charAt(i) < "0" || elm.value.charAt(i) > "9") {
            return false;
        }
    }
    return true;
}
```

isInt( ) first checks to make sure that the element isn't blank (""). Then it uses a for loop to check each character of the element value to make sure that it is a digit between 0 and 9.* isInt( ) uses the charAt( ) method to check each character. If the character is between 0 and 9, the function moves on to the next character. If not, isInt( ) returns false, indicating that the value isn't an unsigned integer. Note that "-" and "+" aren't between 0 and 9, which is how we can be sure that we don't have a signed integer. And since "." isn't between 0 and 9 either, we can be sure we've got an integer, not a floating-point number.

Does it contain only alphabetic characters?

The isAlpha( ) function, shown in Example 4-14, checks the value of a form element to determine whether it contains only alphabetic characters (i.e., "a" through "z" and "A" through "Z").

---

* Don't worry about trying to understand the syntax of the for loop right now; we'll cover it in detail in Chapter 5. For now, all you need to understand is that it lets us check each character in the value entered by the user.

Example 4-14: The isAlpha( ) function

```
function isAlpha(elm) {
    if (elm.value == "") {
        return false;
    }
    for (var i = 0; i < elm.value.length; i++) {
        if ((elm.value.charAt(i) < "a" || elm.value.charAt(i) > "z") &&
            (elm.value.charAt(i) < "A" || elm.value.charAt(i) > "Z")) {
            return false;
        }
    }
    return true;
}
```

isAlpha( ) is very similar to isInt( ). First, isAlpha( ) checks to make sure the element isn't blank, and then it uses a for loop to check that each character of the element value is in the range "a" to "z" or "A" to "Z". If a character is outside of one of these ranges, it isn't an alphabetic character, and isAlpha( ) returns false.

Is it a phone number?

The isPhone( ) function, shown in Example 4-15, returns true for any complete U.S.-style phone number with a three-digit area code (i.e., ###-###-####).

Example 4-15: The isPhone( ) function

```
function isPhone(elm) {
    if (elm.value.length != 12) {
        return false;
    }
    for (var i = 0; i < elm.value.length; i++) {
        if ((i > -1 && i < 3) || (i > 3 && i < 7) || (i > 7 && i < 12)) {
            if (elm.value.charAt(i) < "0" || elm.value.charAt(i) > "9") {
                return false;
            }
        }
        else if (elm.value.charAt(i) != "-") {
            return false;
        }
    }
    return true;
}
```

isPhone( ) first verifies that the length of the element value is 12, because a valid phone number with area code and hyphens has 12 characters. Then the function uses a for loop to validate each character in the element. For certain character positions, it checks that the character is a digit between 0 and 9, while for other characters, it checks for a hyphen character. If any character is out of place, isPhone( ) returns false, but if everything checks out, it returns true.

Regular Expressions

In the validation functions in this chapter, we used various string methods, such as indexOf( ) and charAt( ), to validate aspects of the element value. There's another way to validate a string against a particular pattern, using a feature introduced in JavaScript 1.2 called regular expressions. A regular expression lets you match a word, a number, or any other string of text within another string of text. Regular expressions have a variety of uses, but in JavaScript, validating form data is easily the most common.

The syntax for regular expressions can be a bit scary, so let's look first at a simple example: implementing our isInt( ) validation function using a regular expression. Here's the new version:

```
function isInt(elm) {
    var pattern = /[^0-9]/;
    if (pattern.test(elm.value)) {
        return false;
    }
    else {
        return true;
    }
}
```

The first thing this function does is define a variable named pattern that represents the regular expression we want to match. In this case, we are looking for any character that *isn't* a digit between 0 and 9. If we find such a character, we know that the form element doesn't contain an unsigned integer. Here's the regular expression:

```
var pattern = /[^0-9]/;
```

The forward slashes mark the beginning and end of the regular expression, much like quotes mark the beginning and end of a string. The brackets say that we are specifying a range of characters, in this case 0 to 9. Finally, the caret (^) indicates that we want to negate the range, or, in other words, find any character that is not in the range 0 to 9. You can see that this is a very concise syntax for checking for an unsigned integer.

Now that we have defined our regular expression, we need to test it against the form element value. Every regular expression has a test( ) method you can use to do just that. Here's how we use test( ):

```
pattern.test(elm.value)
```

test( ) returns true if the string argument passed to it (in this case, elm.value) contains the regular expression (pattern). So, if test( ) returns true, meaning it has matched a character outside the range 0 to 9, isInt( ) needs to return false. But if test( ) returns false, we know we've got an unsigned integer, so isInt( ) returns true.

The key to regular expressions is defining the right pattern. Here's the pattern we could use for our isAlpha( ) validation function:

```
var pattern = /[^a-zA-Z]/;
```

This just checks for anything outside of the range "a" to "z" or "A" to "Z".

Regular expressions really shine when you are trying to match a very specific pattern, such as a phone number. Here's the pattern for isPhone():

```
var pattern = /[0-9]{3}-[0-9]{3}-[0-9]{4}/;
```

Note that unlike our previous patterns, where we were looking for an invalid character, this one is checking for a string that contains exactly what we want. In other words, if test( ) returns true, we want isPhone( ) to return true as well. The {3} (or {4}) says we want to match three (or four) occurrences of the digits 0 to 9, and the hyphen (-) outside of any brackets says to match an actual hyphen character.

Finally, here's the pattern for isEmail():

```
var pattern = /^[a-zA-Z0-9\- ]+\@[a-zA-Z0-9 \-\.]
    +\.([a-zA-Z]{2,3})$/;
```

Now that's scary! Although the syntax is frightening, this regular expression does a much better job of looking for an email address than the isEmail( ) function. It looks for one or more alphanumeric characters, including - and _, at the beginning of the string (for the username), followed by an @, then at least one or more alphanumeric characters again, this time including -, _, and . (for the domain and any machine names), and finally two or three alphabetic characters (for the top-level domain, like "com" or "uk").

It is obviously beyond the scope of this book to teach you the ins and outs of regular expression syntax. The point in showing you these patterns is to help you recognize a regular expression when you see one. Ideally, any regular expressions you run into will be well-documented, so you won't have to try to figure out what they match. But if you do run into trouble, see *JavaScript: The Definitive Guide*, by David Flanagan (O'Reilly), for all the details on JavaScript regular expressions.

Chapter 5

Getting in Line with Arrays

Arrays are the great organizers of information. This chapter will introduce you to arrays: what they are, how they work, and how to use them. Then you'll see examples of arrays in action. First, you'll learn to randomize your site: sounds, images, and text will never be the same. Next, you'll see how to use arrays to convert numbers from a Date object to the names of days and months. Finally, you'll combine arrays with forms to create a simple navigational device that will save space and help organize your site.

The array concept

Think of an array as a straight, single-file line of people, each holding something in his hands. Since the line is single-file, each person in it can be addressed by a number. When you ask, "Would the first person in line please show me what's in his hands?" the person at the front of the line will show you what he is holding. When you ask, "Would the 99th person in the line please show me what's in her hands?" the 99th person in line will show you what she is holding. This is very useful, because you don't have to know anyone's name, just her place in line. This is a concept practiced all over the world: ever been to a deli?

To relate this to JavaScript, we have to change the terms around a little. The line of people is an array. Each person in the line is an element of the array, and the object in each person's hands is the data stored in the element.

To create an array in JavaScript, just create a new Array object:

```
var people = new Array();
```

This creates a new array called people. Each element of the array is accessed by placing the number of the element in square brackets ([]). So the first element of the people array looks like this:

```
people[0];
```

Note that 0, not 1, indicates the first element of the array. This is a peculiarity that JavaScript shares with just about every programming language in existence. It may be logical for a computer to start counting with 0, but it can be hard for humans to get used to. In the end, you just have to train yourself to start with 0 when working with arrays (and strings, as we saw in Chapter 4). Of course, when you are new to JavaScript, this is easy to overlook and can lead to bugs in your code. If you are having problems with a script that uses arrays, be sure to check how you are counting.

To give some data to the first element of the people array, simply use the same syntax that you use with a regular variable:

```
people[0] = "my data";
```

Here, the value of the first element in the array is "my data". Simple, right? Now let's apply these array concepts to some real scripts.

Being unpredictable

Would you like to enliven your site with a random quote, image, or sound? You could display randomly selected quotes or a random sentence built out of random nouns, adjectives, and verbs. Besides being a fun way to spiff up your site, creating a randomizing script is a good way to learn about arrays.

Figure 5-1 shows a picture of a community weblog named MetaFilter (*http://www.metafilter.com*). At the top of the page, a randomly selected phrase, or tagline, is displayed under the logo (e.g., "we're all in this together"). A different message is displayed every time you visit. Meta-Filter does this with Perl and server-side programming, but we can do it just as easily with JavaScript.

The array

The first step in the process of creating randomly generated "stuff" is to create an array (or list) of words, quotes, images, or other HTML-related objects. Obviously, you need some information to randomize; this can be anything from simple words to embedded sounds, graphics, or Java applets. Example 5-1 shows the tagline array for MetaFilter. The first line creates a new array, called tagline, and the next five lines give values to each of the five elements in the array.

Example 5-1: Array for MetaFilter's randomly generated tagline

```
var tagline = new Array();

tagline[0] = "the Plastic.com it's okay to like";
tagline[1] = "weblog as conversation";
tagline[2] = "you're wrong. no, you're wrong!";
tagline[3] = "self-policing since 1999";
tagline[4] = "we're all in this together";
```

> ### NOTE
> #### 0, 1, 2, . . .
> Don't forget: the first element of an array is element 0. Miscounting your array elements can give unexpected results—and lead to hard-to-find bugs!

Figure 5-1

MetaFilter's randomly generated tagline

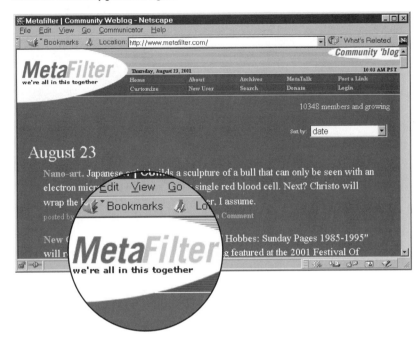

Once we have the taglines in the array, accessing them is easy. Here's how to use document.write( ) to print out the first tagline:

```
document.write(tagline[0]);
```

This outputs "the Plastic.com it's okay to like", the first element in the tagline array. Passing tagline[1] to document.write( ) prints out the tagline "weblog as conversation", passing tagline[2] prints out "you're wrong. no, you're wrong!", and so on.

Making random numbers

Now that we have our taglines in an array, we need to randomize them. For this, we will use something called a random number generator, which does exactly what its name implies: it generates random numbers. We'll use a built-in JavaScript function, Math.random( ), to generate a random value, as shown in Example 5-2.*

Example 5-2: A random number generator

```
function randomNumber(n) {
    number = Math.floor(Math.random( ) * (n + 1));
    return number;
}
```

---

* Math.random( ) is not supported in Netscape Navigator 2, but it is supported in all later versions of Navigator and in every version of Microsoft Internet Explorer.

Arrays are everywhere, except in Netscape Navigator 2

Arrays are not supported in the oldest version of JavaScript, JavaScript 1.0, which is part of Netscape Navigator 2. They are supported, however, in all later versions of Netscape Navigator and every version of Internet Explorer. If you really must provide support for Netscape Navigator 2, you'll need to use the workaround presented here.

The workaround involves user-defined objects, something we'll explore in more detail in Chapter 11. For now, just know that the following code will create and manage arrays like a true array does:

```
function makeArray(len) {
    for (var i = 0; i < len; i++) {
        this[i] = null;
    this.length = len;
}
```

Here's how we can make our array of taglines from Example 5-1, using the makeArray( ) function:

```
var tagline = new makeArray(6);
tagline[0] = "the Plastic.com it's okay to like";
tagline[1] = "weblog as conversation";
tagline[2] = "you're wrong. no, you're wrong!";
tagline[3] = "self-policing since 1999";
tagline[4] = "we're all in this together";
```

The most visible difference is that we are creating a new makeArray object instead of an Array object. There is one other difference: you are required to tell makeArray( ) the number of elements in the array. In this scenario, the array has 5 elements, so the first line is:

```
var tagline = new makeArray(5);
```

The rest of this chapter assumes that we no longer have to provide backwards compatible code for Netscape Navigator 2.

Math.random() generates a random number between 0.0 and 1.0. Math.floor() rounds a number down to the nearest integer.

Our randomNumber( ) function, which returns a random number between 0 and its argument n, makes use of two built-in JavaScript functions. The first, Math.random( ), generates a random number between 0.0 and 1.0. To turn this into a random number between 0 and n, we multiply by n+1 and then use a second built-in JavaScript function, Math.floor( ), to round down to the nearest integer.

The last line of this function is simple but important. It returns the generated random number, which means that the random number is placed where you originally ran the function, as depicted in Figure 5-2. In other words, we can run the random number generator like this to output a random number between 0 and 5:

```
document.write(randomNumber(5));
```

We can also capture the return value from randomNumber( ) in a variable:

```
var number = randomNumber(5);
```

Randomizing the array

Now we need to apply the random number generator to the array of taglines, but how? First, we need to know the number of elements in the array. In JavaScript, every array has a `length` property that indicates the number of elements it contains. Think back to the people-in-line analogy: it's like the total number of people in the line. So, with our `tagline` array, we can get the number of elements with this:

```
tagline.length
```

Using `length`, we can generate a random number to access a random element of the array:

```
randomNumber(tagline.length);
```

We know that `tagline` has 5 elements, so it follows that the previous line of code will give us a random number between 0 and 5. But that isn't quite what we want. Remember that in JavaScript, the first element of an array is element 0; with `tagline`, the last element is `tagline[4]`. Thus, what we want is a random number between 0 and 4. We can get just that with the following:

```
randomNumber(tagline.length - 1);
```

Now we just need to grab the element of the array that corresponds to our random number. We can put the random number code where the number of the array element goes, and presto, we have a random tagline:

```
tagline[randomNumber(tagline.length - 1)];
```

Finally, we can output that tagline with `document.write()`:

```
document.write(tagline[randomNumber(tagline.length - 1)]);
```

Example 5-3 gives the entire source for the randomly generated tagline script.

Example 5-3: A page with a random tagline

```
<html>
<head>
<title>Random Tagline Generator</title>
<script language="Javascript">
// Create the array
var tagline = new Array();

tagline[0] = "the Plastic.com it's okay to like";
tagline[1] = "weblog as conversation";
tagline[2] = "you're wrong. no, you're wrong!";
tagline[3] = "self-policing since 1999";
tagline[4] = "we're all in this together";

// Random number generator
function randomNumber(n) {
    number = Math.floor(Math.random() * (n + 1));
    return number;
}
</script>
</head>
```

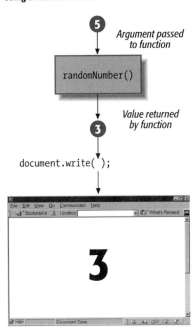

Figure 5-2

Using a random number

5 Argument passed to function

`randomNumber()`

Value returned by function **3**

`document.write( );`

Getting in Line with Arrays

Example 5-3: A page with a random tagline (continued)

```
<body bgcolor="#FFFFFF" text="#000000">
<script language="JavaScript">
// Display the random tagline
document.write(tagline[randomNumber(tagline.length - 1)]);
</script>
</body>
</html>
```

Random sounds and images

You are not limited to using just words in your randomized offerings: you can also use images, Java applets, and other HTML-related objects, or any combination of these. Simply plug your items directly into the array and then use the array elements as appropriate. If you want a random image, for instance, try this:

```
var pix = new Array();
pix[0] = "image1.gif"
pix[1] = "image2.gif"
pix[2] = "image3.gif"
pix[3] = "image4.gif
```

This creates an array of four image files. To display them randomly, you just need to modify the script in Example 5-3 to output an img tag that displays a random element of the pix array:

```
document.write("<img src='" + pix[randomNumber(pix.length -1)] + "'>");
```

Doing the date right

Back in Chapter 1, you learned about the Date object. We discussed how to access different units of time, display the current day, and find the difference (in days) between two dates. What we didn't cover, however, was how to display a fully formatted date on the page (e.g., Monday, July 30, 2001). Example 5-4 uses the "associative" powers of arrays to solve this little problem.

Example 5-4: Printing fully formatted dates

```
<html>
<head>
<title>Doing the Date Right</title>
</head>

<body>
<script language="JavaScript">

// Array of day names
var dayNames = new Array();
dayNames[0] = "Sunday";
dayNames[1] = "Monday";
dayNames[2] = "Tuesday";
dayNames[3] = "Wednesday";
dayNames[4] = "Thursday";
dayNames[5] = "Friday";
dayNames[6] = "Saturday";
```

Example 5-4: Printing fully formatted dates (continued)

```
// Array of month Names
var monthNames = new Array( );
monthNames[0] = "January";
monthNames[1] = "February";
monthNames[2] = "March";
monthNames[3] = "April";
monthNames[4] = "May";
monthNames[5] = "June";
monthNames[6] = "July";
monthNames[7] = "August";
monthNames[8] = "September";
monthNames[9] = "October";
monthNames[10] = "November";
monthNames[11] = "December";

// Elements of Date object assigned to variables
var now = new Date( );
var day = now.getDay( );
var month = now.getMonth( );
var year = now.getFullYear( );
var date = now.getDate( );

// Code to print fully formatted date (e.g., Monday, July 30, 2001)
document.write("<h1>" + dayNames[day] + ", " + monthNames[month] + " ");
document.write(date + ", " + year + "</h1>");
</script>
</body>
</html>
```

Essentially, the script associates JavaScript's numerically formatted dates with ones that you and I understand. The day of the week, for instance, is a number 0 through 6 when taken directly from the Date object with getDay( ). The script in Example 5-4 has an array named dayNames that contains the full name of each day of the week. The first element, dayNames[0], contains the word "Sunday"; the second element, dayNames[1], contains the word "Monday"; and so on through "Saturday", daynames[6].

When the script asks JavaScript for the day of the week, now.getDay( ) returns a number 0 through 6, which is stored in the variable day. So if it's Thursday, day is 4. If we plug 4 into dayNames, we access dayNames[4], which contains "Thursday", exactly what we want to display.

This process is also used for month names, which have their own array, monthNames. If it's July, now.getMonth( ) returns 6 (not 7 because January is month 0, not 1), which is stored in variable month. Plugging 6 into the monthNames array gives us "July".

The last two lines are the most important; they display the formatted date on the page by inserting the numeric date values into their corresponding arrays, as previously explained. Thus, if the value of day is 1, the value of month is 6, the value of date is 30, and the value of year is 2001, the script displays "Monday, July 30, 2001", as shown in Figure 5-3. Note that the year and the day of the month do not need special formatting.

Figure 5-3

A fully formatted date created using arrays of day and month names

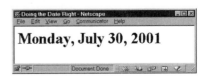

Getting in Line with Arrays

Jumpin' jive

The select menu (a pop-up menu in a form) is a great tool when you need to save space on a web site. (Be sure to label it clearly, though—you don't want to hide choices from the user.) As shown in Figure 5-4, select menus can contain lots of options, but they take up very little space when they're not being used.

Netscape's search page features a JavaScript select menu in the upper right corner that lets users see all available areas of the Netscape web site and quickly navigate to one. With JavaScript, it's all done locally, and there's no waiting for the server to process the information.

Figure 5-4

Netscape's select menu to the major areas of their site

In this section, we'll learn how to use JavaScript to add this "jumpin' jive" functionality to a page. There are three steps to this script:

- Creating arrays for the names and URLs of the pages
- Displaying the form on the page
- Creating the "jump" code

Creating the arrays

To begin, we need to create two arrays. The first array contains the names of the pages we want to appear in the select menu. The second array, used in tandem with the first, contains the URLs of those pages.

Unlike the arrays in the random tagline script, the arrays in the jump menu script are created all at once, not element by element. This is just a shortcut that makes our code more concise. In Example 5-5, examine the pages array closely. The data for this array is passed directly to the array creation function. "Select a Page" is the data in the first element of the array, pages[0]; "Autos" is the data in the second element of the array, pages[1]; and so on.

Example 5-5: The two arrays used in the jump menu script

```
// The pages array holds the descriptions of the pages
var pages = new Array(
    "Select a Page",
    "Autos",
    "Business and Careers",
    "Computing",
    "Entertainment",
    "Games");

// The urls array holds the URLs of the pages
var urls = new Array(
    "",
    "autos.html",
    "business.html",
    "computing.html",
    "entertainment.html",
    "games.html");
```

This all-at-once creation of the array and its elements is a shortcut to the technique used in Example 5-1. That technique would have worked here as well.

The pages array contains the page names, or descriptions, to be displayed in the select menu. The urls array contains the URLs that correspond to those descriptions. For example, "Autos" is the second element in the pages array; selecting "Autos" in the select menu will load the page at *autos.html* because it is the second element in the urls array. It is important to make sure that the positions of the elements in the pages array match up appropriately with the positions of the elements in the urls array. Note that the first element in the pages array, "Select a Page," does nothing, because the corresponding element in the urls array is empty (""). "Select a Page" simply serves to notify visitors, "Yes, you *can* click here."

Displaying it on the page

Now we need to display the select menu on the page. What better way to do this than with JavaScript? We can even automate the process so we don't need to rewrite the names of all those pages. Example 5-6 shows the code.

Example 5-6: Creating the select menu

```
<script language="JavaScript">
document.write('<form>');
document.write('<select name="jumpMenu" onChange="goPage(this.form);">');
for (var i = 0; i < pages.length; i++) {
    document.write('<option>' + pages[i] + '</option>');
}
document.write('</select>');
document.write('</form>');
</script>
```

The onChange event handler is invoked when a user selects an item in the select menu.

This may be confusing at first glance, so let's go through it step by step. The first line of the script begins to display the form on the page, and the second line starts to create the select menu, giving it the name jumpMenu. This line also specifies an onChange event handler for the select menu. Whenever the user selects an item in the menu, the script runs a function called goPage( ), which loads the selected page in the browser window.

Next comes a for loop to display all the options (page names) in the select menu. A for loop is a common programming construct that repeats a specified block of code over and over until a condition is met. In JavaScript, a for loop looks like this:

```
for (setup; conditional; modify something in the conditional) {
    run this code
}
```

There are four main pieces of a for loop: some setup code, a conditional, some code that modifies something in the conditional, and some code to be run. The first three are in parentheses after for and are separated by semicolons, and the fourth piece comes next, in curly brackets ({}).

The setup code is run just once; it is the first thing that the for loop does. Next, the for loop checks the conditional. If it is true, the loop runs the code in curly brackets and then goes back up to the last item in the parentheses (the modification code) and runs that code. Then the process repeats, with the for loop checking the conditional to see if the code in brackets should be run again. If the conditional is true, the code in curly brackets is run, the modification code is run, the conditional is checked, and so on. At some point, the conditional should be false, which ends the repetition. Figure 5-5 depicts how a for loop works.

Let's make this concrete by looking at our for loop in Example 5-6:

```
for (var i = 0; i < pages.length; i++) {
    document.write('<option>' + pages[i] + '</option>');
}
```

This loop begins by creating a variable, i, and setting it equal to 0. This is the setup code for the for loop. Then the for loop asks: "Is i less than the length of the pages array?" The length of pages is 6 and i is 0, so the condition is true, and the for loop runs the code inside the curly brackets. Now the for loop increases the value of i by 1 (i++), asks if i is still less than the length of the pages array, and runs the code in brackets again if

Figure 5-5

How a for loop works

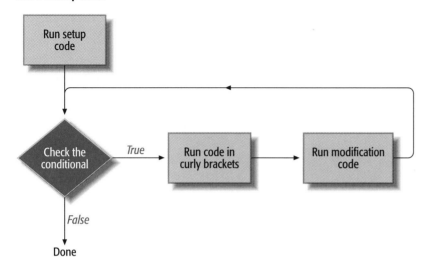

A for loop is a common programming construct that repeats a specified block of code over and over until a condition is met.

it is. This process repeats until i is equal to the length of the pages array, at which point the loop is done because the condition is no longer true.

So how are the page descriptions displayed? Each time the loop repeats, document.write( ) creates an option element that displays one of the page descriptions from the pages array. For example, the first time the for loop runs, i is equal to 0. When i is plugged into the pages array, as in pages[i], we get the first element of the array, "Select a Page". The second time through the loop, we get the second element, "Autos". Each time the loop repeats, i is increased by 1, so each description gets placed in its own option element, until the end of the pages array is reached. Finally, after all the options for the select menu are displayed on the page, the select menu and the form are closed off. Figure 5-6 shows our select list.

Figure 5-6

Our jump menu

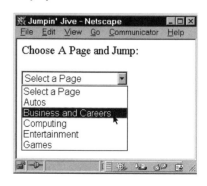

Jumping to the page

The last step in building our select menu is to create the function that jumps to the selected page. As you learned in Chapter 4, a form can pass itself to a function. We did exactly that in Example 5-6, when we passed this.form to the goPage( ) function as part of the onChange event handler for the select menu. The goPage( ) function is shown in Example 5-7.

Example 5-7: The goPage( ) function

```
function goPage(form) {
    var i = form.jumpMenu.selectedIndex;
    if (i != 0) {
        window.location = urls[i];
    }
}
```

NOTE

How do I get this to work with frames?

In the goPage() function, change the following line:

```
window.location = urls[i];
```

to reference a frame instead of the current window:

```
parent.frame.location = urls[i];
```

where *frame* is the name of the frame that you want changed.

The goPage() function uses the selectedIndex property of the select menu (named jumpMenu) to determine which option is selected. For example, if the first option is selected, the value of selectedIndex is 0. If the second option is selected, the value is 1. The function uses this information to determine which URL to deliver.

Since the first option in the select menu, "Select a Page", does nothing, the function does not change the page if selectedIndex is 0. Placing this line within an if statement lets us tell the function to change the window location only if i does not equal 0.

The last line is the most important, since it brings the user to the URL for the selected page, using window.location. This is where the urls array comes into play. By matching the selected option with an entry from the urls array, the script determines which document to load. For instance, if the user selects the second option ("Autos"), the select menu returns a selectedIndex of 1. And since the urls array and the pages array mirror each other, "Autos" corresponds to *autos.html*, and the script jumps to that URL.

Example 5-8 shows the complete code for the Jjumpin' jive script. To use this in your own pages, specify your own pages and URLs and just be sure that their elements in the arrays correspond appropriately.

Example 5-8: Source code for the complete jumpin' jive script

```html
<html>
<head>
<title>Jumpin' Jive</title>
<script language="JavaScript">
// The pages array holds the descriptions of the pages
var pages = new Array(
    "Select a Page",
    "Autos",
    "Business and Careers",
    "Computing",
    "Entertainment",
    "Games");

// The urls array holds the URLs of the pages
var urls = new Array(
    "",
    "autos.html",
    "business.html",
    "computing.html",
    "entertainment.html",
    "games.html");

// The goPage() function determines which page is selected and goes to it
function goPage(form) {
    var i = form.jumpMenu.selectedIndex;
    if (i != 0) {
        window.location = urls[i];
    }
}
</script>
</head>
```

Example 5-8: Source code for the complete jumpin' jive script (continued)

```
<body>
<p>Choose a Page and Jump:</p>
<script language="JavaScript">
// The select menu is displayed wherever you place this code
document.write('<form>');
document.write('<select name="jumpMenu" onChange="goPage(this.form);">');
for (var i = 0; i < pages.length; i++) {
    document.write('<option>' + pages[i] + '</option>');
}
document.write('</select>');
document.write('</form>');
</script>
</body>
</html>
```

Chapter 6

Too Many Browsers? Not Really

A long time ago, life was simple: there was standard HTML and NCSA Mosaic. Then came Netscape Navigator, with its HTML "extensions," and suddenly sites started labeling themselves "Enhanced for Netscape," meaning, of course, "this site looks lousy in Mosaic." By the time Microsoft came along with Internet Explorer, Mosaic was effectively dead, and Netscape and Microsoft were locked in a war to extend HTML in ways that would make one of their products the dominant browser. Fortunately, they both handled JavaScript, albeit to different extents, so it became the job of JavaScript to differentiate between the two.

As of this writing, that war is just about over. Microsoft Internet Explorer (IE) is by far the dominant browser, though Netscape has finally released an updated browser, Netscape 6, years after being bought by America Online. Of course, many people still use Netscape Navigator, and many others use older versions of Internet Explorer, so the basic problem remains: how do you find out which browser a given user is using and tailor your site accordingly?

This chapter is all about making your site as friendly as possible to each browser, as well as to different versions of those browsers.

IN THIS CHAPTER

Detecting different browsers using the navigator object

Tailoring content to specific browsers

Checking for plug-ins

What browser is that knocking at my door?

Before you learn how JavaScript differentiates between one browser and another, you need to understand how JavaScript gets information from the browser. This applies to both Netscape Navigator and Internet Explorer.

The navigator object

JavaScript identifies browsers through the navigator object. Although "navigator" is the name of Netscape's browser, it serves the same function in IE's implementation of JavaScript. You can get a lot of information

The navigator object provides information about the browser, regardless of whether the browser is Netscape Navigator, Internet Explorer, or any other browser.

from the `navigator` object, and we'll cover it all in this chapter. Table 6-1 shows three of the more useful properties for getting information about browsers, versions, and operating systems.

Table 6-1: Properties of the browser object

Property	What it refers to
navigator.appName	The browser's name
navigator.appVersion	The browser's version
navigator.userAgent	The browser's "user agent"—the official term for a web browser or a web-capable reader, like a hand-held device or WebTV

Without any context, the significance of these properties may not be clear. Table 6-2 shows some examples of what you actually get when you use these properties on different browsers. Note that this list isn't comprehensive; it just shows the properties for a handful of configurations, including some that are mostly of historical interest.

Now you begin to see the power behind these properties: they can determine the application name, version, and platform for any browser.

The first of these, `navigator.appName`, is the most straightforward; it tells you the name of the browser and nothing more. If you are using Netscape Navigator, the value of `appName` is "Netscape". If you are using Internet Explorer, the value is "Microsoft Internet Explorer".

The second property, `navigator.appVersion`, returns both the version number and the browser's platform. According to Table 6-2, when you ask Netscape Navigator 4.0 for its `appVersion`, the browser returns "4.0

Table 6-2: Navigator properties on different browsers

Browser	appName	appVersion	userAgent
Netscape 3.01 on a Mac	Netscape	3.01 (Macintosh; I; PPC)	Mozilla/3.01 (Macintosh; PPC)
Netscape 4.0 on Windows 95	Netscape	4.0 (Win95; I)	Mozilla/4.0 (Win95; I)
Netscape 4.72 on Windows 98	Netscape	4.72 [en] (Win98; U)	Mozilla/4.72 [en] (Win98; U)
Netscape 6.01 on Windows Me	Netscape	5.0 (Windows; en-US)	Mozilla/5.0 (Windows; U; Win 9x 4.90; en-US; m18) Gecko/ 20010131 Netscape6/6.01
Internet Explorer 3.0 on Windows 95	Microsoft Internet Explorer	2.0 (compatible; MSIE 3.01; Windows 95)	Mozilla/2.0 (compatible; MSIE 3.01; Windows 95)
Internet Explorer 4.0 on Windows 95	Microsoft Internet Explorer	4.0 (compatible; MSIE 4.0; Windows 95)	Mozilla/4.0 (compatible; MSIE 4.0; Windows 95)
Internet Explorer 5.0 on a Mac	Microsoft Internet Explorer	4.0 (compatible; MSIE 5.0; Macintosh; I; PPC)	Mozilla/4.0 (compatible; MSIE 5.0; Mac_PowerPC)
Internet Explorer 5.5 on Windows Me	Microsoft Internet Explorer	4.0 (compatible; MSIE 5.5; Windows 98; Win 9x 4.90)	Mozilla/4.0 (compatible; MSIE 5.5; Windows 98; Win 9x 4.90)
Internet Explorer 6.0 on Windows 2000	Microsoft Internet Explorer	4.0 (compatible; MSIE 6.0; Windows NT 5.0)	Mozilla/4.0 (compatible; MSIE 6.0; Windows NT 5.0)

(Win95; I)". While this value makes sense, many of the values listed for appVersion in Table 6-2 don't seem very intuitive. See the "Browser versions" sidebar for details.

The third property, navigator.userAgent, essentially combines the first two properties. The userAgent property is not new to the browser world; it was around long before JavaScript. Many servers use the information gathered from userAgent to determine which browsers are being used to access their sites. For the most part, however, we will use appName and appVersion, because they contain all the information we need.

You can access the properties of the navigator object just as you would those of any other object. For example, to print out the name of a browser, just pass navigator.appName to document.write():

```
document.write("Welcome all " + navigator.appName + " users.");
```

There's not much reason to do this, however. The point of checking browser identities is to tailor your pages (or your entire site) for different browsers. The rest of this chapter is all about doing just that.

Browser name and number

The browser's name and major version number (2, 3, 4, etc.) almost always determine which features a browser supports. For example, IE 3 does not support Microsoft's version of Dynamic HTML, but IE 4 and later versions do. Navigator 2 and IE 3 do not support JavaScript image replacement, but all later versions of both browsers do. If you know what browser and version you're dealing with, you know a lot about what kind of documents you can serve.

To determine the browser's name and version, we'll use two of the properties you just learned about: appName and appVersion. To make our browser detection script shorter, we start by assigning the values of these properties to two variables, as shown in Example 6-1.

Example 6-1: Assigning the values of appName and appVersion to variables

```
var browserName = navigator.appName;
var browserVersion = parseInt(navigator.appVersion);
```

First, the browser's name is assigned to the variable browserName. The second line assigns the browser's version to the variable browserVersion. Note that this line uses a built-in JavaScript function, parseInt(), to extract the integer value (whole number) from navigator.appVersion. It works like this: the appVersion of Netscape 6.01 on Windows Me is "5.0 (Windows; en-US)". When this is passed to parseInt(), the returned value is simply 5, an integer. The appVersion of Internet Explorer 4.0 for Windows 95 is "4.0 (compatible; MSIE 4.0b1; Windows 95)". When this is passed to parseInt(), the returned value is 4.

Browser versions

You might notice something odd about the values of appVersion for Internet Explorer in Table 6-2. For example, IE 3.0 doesn't give the value you would expect: "3.01 (Win95)", for Version 3.01 running on Windows 95. Instead, you get "2.0 (compatible; MSIE 3.01; Windows 95)". This is because, when Internet Explorer 3.0 originally came out, it tried to be compatible with Navigator 2.0 and its implementation of JavaScript. This meant that it needed an appVersion that returned the same value as Navigator 2.0. (Of course, the 3.01 is still in the appVersion string, just not as the primary version number.)

The same situation occurs with Internet Explorer 5, 5.5, and 6, which all report an appVersion of 4.0.

It's also important to pay attention to Netscape 6's reported appVersion. Netscape 6 is based on Mozilla, an open-source browser that was rewritten from scratch. However, early Mozilla work was based on Netscape's old browser code, what would have been Netscape Navigator 5. Although there never was a Navigator 5, the version number stuck, so Mozilla—and, thus Netscape 6—returns an appVersion of 5.0.

Matching up names and numbers

Now that we have the browser name and its major version number, we need to match up the names and numbers. This is done with if statements. Example 6-2 shows an if statement that detects the presence of Netscape 6 using the browserName and browserVersion variables defined in Example 6-1.

Example 6-2: Checking for Netscape 6 and printing the results

```
if (browserName == "Netscape" && browserVersion == 5) {
    document.write("This is Netscape 6");
}
else {
    document.write("This is not Netscape 6");
}
```

This if statement compares both the browser's name and version: if the browser name is "Netscape" and the version is 5, it must be Netscape 6, so the code within the curly braces after the if is run, printing "This is Netscape 6" to the page. If the browser is not Netscape 6, the code in the curly braces following the else is run, printing "This is not Netscape 6".

By combining a series of if statements, we can detect any browser that supports JavaScript.

By combining a series of if statements similar to the one in Example 6-2, we can detect any browser that supports JavaScript. Example 6-3 shows how to use if statements to piece together the identity of the browser. This script detects the latest two versions of Navigator and the latest four versions of Internet Explorer.

Example 6-3: Detecting recent browsers from Netscape and Microsoft

```
var browser;

if (browserName == "Netscape" && browserVersion == 5) {
    browser = "nn6";                                        // Netscape 6
}
else if (browserName == "Netscape" && browserVersion == 4) {
    browser = "nn4";                                        // Navigator 4
}
else if (browserName == "Microsoft Internet Explorer" &&
        browserVersion == 4 &&
        navigator.appVersion.indexOf("MSIE 6.0") != -1) {
    browser = "ie6";                                        // IE 6.0
}
else if (browserName == "Microsoft Internet Explorer" &&
        browserVersion == 4 &&
        navigator.appVersion.indexOf("MSIE 5.5") != -1) {
    browser = "ie55";                                       // IE 5.5
}
else if (browserName == "Microsoft Internet Explorer" &&
        browserVersion == 4 &&
        navigator.appVersion.indexOf("MSIE 5.0") != -1) {
    browser = "ie5";                                        // IE 5.0
}
else if (browserName == "Microsoft Internet Explorer"
        && browserVersion == 4) {
    browser = "ie4";                                        // IE 4
}
```

Based on the browser's name and version, this script sets the variable `browser` to one of six strings: "nn6", "nn4", "ie6", "ie55", "ie5", or "ie4", corresponding to Netscape Navigator 6 and 4 and Internet Explorer 6, 5.5, 5, and 4, respectively. Detecting the different versions of IE is more complicated than detecting different versions of Navigator, because IE 4, IE 5, IE 5.5, and IE 6 all report a browser version of 4. Thus, we have to use `indexOf( )` to detect the "MSIE #.#" portion of `appVersion` in order to distinguish among these browsers.

Detecting the different versions of Internet Explorer is complicated, because IE 4, IE 5, IE 5.5, and IE 6 all report a browser version of 4.

To infinity and beyond

By now, you should understand the concept behind `if` statements and how they use `browserName` and `browserVersion`. One smart thing to do in your own scripts is to use the "greater than or equal to" operator when checking for the latest browser versions. For example, here's how to check if the browser is Netscape 6 or later:

```
if (browserName == "Netscape" && browserVersion >= 5) {
    browser = "nn6up"
}
```

The advantage of this approach is that if you check for Netscape 6 or later, your pages will work with later versions of the Netscape browser, whenever they are released.

Of course, this technique also works with earlier browser versions. Say you need to know if the browser is IE 4 or later. This is easy, as shown in the following `if` statement:

```
if (browserName == "Microsoft Internet Explorer" &&
    browserVersion >= 4) {
    browser = "ie4up";
}
```

Running browser-specific code

With this information, we can begin tailoring our pages to fit the needs of the various browsers. Example 6-4 shows the skeleton for an HTML document that detects the browser being used and runs the appropriate JavaScript code for that browser.

Example 6-4: Partial HTML document with version detection

```
<html>
<head>
<title>A Smart Page</title>
<script language="JavaScript">
// Check browser name and version and assign info to variable
var browserName = navigator.appName;
var browserVersion = parseInt(navigator.appVersion);
var browser;

if (browserName == "Netscape" && browserVersion == 5) {
    browser = "nn6";
}
else if (browserName == "Netscape" && browserVersion == 4) {
    browser = "nn4";
}
```

Example 6-4: Partial HTML document with version detection (continued)

```
else if (browserName == "Microsoft Internet Explorer" &&
        browserVersion == 4 &&
        navigator.appVersion.indexOf("MSIE 6.0") != -1) {
    browser = "ie6";
}
else if (browserName == "Microsoft Internet Explorer" &&
        browserVersion == 4 &&
        navigator.appVersion.indexOf("MSIE 5.5") != -1) {
    browser = "ie55";
}
else if (browserName == "Microsoft Internet Explorer" &&
        browserVersion == 4 &&
        navigator.appVersion.indexOf("MSIE 5.0") != -1) {
    browser = "ie5";
}
else if (browserName == "Microsoft Internet Explorer"
        && browserVersion == 4) {
    browser = "ie4";
}

// Handle browser-specific code
if (browser == "nn6" || browser == "ie6" ||
    browser == "ie55" || browser == "ie5") {
    // Latest JavaScript code goes here
}
else if (browser == "nn4") {
    // Specific code for Netscape Navigator 4 goes here
}
else if (browser == "ie4") {
    // Specific code for Internet Explorer 4 goes here
}
</script>
</head>

<body>
<!-- This is where standard HTML goes -->
</body>
</html>
```

> **NOTE**
>
> ## The be-all and end-all of browser detection
>
> As you can tell just by looking at Table 6-2, there are lots of nuances to browser detection. Fortunately, there are a number of different browser detection scripts available on the Web, so you don't have to create your own. You can find a very thorough one, along with a helpful discussion of its use, at: *http://www.mozilla.org/docs/web-developer/sniffer/browser_type.html.*

This page has a working knowledge of which browser is being used, so it can use that information to run particular code on specific browsers. Of course, Example 6-4 is just a template (it doesn't display anything), but you may find it useful in your own web pages. In the next section, we'll look at a few specific examples of using browser detection to control particular features on a web page.

Different browsers, different needs

Telling your visitors to "choose the Netscape-enhanced site" or "click here if you have Internet Explorer" isn't very elegant. With JavaScript, you can choose automatically for your visitors and save them the trouble. The technique you should use for handling browser-specific features depends on how much your pages rely on those features. Sometimes you'll just need to wrap browser detection code around an isolated element on a page. In other cases, you may want to create completely different pages for different browsers.

Bits and pieces

Back in the early days of JavaScript, browser detection was often used to determine whether to take advantage of image rollovers on a web page (we'll be discussing this feature in more detail in Chapter 7). Rollover images were supported as of Navigator 3 and IE 4, but not in earlier browsers, so web sites that used these dynamic images needed to check the browser version and behave accordingly. Today, of course, it is pretty safe to assume at least a Version 4 browser, so browser detection for rollovers isn't really necessary, unless you need to support very old browsers (e.g., Navigator 2 and IE 3).

If you want to use rollovers and you do need to support very old browsers, you can use browser detection to tailor your page to do the right thing. This approach works well with rollovers, because if they aren't supported, you can show a static image without affecting the overall layout of your page.

Figure 6-1 shows a page that uses simple rollovers. When the user moves the mouse over the circular images at the bottom of the page, the shadows are reversed, making it clear that these are active buttons. This script starts by checking for Navigator 3 or later, or IE 4 or later. If the browser meets these criteria, `browser` is set to "rollover"; otherwise, it is set to "norollover". Example 6-5 demonstrates how browser detection can be wrapped around a single rollover.

Figure 6-1

Circular images that use rollovers, if supported by the browser

Example 6-5: Browser detection for a simple rollover script

```
<html>
<head>
<title>A Smart Rollover Page</title>
<script language="JavaScript">
var browserName = navigator.appName;
var browserVersion = parseInt(navigator.appVersion);
var browser;

// Determine whether rollovers are supported
if ((browserName == "Netscape" && browserVersion >= 3) ||
    (browserName == "Microsoft Internet Explorer" && browserVersion >= 4)) {
    browser = "rollover";
}
else {
    browser = "norollover";
}
</script>
</head>

<body>
<a href="travel.html"
   onMouseOver="if (browser=='rollover')
                document.travel.src='travel_on.gif';">
<img name="travel" src="travel_off.gif" border="0" height="77"
     width="83"></a>
</body>
</html>
```

For the sake of simplicity, the body of the page is very brief. When the mouse moves over the image link, the code inside the onMouseOver event handler is run. This code uses the dynamic image feature of JavaScript to change the image (named travel) so that it appears highlighted. The important part of this event handler is the if statement; it allows the image to be highlighted only if browser is equal to "rollover", that is, the browser is capable of handling dynamic images. (Don't worry about understanding how the rollover works right now; we'll be discussing rollovers in detail in Chapter 7. For now, all you need to understand is how the browser detection works.)

A much more common use of browser detection these days is for pages that use Dynamic HTML (DHTML), which has a number of dependencies on browser version. (We'll be discussing DHTML in more detail in Chapter 9 and Chapter 10.) If your page uses a single DHTML element that can easily be replaced by standard HTML for browsers that don't support DHTML, you might consider using browser detection around that element to handle different browsers. At a minimum, you need four different branches, for Netscape 6, for IE 4 and later, for Navigator 4, and for all earlier browser versions, as shown in Example 6-6.

Example 6-6: Simple browser detection for DHTML

```
<html>
<head>
<title>A Smart DHTML Page</title>
<script language="JavaScript">
```

Example 6-6: Simple browser detection for DHTML (continued)

```
var browserName = navigator.appName;
var browserVersion = parseInt(navigator.appVersion);
var browser;

if (browserName == "Netscape" && browserVersion >= 5) {
    browser = "nn6up";
}
else if (browserName == "Netscape" && browserVersion == 4) {
    browser = "nn4";
}
else if (browserName == "Microsoft Internet Explorer" &&
        browserVersion >= 4) {
    browser = "ie4up";
}
</script>
</head>

<body>
<script language="JavaScript">
// Branches for different DHTML implementations plus standard HTML version
if (browser == "nn6up") {
    // Netscape 6 (DOM standard) DHTML goes here
}
else if (browser == "nn4") {
    // DHTML specific to Netscape Navigator 4 goes here
}
else if (browser == "ie4up") {
    // Microsoft-specific DHTML goes here
}
else {
    // Standard HTML replacement goes here
}
</script>
</body>
</html>
```

After determining which browser is being used, this script provides locations for three different implementations of a DHTML element, plus a place to put the standard HTML replacement. As you can imagine, if you are integrating DHTML throughout your page design, supporting these four branches will quickly cause your pages to get quite messy. In that case, you should probably use a different technique for browser detection, like the single-frame method that is discussed in the next section.

The single-frame method

If you use a lot of browser-specific features on your site, you may want to use totally different pages for different browsers, especially if you're employing features that significantly affect the layout and function of your pages. If this is the case, the single-frame method is for you. With the single-frame method, a script detects the browser type, creates a single frame for the user, and displays a page with content appropriate for that browser inside the frame.

With the single-frame method, a script detects the browser type, creates a single frame for the user, and displays a page with content appropriate for that browser inside the frame.

The single-frame method is the easiest and most reliable way to direct different browsers to different pages. It is also transparent: because it uses a

The back-up black hole

You may be wondering: "Why not just direct browsers to different pages using window.location?" The reason is what I call the back-up black hole. If you create a special page to direct browsers to browser-specific pages, when a user presses the Back button from any of those pages, he will be directed right back to the referring page. This is quite unprofessional and can confuse your visitors.

single frame, the user doesn't see any frame borders, just the page. Thus, for instance, a page full of ActiveX controls and other IE-related technologies can be kept "safe" from Navigator with this method. If the user is running Navigator, she can be shown a page that doesn't contain any IE-specific content.

If your web pages make heavy use of DHTML, you may want to consider using the single-frame method. In this example, we direct users of IE 4 and later to a page that makes extensive use of Microsoft's implementation of DHTML. For Netscape 6, we use a page that supports DHTML based on the W3C-standard DOM, since Netscape 6 (mostly) supports the standard DOM.* Users of Netscape 4 are directed to a page that provides limited DHTML functionality, as supported by that browser. For any older browsers, users are directed to a page that doesn't use DHTML at all. The full HTML is shown in Example 6-7.

Example 6-7: HTML for the single-frame method for a DHTML page

```html
<html>
<head>
<title>A Smart DHTML Page</title>
<base target="_top">
<script language="JavaScript">
var browserName = navigator.appName;
var browserVersion = parseInt(navigator.appVersion);
var browser;

if (browserName == "Netscape" && browserVersion >= 5) {
    browser = "nn6up";
}
else if (browserName == "Netscape" && browserVersion == 4) {
    browser = "nn4";
}
else if (browserName == "Microsoft Internet Explorer" &&
        browserVersion >= 4) {
    browser = "ie4up";
}

// Frame for IE 4 or later with Microsoft-specific Dynamic HTML
if (browser == "ie4up") {
    document.write('<frameset rows="100%,*" frameborder="no" border="0"');
    document.write('marginheight="5" marginwidth="5">');
    document.write('<frame src="ms_dhtml.html" scrolling="auto">');
    document.write('</frameset>');
}

// Frame for Netscape 6 with DOM-standard DHTML
else if (browser == "nn6up") {
    document.write('<frameset rows="100%,*" frameborder="no" border="0"');
    document.write('marginheight="5" marginwidth="5">');
    document.write('<frame src="dom_dhtml.html" scrolling="auto">');
    document.write('</frameset>');
}
```

* IE 5 has some support for the W3C-standard DOM, and IE 5.5 and IE 6 have great support for it, so we could use the DOM-standard DHTML for these pages. But these browser versions also support Microsoft's implementation of DHTML, so there's no reason not to use the Microsoft-specific page for these browsers.

Example 6-7: HTML for the single-frame method for a DHTML page (continued)

```
// Frame for Navigator 4 with limited DHTML
else if (browser == "nn4") {
    document.write('<frameset rows="100%,*" frameborder="no" border="0"');
    document.write('marginheight="5" marginwidth="5">');
    document.write('<frame src="nn4_dhtml.html" scrolling="auto">');
    document.write('</frameset>');
}
</script>
</head>

<body bgcolor="#FFFFFF">
<!-- This is what earlier browsers see; it shouldn't contain any DHTML -->
</body>
</html>
```

The JavaScript code resides in the head of the document that defines the single frame. First, the browser's name and version are determined. There are three cases that we care about: Netscape 6 or later, Navigator 4, and IE 4 or later. These correspond to the values "nn6up", "nn4", and "ie4up" for the browser variable. If the user isn't using one of these browsers, the browser variable is not set.

Next, a single frame is created for each browser type. If the browser is IE 4 or later, the script creates a single frame that displays *ms_dhtml.html* (the page that uses Microsoft's implementation of DHTML). If the browser is Netscape 6 or later, the script creates a frame that displays *dom_dhtml.html*. And with Navigator 4, the frame displays *nn4_dhtml.html*. Since we aren't redirecting the browser to a different page, but instead creating a single frame for each page, all of this is transparent to the visitor.

What about the frame borders? Not a problem. When the frameset is created, the first row is set to 100% and the second to nothing. Therefore, when the single frame is defined, it will take up the full browser window. Surprisingly, leaving out the second frame does not result in any adverse effects. There's another advantage to the single-frame method: since you're using frames, though only one, you now have the ability to set the margin height and width for your page.

When using this method, it is advisable to include the following line in the head of your HTML documents:

```
<base target="_top">
```

This bit of HTML ensures that any links that aren't specifically targeted to a frame or window are loaded in the top-level browser window.

Setting target to "_top" in the base element ensures that any links that aren't specifically targeted to a frame or window are loaded in the top-level browser window.

Style differences

Another area where browser detection can improve your web pages is in helping you present a consistent page design across different browsers. As you probably already know from experience, different default font sizes, margins, and even color rendering can warp what is an attractive page in one browser into an unreadable mess in the next.

One of the most noticeable examples of how browsers render pages differently is in the variety of default font sizes among different versions of Netscape Navigator and Internet Explorer. Form elements are another common culprit; they are rendered at wildly differing sizes and margins in the various browsers. Even the use of Cascading Style Sheets (CSS) doesn't solve these problems, because different browsers apply styles in slightly different ways. Combined, these differences force designers to continually test all target browsers to create pages that look decent across all platforms.

By combining a little JavaScript browser detection code with style sheets that are targeted at different browsers, we can produce consistent pages across all browsers.

With JavaScript, you don't have to settle for decent. By combining a little browser detection code with style sheets that are targeted at different browsers, we can produce consistent pages across all browsers. First, let's take a look at the problem we are trying to solve. Example 6-8 shows a simple form that uses a single style sheet, *styles.css*.

Example 6-8: A simple form that uses a single style sheet

```
<html>
<head>
<title>A Form</title>
<link rel="stylesheet" href="styles.css" type="text/css">
</head>

<body>
<form name="form1" method="post" action="">
  <table border="0" width="100%" cellpadding="3">
    <tr>
      <th bgcolor="#00FF00">
        <span>Please Fill Out the Following Form:</span>
      </th>
    </tr>
    <tr>
      <td>
        <input type="text" name="textfield" value="Enter Keywords Here"
               size="20">
        <select name="select">
          <option>Default Selection</option>
          <option selected>Selection 2</option>
          <option>Selection 3</option>
        </select>
        <input type="submit" name="Submit" value="Submit">
      </td>
    </tr>
    <tr>
      <td>
        <p>Shall we place you on our mailing list?</p>
          <input type="radio" name="radiobutton" value="radiobutton">Yes<br>
          <input type="radio" name="radiobutton" value="radiobutton">No
      </td>
    </tr>
    <tr>
      <td>
        <input type="checkbox" name="checkbox"
               value="checkbox">Remember Me</td>
    </tr>
  </table>
</form>
</body>
</html>
```

Notice the use of the `link` tag to link the *styles.css* style sheet into the HTML document. Figure 6-2 shows how different this form appears in Navigator 4 and IE 5.5, despite the use of a single style sheet.

Figure 6-2

A simple form displayed in Navigator 4 and IE 5.5

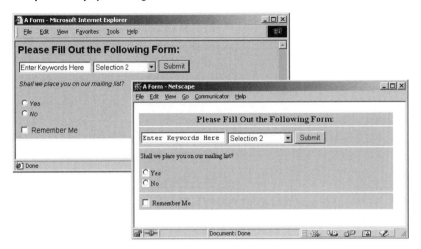

To solve this problem, we can use browser detection to link different CSS files to our HTML document, depending on the browser that's viewing it. Then we can tailor our design to the browser and apply our own styles to the browser defaults. Creating custom style sheets is much easier and faster than creating entire custom HTML documents, and it lets us deal with just the design tweaks we want. Example 6-9 shows the JavaScript that links different style sheets for Navigator 4 and IE 5.5 into our form.

Example 6-9: Using browser detection to apply the appropriate style sheet

```
<html>
<head>
<title>A Smart Form</title>
<script language="JavaScript">
var browserName = navigator.appName;
var browserVersion = parseInt(navigator.appVersion);
var browser;

if (browserName == "Netscape" && browserVersion == 4) {
    browser = "nn4";
}
else if (browserName == "Microsoft Internet Explorer" &&
        browserVersion == 4 &&
        navigator.appVersion.indexOf("MSIE 5.5") != -1) {
    browser = "ie55";
}

// Write link tag to include browser-specific style sheet
document.write('<link rel="stylesheet" href="' + browser + '.css" ');
document.write('type="text/css">');
</script>
</head>
```

If the browser is Navigator 4, the script links in *nn4.css*; with IE 5.5, the style sheet is *ie55.css*. For simplicity, this example detects just two browsers, but you can see how it could be extended to handle others. Figure 6-3 shows how much more consistent our form looks in Navigator 4 and IE 5.5 with the browser-specific styles applied.

Figure 6-3

A form using browser-specific style sheets, displayed in Navigator 4 and IE 5.5

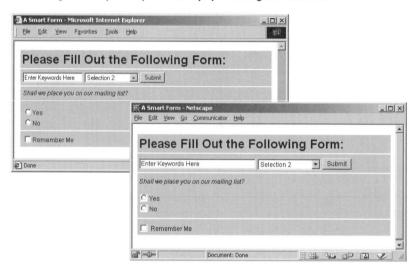

NOTE

How do I find the MIME type for . . . ?

In Navigator, select Edit → Preferences → Navigator → Applications to get a list of plug-ins installed for your browser, along with their MIME types. You can also type "about:plugins" into the Location field or select Help → About Plug-ins; this displays a page that lists the installed plug-ins and their respective MIME types.

With IE on the Mac, select Edit → Preferences → Receiving Files → File Helpers to find the MIME types for different documents. On Windows systems, you'll need to use View → Folder Options → File Types from Windows Explorer, rather than Internet Explorer, to get a list of supported file types.

Checking for plug-ins

With the proliferation of plug-ins for various kinds of content on the Web, you never know whether a user will have just the right version of a plug-in for your content. Although most browsers try to help—by noticing when content requires an unavailable plug-in and asking if the user wants to install the plug-in—we can do better with JavaScript.

In Navigator 3 and later and IE 5 and later on the Mac, JavaScript has the ability to detect which plug-ins are installed in a browser and which file types (PDF, MP3, etc.) a browser supports. The two objects that allow for this are `nagivator.plugins` and `navigator.mimeTypes`. The first object, `nagivator.plugins`, contains the names and descriptions of all the plug-ins installed in the browser. The second, `navigator.mimeTypes`, indicates which file types the browser can handle.

With IE on Windows systems, the process of determining whether a particular plug-in is supported is quite different, but, as you'll see shortly, we can still use some JavaScript to support these browsers.

File types

When a web server sends a document to a web browser, it includes some information about the type of file it is sending. The browser uses this information, called a MIME type, to determine how to handle the file—whether to display the contents in the window or launch the appropriate plug-in or helper application. For example, a PDF document has the MIME type application/pdf, and a Flash movie's MIME type is application/x-shockwave-flash. The MIME types that a browser supports almost always determine which plug-ins are installed. In other words, if a browser supports the MIME type application/x-shockwave-flash, the Flash plug-in is most likely installed.

To make use of JavaScript's ability to detect MIME types, we simply give nagivator.mimeTypes the file type that we are looking for, as shown in Example 6-10. If the file type is found, the object returns true; otherwise, it returns false.

Example 6-10: Checking for the Flash MIME type

```
if (navigator.mimeTypes["application/x-shockwave-flash"]) {
    document.write("You have Flash!");
}
else {
    document.write("You do not have Flash.");
}
```

Notice that the MIME type in question, application/x-shockwave-flash, is specified in double quotes, inside square brackets, after we refer to navigator.mimeTypes. That's because mimeTypes is actually an array that lists all the supported MIME types in the browser. But unlike the arrays we saw in Chapter 5, which used numbers to access their elements, mimeTypes uses string values instead. This kind of array is called an associative array. Associative arrays are useful because they provide a more descriptive way to keep track of the elements in an array, by name rather than by number.

An associative array uses string values instead of numbers to access its elements.

The if statement in Example 6-10 determines whether the Flash MIME type is present in the mimeTypes array. If there is an element defined for application/x-shockwave-flash, the if statement is true and the message "You have Flash!" is written to the screen. If there is no such element in the array, however, the if statement is false and the message is "You do not have Flash."

Would you like Flash with that?

Of course, what we really want to do is show a Flash movie if the Flash MIME type is found and, if it's not found, display a link to download the Flash plug-in. This is what most sites that use Flash do, as shown in Figure 6-4 and Figure 6-5.

Figure 6-4

Shockwave.com showing Flash content when the Flash Player is available

Figure 6-5

Shockwave.com displaying a page allowing the user to download Flash Player if it isn't installed

At Shockwave.com, visitors need to have the Flash plug-in, as shown in Figure 6-5. This is pretty reasonable, of course, since the site is all about Flash. Depending on the goals of your site, you may want to take a more flexible approach and support both Flash and non-Flash variations, to accommodate more users.

Let's write a script that creates dramatically different pages depending on the user's configuration. Here are the possibilities:

- If the browser supports the navigator.mimeTypes array (Navigator 3 and later or IE 5 and later on the Mac) and Flash is found, display the Flash movie.

- If the browser supports the mimeTypes array and Flash is not found, display a page that links to the Flash download page and to a non-Flash version of the site.

- If the browser is IE on Windows (which doesn't support the mimeTypes array), show the movie if Flash is found, or download the Flash ActiveX control if Flash is not found (see Figure 6-6).

- If none of the previous cases applies, simply display a page that gives the user the option to enter either the Flash or the non-Flash version of the site or to download the Flash plug-in.

Figure 6-6

Enabling IE on Windows users to download the Flash ActiveX control

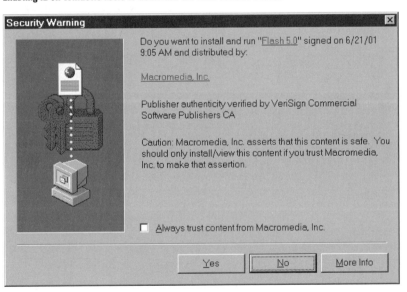

With this script, Navigator and IE/Mac users are taken care of, IE/Windows users have Flash automatically downloaded as a control, and anybody else can decide what they want to do. The script is shown in Example 6-11.

Example 6-11: Code for a Flash detection script

```html
<html>
<head>
<title>A Smart Flash Page</title>
<script language="JavaScript">
var browser;

// Determine if browser supports mimeTypes array
if (navigator.mimeTypes && navigator.mimeTypes.length != 0) {
  browser = "mimeTypes"
}
else {
  browser = "noMimeTypes"
}

</script>
</head>

<body>
<script language="JavaScript">
// If browser supports mimeTypes...
if (browser == "mimeTypes") {
  // Display Flash plug-in on page if detected
  if (navigator.mimeTypes["application/x-shockwave-flash"]) {
    document.write('<embed src="movie.swf" height="320" width="240">');
  }
  // Otherwise display links to download plug-in or view non-Flash site
  else {
    document.write('<p><a href="http://www.macromedia.com/downloads/">');
    document.write('Download Flash Player</a>');
    document.write('<p><a href="noflash.html">Enter Non-Flash Site</a>');
  }
}
// For IE, use object tag to open movie in Flash ActiveX control or
// download it if it isn't available
else if (navigator.appName == "Microsoft Internet Explorer") {
  document.write('<object ');
  document.write('classid="clsid:D27CDB6E-AE6D-11cf-96B8-444553540000"');
  document.write('codebase=');
  document.write('"http://download.macromedia.com/pub/shockwave/cabs/flash/
swflash.cab#version=4,0,2,0"');
  document.write('width="240" height="320" name="Flash" id="movie">');
  document.write('<param name="src" value="movie.swf">');
  document.write('<param name="bgcolor" value="#000000">');
  document.write('</object>');
}

// Otherwise, display links to enter Flash and non-Flash sites, as
// well as download the plug-in
else {
  document.write('<p><a href="flash.html">Enter Flash site</a>');
  document.write('<p><a href="noflash.html">Enter Non-Flash Site</a>');
  document.write('<p><a href="http://www.macromedia.com/downloads/">');
  document.write('Download Flash Player</a>');
}
</script>
</body>
</html>
```

NOTE

Pesky details

In Example 6-11, we actually check for the presence of navigator.mimeTypes and verify that the length of the mimeTypes array isn't zero:

```
if (navigator.mimeTypes &&
navigator.mimeTypes.length != 0)
```

This is because IE on Windows systems actually defines a mimeTypes object but leaves it empty. Checking the length allows us to handle IE on Windows appropriately.

The script starts by checking whether the browser supports the navigator. mimeTypes array. The technique shown here is another form of browser version checking called object detection. Instead of checking the specific browser name and version, object detection checks for the presence of a particular object, in this case, the mimeTypes object. This is much easier than checking to see if the browser is Navigator 3 or later or IE 5 or later for the Mac, and it has the same results. If the mimeTypes object is supported, the browser variable is set to "mimeTypes" to indicate this; otherwise, the variable is set to "noMimeTypes".

If the browser supports mimeTypes, the script determines if the Flash plug-in is available, by checking for the application/x-shockwave-flash MIME type. If that MIME type is detected, we display the Flash movie using the embed tag. If the MIME type is not detected, we display links to download the Flash plug-in and to enter the non-Flash site.

If the browser is IE (on Windows), we display the Flash ActiveX control using the object tag. If this control is not available on the user's system, we give the user the option to download it, as shown in Figure 6-6.

Finally, if there's no way for JavaScript to detect the presence of Flash, we display a page with all possible options—enter the Flash site, enter the non-Flash site, or download the Flash plug-in—so users can decide on their own what to do.

Different versions of Flash?

What if you need to check for a particular version of the Flash plug-in? You might, for example, need to look for Flash Player 5, because your Flash movie makes extensive use of ActionScript. Rather than checking for application/x-shockwave-flash in the mimeTypes array, you can search the navigator.plugins array instead. The first step is to give "Shockwave Flash" to the plugins array to see if any Flash plug-in is available:

```
var plugin = navigator.plugins["Shockwave Flash"];
```

If a Flash plug-in is available, this statement returns an object that has a description property that contains the version number for the plug-in. Here's how we can get at that information:

```
if (plugin.description.indexOf("Flash 5") != -1)
    document.write("You have Flash 5!");
```

Note that the the plugins array has the same behavior as the mimeTypes array under IE on Windows systems: the plugins object is defined, but it doesn't contain anything.

Beyond the browser

JavaScript is not limited to detecting just browsers and plug-ins; it can also determine the operating system on which a browser is running. As we saw back in Table 6-2, the navigator.appVersion property includes information about the operating system as well. Table 6-3 shows appVersion values for some common operating systems (the browser version information has been taken out, because it is irrelevant to our purpose here).

Table 6-3: appVersion values for common operating systems

Operating system	appVersion
Windows 2000	Windows NT 5.0; U
Windows 98	Win98; U
Windows 95	Win95; I
Windows 3.1	Win16; I
Macintosh PPC	Macintosh; I; PPC
Linux (Unix)	X11; U; Linux

With this knowledge, you can create simple functions to determine which operating system a visitor is using. Example 6-12 shows a function that uses indexOf( ) to determine if a browser is running on Windows 98.

Example 6-12: Is the platform Windows 98?

```
function isWin98( ) {
    if (navigator.appVersion.indexOf("98") != -1) {
        return true;
    }
    else {
        return false;
    }
}
```

NOTE

Pesky details

Navigator and IE report Windows 98 as "Win98" and "Windows 98", respectively. Searching for "98" bridges the gap.

You can use this function, which returns true if the browser is running on Windows 98, to tailor parts of your page, just as you did with the browser detection script. For example:

```
if (isWin98( )) {
    document.write("You're running Windows 98");
}
```

If the platform is Windows 98, the script prints "You're running Windows 98".

Think of it this way: if it's in the appVersion, you can detect it. This ability opens up many doors. For example, say your company develops software for a number of different operating systems. When visitors come to your site to download software, you can save them the trouble of specifying their operating system by doing it for them with JavaScript.

You can also easily combine operating system detection and browser detection, or operating system detection and plug-in detection. They're all interchangeable. Never again will your visitors have to make decisions based on their software (and hardware); you can do it for them.

Chapter 7

Dynamic Images

Static images aren't a great deal of fun: they're pretty and functional, but they don't *do* anything. With JavaScript, you can bring to life all the static images on your web site using a feature called dynamic images. Though dynamic images were not introduced until Navigator 3 and Internet Explorer 4, creative uses of this feature are found on sites all over the Web.

As the name "dynamic images" suggests, JavaScript can change an image right on the page. An image of a sprawling metropolis can be replaced with a serene forest instantly. Any image on your site can be made dynamic with a little bit of JavaScript code and some imagination.

Image basics

Like forms, JavaScript considers images to be objects. Let's illustrate this by creating an image in HTML and controlling it through JavaScript:

```
<img src="cupajoe.gif" name="cupholder" height="85" width="86"
    border="0">
```

This is your basic img tag, with name, height, width, border, and src attributes. For now, we'll be focusing on two of these: src and name. As you already know, src contains the name of the image file that you want displayed. The second attribute may seem a little odd. Normally, you don't put a name in an img tag, but to access this image through Java-Script, it's helpful to assign it a name. Once this image is assigned the name cupholder, we can refer to it in JavaScript like this:

```
document.cupholder
```

As you can see, the image object, cupholder, is a property of the document object in the JavaScript tree. Now for the fun part: because we have access to the image object through JavaScript, we also have access to its attributes, which become properties of the image object. For example, to change the actual image file that's being displayed in the image, we can just change its src property:

```
document.cupholder.src = "cupajoesteam.gif";
```

If we do this, the old image file, *cupajoe.gif*, is no longer displayed, and *cupajoesteam.gif* appears in its place. The image changes directly on the page, no redrawing required.

Preloading images with the Image object prevents a long wait when displaying a new image.

There's only one problem: before the new image is displayed, it has to load, and as anybody without a high-speed Internet connection will tell you, that takes time. Fortunately, JavaScript provides a way to preload images, so they'll be displayed as soon as we ask for them. To do this, we have to create a new image object. Instead of creating the image in HTML with the img tag, we use the JavaScript Image object to create an image in memory that the browser loads and stores in its cache:

```
var cupsteam = new Image( );
cupsteam.src = "cupajoesteam.gif";
```

This creates a new image object named cupsteam with its src property set to *cupajoesteam.gif*. Instead of loading *cupajoesteam.gif* and displaying it on the page, however, the browser loads the image and stores it in its cache. Now that the image has been preloaded, we can replace the image in cupholder (the image object that's physically on the page) with the image in cupsteam (the image in the cache) without any delay:

```
document.cupholder.src = cupsteam.src;
```

This sets the src property of cupholder equal to the src property of cupsteam, thereby replacing the image on the page with the one that's preloaded. If you combine this with some event handlers, these image changes can become interactive. Let's create a small HTML document, shown in Example 7-1, that demonstrates how this can be done. The two different images are shown in Figure 7-1.

Figure 7-1

Changing the source of the image object to replace one image with another

A Cup of Joe   A Cup of Joe

Example 7-1: Changing an image using onMouseOver and onMouseOut

```
<html>
<head>
<script language="JavaScript">
if (document.images) {
    var cup = new Image( );
    cup.src = "cupajoe.gif";
    var cupsteam = new Image( );
    cupsteam.src = "cupajoesteam.gif";
}
</script>
</head>

<body bgcolor="#FFFFFF">
<a href="#"
    onMouseOver="if (document.images)
                document.cupholder.src = cupsteam.src;"
    onMouseOut="if (document.images)
                document.cupholder.src = cup.src;">
<img name="cupholder" height="124" width="91" border="0"
    src="cupajoe.gif"></a>
<br>
</body>
</html>
```

First we create two new `Image` objects—one called cup and one called cupsteam—and preload their image files, *cupajoe.gif* and *cupajoesteam.gif*, respectively. Note that these activities are wrapped in an `if` statement that checks for the existence of `document.images`. Dynamic images are available only with Navigator 3 and later and IE 4 and later, so we need to prevent earlier browsers from running this code. Rather than checking specifically for these browsers using the techniques we discussed in Chapter 6, we can use object detection. If the `document.images` object is available, we know we're dealing with a browser that supports dynamic images.

Once we've created our two `Image` objects in memory, we need to create a physical image object on the page using the `img` tag. The preloaded images will be displayed where we place this image tag. Let's name it cupholder and use the coffee cup image, *cupajoe.gif*, as its (initial) image file. To make the image change when the mouse moves over it, we surround it with a link and add some event handlers.

Versions of Netscape Navigator earlier than 3 and of Internet Explorer before Version 4 do not handle dynamic images.

The first of these event handlers, `onMouseOver` (which is triggered when the mouse moves over the image), changes cupholder's source to cupsteam's source (*cupajoesteam.gif*), again if the `document.images` object exists. If the user moves the mouse over the coffee cup image, steam starts to rise from it. The second event handler, `onMouseOut` (which is triggered when the mouse moves off the image), changes cupholder's image back to cup's source (*cupajoe.gif*). So, when the user moves the mouse off the image, the steam rising from the coffee cup suddenly disappears.

This is a basic example of dynamic images in action; the scripts in the rest of this chapter expand upon this technique and show you some real-world examples.

Image rollovers

For some reason, people love images that change when the mouse is moved over them. Maybe it's because the "rollover" effect is used in so many desktop programs and multimedia titles, or perhaps it signifies to users, "Yes, something will happen if you click here." Or maybe people just like eye candy. Whatever the reason, image rollovers are an interesting effect to add to your site.

One of the most compelling examples of the rollover is the combination of a static image and an animated image (an animated GIF). To illustrate this, let's take a look at Kids Domain (*http://www.kidsdomain.com*), a children's web site that does a great job of making their pages fun, as shown in Figure 7-2.

When the user first enters the site, all the image links are static. When the user rolls over the image links, however, that quickly changes. If the mouse is moved over the Download link, for example, the stars behind the spaceship suddenly start spinning. Move over to the KD UK link, and

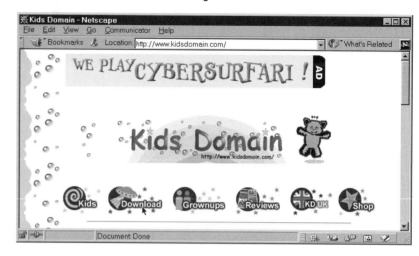

Figure 7-2

The Kids Domain web site's animated GIF image rollovers

the stars behind the Union Jack start to spin. The other links are animated in a similar way, reinforcing that they are all active and clickable.

How does this work? The basic technique is the one we already saw in
Example 7-1, but there are more images involved. There are a total of six
rollovers, each consisting of two image files, one active image and one
inactive. And each active image is actually an animated GIF, so it's *really*
active.

Creating the images

Let's create a page that can display six rollovers, like the Kids Domain
page. As in the previous example, we need to preload all the images,
active and inactive alike, by creating Image objects for all our images, as
shown in Example 7-2.

Example 7-2: Creating the Image objects

```
if (document.images) {
    // Six image objects for the active images
    var img1on = new Image( );
    img1on.src = "kidson.gif";
    var img2on = new Image( );
    img2on.src = "downloadson.gif";
    var img3on = new Image( );
    img3on.src = "grownupson.gif";
    var img4on = new Image( );
    img4on.src = "reviewson.gif";
    var img5on = new Image( );
    img5on.src = "ukon.gif";
    var img6on = new Image( );
    img6on.src = "shopon.gif";
```

Example 7-2: Creating the Image objects (continued)

```
    // Six image objects for the inactive images
    var img1off = new Image( );
    img1off.src = "kidsoff.gif";
    var img2off = new Image( );
    img2off.src = "downloadsoff.gif";
    var img3off = new Image( );
    img3off.src = "grownupsoff.gif";
    var img4off = new Image( );
    img4off.src = "reviewsoff.gif";
    var img5off = new Image( );
    img5off.src = "ukoff.gif";
    var img6off = new Image( );
    img6off.src = "shopoff.gif";
}
```

As in Example 7-1, we check for the existence of document.images before creating our images. The first set of Image objects, beginning with img1on, preloads the image files that are displayed when the mouse moves over a given rollover. Notice that the variable names for these Image objects have the same suffix: "on". The actual image files that correspond to these Image objects also have similar names (e.g., *kidson.gif* with img1on), but they don't need to.

The second set of Image objects, beginning with img1off, preloads the image files that are displayed when the mouse is moved off a given rollover. Notice they share a similar suffix as well: "off". As you can see, the source for img1on is *kidson.gif;* the source for img1off is *kidsoff.gif*, and so on. The names of all the variables for the Image objects (img1on, img1off, etc.) should be left unchanged, because they are critical to the operation of the rollover script, as you'll see shortly.

Displaying the images

After we've preloaded all the images, we need to place them and their links on the page, as shown in Example 7-3.

Example 7-3: Creating an image and its link with event handlers

```
<a href="kids.html"
    onMouseOver="imgOn('img1');"
    onMouseOut="imgOff('img1');">
<img name="img1" border="0" height="52" width="86" src="kidsoff.gif"></a>
```

Because "Kids" is the first rollover in the menu, its name attribute is set to img1. Notice that the onMouseOver and onMouseOut event handlers pass the name of the image to two functions, imgOn( ) and imgOff( ), which we'll get to in the next section. Also note that the src attribute in the img tag is set to inactive image, since we want to display the inactive state when the page loads. We obviously need five more images (and links), named img2, img3, etc., to complete the page.

Please, sir, may I have some more?

If you want to add more rollovers to a page, you need to follow the naming scheme for adding more on and off Image objects. For example, if you need seven rollovers instead of six, you can add one like this:

```
var img7on = new Image( );
img7on.src =
    "anotherimageon.gif";
var img7off = new Image( );
img7off.src =
    "anotherimageoff.gif";
```

Dynamic Images

Roll over!

When the user moves the mouse over an image, the onMouseOver event handler for that image runs the imgOn( ) function, shown in Example 7-4.

Example 7-4: The imgOn( ) function

```
function imgOn(imgName) {
    if (document.images) {
        document.images[imgName].src = eval(imgName + "on.src");
    }
```

This function takes one argument, imgName, which is the name of the image to be activated (e.g., img1). If the browser supports document. images, the function changes the source of the image specified in imgName by adding the "on" suffix to it. For example, when the mouse is moved over the first rollover, "Kids", imgOn( ) is passed the name img1. When the "on" suffix is added to that name, the result is img1on, which is the name of the active image object for the "Kids" rollover (see Example 7-2). Note that we actually use the eval( ) function to combine the image name and the "on" suffix; this is just a bit of required JavaScript magic that makes this script work properly.

Once the name of the Image object is determined, the physical image on the page, document.images[img1], is changed to that image file. document. images is an array of all the images on the page; by specifying img1 as the array index, we can access the image named img1. So, in the case of the "Kids" link, imgOn( ) changes the image source of img1 to the image that is stored in img1on.src, which is *kidson.gif*.

Conversely, when the mouse pointer is moved off the image, the function imgOff( ) is run. This function is shown in Example 7-5.

Example 7-5: The imgOff( ) function

```
function imgOff(imgName) {
    if (document.images) {
        document.images[imgName].src = eval(imgName + "off.src");
    }
}
```

The function imgOff( ) does the same thing that imgOn( ) does, except that it adds the "off" suffix to the name that it is passed, thus displaying the inactive image file—*kidsoff.gif*, in this case.

To put it all together, let's look at the complete source file, shown in Example 7-6.

Example 7-6: Complete source for the rollover page

```
<html>
<head>
<title>Image Rollovers</title>
<script language="JavaScript">
// Create image objects and preload all active and inactive images
```

Example 7-6: Complete source for the rollover page (continued)

```
if (document.images) {
    // Six image objects for the active images
    var img1on = new Image( );
    img1on.src = "kidson.gif";
    var img2on = new Image( );
    img2on.src = "downloadson.gif";
    var img3on = new Image( );
    img3on.src = "grownupson.gif";
    var img4on = new Image( );
    img4on.src = "reviewson.gif";
    var img5on = new Image( );
    img5on.src = "ukon.gif";
    var img6on = new Image( );
    img6on.src = "shopon.gif";

    // Six image objects for the inactive images
    var img1off = new Image( );
    img1off.src = "kidsoff.gif";
    var img2off = new Image( );
    img2off.src = "downloadsoff.gif";
    var img3off = new Image( );
    img3off.src = "grownupsoff.gif";
    var img4off = new Image( );
    img4off.src = "reviewsoff.gif";
    var img5off = new Image( );
    img5off.src = "ukoff.gif";
    var img6off = new Image( );
    img6off.src = "shopoff.gif";
}

// Function to activate an image
function imgOn(imgName) {
    if (document.images) {
        document.images[imgName].src = eval(imgName + "on.src");
    }
}

// Function to deactivate an image
function imgOff(imgName) {
    if (document.images) {
        document.images[imgName].src = eval(imgName + "off.src");
    }
}
</script>
</head>

<body bgcolor="#FFFFFF">
<a href="kids.html"
   onMouseOver="imgOn('img1');" onMouseOut="imgOff('img1');">
<img name="img1" border="0" height="52" width="86"
     src="kidsoff.gif"></a>
<a href="downloads.html"
   onMouseOver="imgOn('img2');" onMouseOut="imgOff('img2');">
<img name="img2" border="0" height="52" width="86"
     src="downloadsoff.gif"></a>
<a href="grownups.html"
   onMouseOver="imgOn('img3');" onMouseOut="imgOff('img3');">
<img name="img3" border="0" height="52" width="86"
     src="grownupsoff.gif"></a>
<a href="reviews.html"
   onMouseOver="imgOn('img4');" onMouseOut="imgOff('img4');">
<img name="img4" border="0" height="52" width="86"
     src="reviewsoff.gif"></a>
```

Example 7-6: Complete source for the rollover page (continued)

```
<a href="uk.html"
    onMouseOver="imgOn('img5');" onMouseOut="imgOff('img5');">
<img name="img5" border="0" height="52" width="86"
    src="ukoff.gif"></a>
<a href="shop.html"
    onMouseOver="imgOn('img6');" onMouseOut="imgOff('img6');">
<img name="img6" border="0" height="52" width="86"
    src="shopoff.gif"></a>
</body>
</html>
```

First, we use object detection to see if the browser supports dynamic images. Next, we create `Image` objects for the six "active" images and the six "inactive" images. Then we define the `imgOn( )` and `imgOff( )` functions, and, finally, we create the links. In each link, `imgOn( )` is run when the user places the mouse over the image, and `imgOff( )` is run when the mouse leaves the image. The first link passes `img1` to these functions; the second link passes `img2` to the functions, and so on.

The function `imgOn( )`, which is invoked by the `onMouseOver` handler, changes the image to the source for the "on" `Image` object (`img1on.src`, `img2on.src`, etc.). The function `imgOff( )`, which is triggered by the `onMouseOut` event handler, changes the image to the source for the "off" `Image` object (`img1off.src`, `img2off.src`, etc.). Thus, putting the mouse over the link displays the active image and moving the mouse off the image displays the inactive image.

Multiple rollovers

Playing around with one image at a time is okay, but how about two images, or three, or more? A good example of multiple images reacting to one action can be found at T.G.I. Friday's web site (*http://www.tgifridays. com*). The menu along the left of T.G.I. Friday's page represents the different areas of their site. As the user moves the mouse over each menu item, the image lights up, highlighting it as in our previous rollover example. So far, so good. T.G.I. Friday's takes this concept one step further, however, by having each rollover change two images: the menu item itself and a banner in the middle of the page that describes where that menu item leads, as shown in Figure 7-3.

So how does it work? As you can probably guess, it's similar to the rollover script, but with a few enhancements. In addition to the active and inactive images, the banner images also have to be preloaded. When the mouse is over one of the menu items, the appropriate banner graphic replaces the "In here it's always Friday" image in the middle of the page.

To handle two rollovers at once, all we need to do is add a few lines to our previous script. Example 7-7 shows a simple script that produces the effect seen on T.G.I. Friday's site.

Figure 7-3

A rollover triggering changes in two images

Example 7-7: Changing two images with one event

```
<html>
<head>
<title>Multiple Rollovers</title>
<script language="JavaScript">
// Create image objects and preload all active, inactive, and
// banner images
if (document.images) {
    // Active images
    var img1on = new Image();
    img1on.src = "hotstuffon.gif";
    var img2on = new Image();
    img2on.src = "webwisheson.gif";

    // Inactive images
    var img1off = new Image();
    img1off.src = "hotstuffoff.gif";
    var img2off = new Image();
    img2off.src = "webwishesoff.gif";

    // Banner images
    var img1banner = new Image();
    img1banner.src = "hotstuffbanner.gif";
    var img2banner = new Image();
    img2banner.src = "webwishesbanner.gif";
}

// Function to activate image and banner
function imgOn(imgName) {
    if (document.images) {
        document.images[imgName].src = eval(imgName + "on.src");
        document.banner.src = eval(imgName + "banner.src");
    }
}

// Function to deactivate image and banner
function imgOff(imgName) {
    if (document.images) {
```

Dynamic Images

Example 7-7: Changing two images with one event (continued)

```
          document.images[imgName].src = eval(imgName + "off.src");
          document.banner.src = "alwaysfriday.gif";
     }
}
</script>
</head>

<body bgcolor="#FFFFFF">
<!-- Hot Stuff Rollover -->
<a href="hotstuff.html"
   onMouseOver="imgOn('img1');" onMouseOut="imgOff('img1');">
<img name="img1" border="0" height="23" width="180"
     src="hotstuffoff.gif"></a>
<!-- Webwishes Rollover -->
<a href="webwishes.html"
   onMouseOver="imgOn('img2');" onMouseOut="imgOff('img2');">
<img name="img2" border="0" height="23" width="180"
     src="webwishesoff.gif"></a>
<!-- Default Banner Image -->
<img name="banner" height="115" width="322" src="alwaysfriday.gif">
</body>
</html>
```

First, we create Image objects for the active, inactive, and banner image files. For the sake of space, this script simulates only the first two rollovers in T.G.I. Friday's menu, "Hot Stuff" and "Friday's Webwishes." Like the active and inactive images, the variable names for the banner images all have the same suffix, "banner".

After we've created all the Image objects, we need to create the physical images on the page, using img tags and links. In addition to the inactive "Hot Stuff" and "Friday's Webwishes" images, we also have to create the default "In here it's always Friday" banner image. (In the real layout, these images are carefully organized with a table, but for our purposes it's not important.) Notice that the placeholder image is named banner; this is important for the new versions of imgOn( ) and imgOff( ) that support the banner rollovers.

The only difference between the new and old versions of imgOn( ) is the addition of one line:

```
document.banner.src = eval(imgName + "banner.src");
```

This line changes the banner image source, document.banner.src, to the banner image that corresponds to the menu item being rolled over. For instance, when the user moves the mouse over the "Hot Stuff" link, it passes its name, img1, to imgOn( ). As before, the "on" suffix is added to the name, and the active image is displayed. To change the banner image, the new line appends the "banner" suffix to the rollover's name (now it's img1banner), and the appropriate image is displayed in the middle of the page.

The modified imgOff( ) function has an added line that simply changes the banner image back to the default image, *alwaysfriday.gif*:

```
document.banner.src = "alwaysfriday.gif";
```

An image billboard

Take image replacement, a link, and three arrays, and what do you get? A JavaScript billboard. The billboard saves space and is useful and fun to look at. The JavaScript billboard is reminiscent of the billboards you pass as you drive home from work, except that it rotates and it's on your web site.

Figure 7-4 shows the images for a billboard that displays three different images, with a two-second delay between each image. Depending on which image users click on, they'll be brought to a different page.

There are three main parts to the billboard script: the images, the URLs, and the rotation function. Let's begin, as usual, by defining some variables for the billboard, as shown in Example 7-8. As with all of our dynamic images examples, the code is wrapped in an if statement that tests for the existence of document.images.

Example 7-8: Creating variables for the billboard

```
if (document.images) {
    var boardNum = 0;
    var boardSpeed = 2000;

    var billboard = new Array();
    billboard[0] = new Image();
    billboard[0].src = "java.gif";
    billboard[1] = new Image();
    billboard[1].src = "javascript.gif";
    billboard[2] = new Image();
    billboard[2].src = "mac.gif";

    var url = new Array();
    url[0] = "java/index.html";
    url[1] = "javascript/index.html";
    url[2] = "mac/index.html";
}
```

The first variable, boardNum, keeps track of which image/link combination the billboard is currently displaying. The second variable, boardSpeed, determines how long (in milliseconds) the billboard should display an individual image before switching to the next one. You can change this as you like.

Next, all of the billboard's images are preloaded in the form of an array of Image objects called billboard. These images are the essence of the billboard. You can use any number of images you want; this example uses only three. (If you want to add transitions to the display of each image, animated GIFs are your best bet.)

Once we've preloaded the images, we need to specify where we want them to link to when they are displayed in the billboard. As shown in Example 7-8, we've used another array, called url. Each of these URLs corresponds to an image in the billboard array; for instance, *java.gif* links to *java/index.html*.

Figure 7-4

Three images for a rotating billboard

Dynamic Images

Now that we have all of our data in arrays, it's time to create the rotation function that automates the billboard, as shown in Example 7-9.

Example 7-9: The rotation function

```
function rotateBoard( ) {
    if (boardNum < (billboard.length - 1)) {
        boardNum++;
    }
    else {
        boardNum = 0;
    }
    document.billboard.src = billboard[boardNum].src;
    setTimeout('rotateBoard( )', boardSpeed);
}
```

This function first checks whether the last image in the billboard array is currently displayed. The current billboard image is defined by boardNum. For example, if boardNum is 0, we are displaying the first billboard image; if it's 1, we're displaying the second, and so on. We can see if we're displaying the last image by checking boardNum against the length of the billboard array, minus 1 (to deal with the fact that we start counting at 0).

If we're not displaying the last image, boardNum is increased by 1, to point at the next image in the array. If we are displaying the last image, however, boardNum is set back to 0, so we can start the cycle again.

Now rotateBoard( ) uses the freshly calculated boardNum as an index into the billboard array, to assign the next image to document.billboard.src. This results in the display of the next billboard image.

Finally, the function uses setTimeout( ) to pause for a specified number of milliseconds (the value is in boardSpeed), after which the function is run again, repeating the process of changing the billboard image.

The last function, jumpBillboard( ), shown in Example 7-10, is very simple; it just brings the user to the proper URL when he clicks on the billboard.

Example 7-10: Function to load the correct URL when the user clicks on an image

```
function jumpBillboard( ) {
    window.location = url[boardNum];
}
```

The final step is to create an image for the billboard on the page, using the img tag and a link. The image must be named billboard, as shown in Example 7-11.

Example 7-11: Creating the image

```
<a href="javascript:jumpBillboard( );">
<img name="billboard" border="0" height="100" width="150"
    src="java.gif"></a>
```

Note that the href attribute of the link runs jumpBillboard( ) using the JavaScript pseudo-protocol. Thus, when a visitor clicks on the billboard, she is brought to the appropriate page (the one that corresponds to the currently displayed image).

Once we have the billboard on the page, all we need is a way to start it rotating. The best way to do this is to place an onLoad event handler inside the body tag, so that as soon as the document loads, the rotateBoard( ) function is run and the billboard starts rotating. The code for the entire billboard system is shown in Example 7-12.

Example 7-12: Complete code for the billboard rotation system

```
<html>
<head>
<title>The Billboard</title>
<script language="JavaScript">
if (document.images) {
    var boardNum = 0;
    var boardSpeed = 2000;

    // Create an array of images for the billboard
    var billboard = new Array( );
    billboard[0] = new Image( );
    billboard[0].src = "java.gif";
    billboard[1] = new Image( );
    billboard[1].src = "javascript.gif";
    billboard[2] = new Image( );
    billboard[2].src = "mac.gif";

    // Create an array of URLs that correspond to the images
    var url = new Array( );
    url[0] = "java/index.html";
    url[1] = "javascript/index.html";
    url[2] = "mac/index.html";
}

// Function to rotate the images on the billboard
function rotateBoard( ) {
    if (boardNum < (billboard.length - 1)) {
        boardNum++;
    }
    else {
        boardNum = 0;
    }
    document.billboard.src = billboard[boardNum].src;
    setTimeout('rotateBoard( )', boardSpeed);
}

// Function to load the appropriate URL when the user clicks on an image
function jumpBillboard( ) {
    window.location = url[boardNum];
}
</script>
</head>

<body bgcolor="#FFFFFF"
    onLoad="if (document.images) setTimeout('rotateBoard( )', boardSpeed);">
<!-- The billboard image and link -->
<a href="javascript:jumpBillboard( );">
<img name="billboard" border="0" height="100" width="150" src="java.gif"></a>
</body>
</html>
```

Chapter 8

Customizing a Site with Cookies

The infamous cookie. The cookie originated as an innocent device that web sites could use to remember things about an individual visitor. With cookies, site visitors were not just an anonymous crowd; they were individuals. A site could remember a user's name, his last visit, and even his favorite color. But soon the denizens of the Web realized they preferred to remain "anonymous surfing entities." In some circles, the cookie became as taboo as spam. It's up to you whether you wish to use cookies on your site. Either way, this chapter teaches you the basics and gets you started with a tasty group of examples.

What's a cookie?

A cookie is a small, customized piece of information that a web site stores on a visitor's hard drive. Through a web browser, a web page can store, retrieve, and delete cookies. A cookie has only one purpose: to remember information about an individual visitor.

Before you start working with cookies, there are a few rules of which you should be aware. First, web browsers are not required to store more than 300 cookies total, nor more than 20 cookies per web server (for the entire server, not just for your page or site on the server). Storage is also limited to a maximum of 4 kilobytes per cookie, so you have to be careful not to try to store too much information in a cookie.

By default, a cookie lasts for the duration of the web browser session; it is lost when the user exits the browser. To make a cookie last beyond a single browsing session, we can set an expiration date, which is what actually causes the browser to store the cookie on the user's hard drive. Figure 8-1 shows what the contents of a cookie file look like, in case you are curious.

A cookie is a small, customized piece of information that a web site stores on a visitor's hard drive.

Figure 8-1

Contents of a cookie file

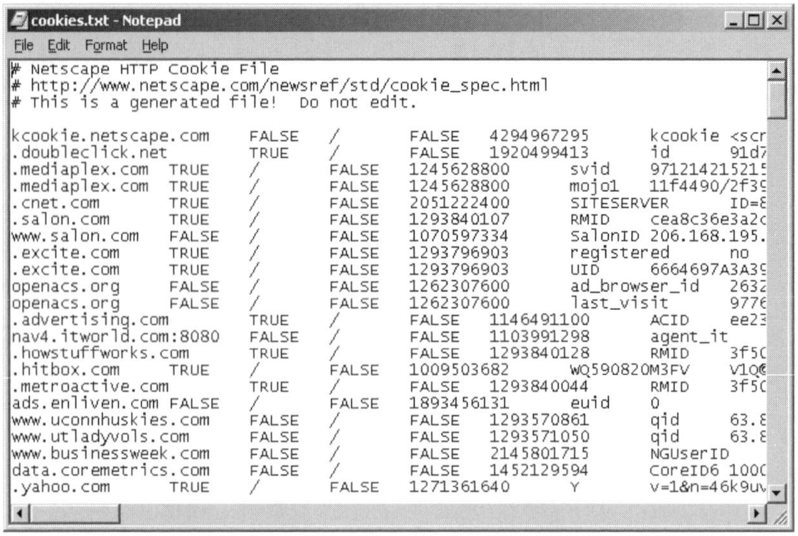

```
cookies.txt - Notepad                                          _ □ ×
File   Edit   Format   Help
# Netscape HTTP Cookie File
# http://www.netscape.com/newsref/std/cookie_spec.html
# This is a generated file!   Do not edit.

kcookie.netscape.com    FALSE    /       FALSE   4294967295           kcookie  <scr
.doubleclick.net        TRUE     /       FALSE   1920499413           id        91d7
.mediaplex.com  TRUE    /       FALSE   1245628800      svid      97121421521£
.mediaplex.com  TRUE    /       FALSE   1245628800      mojo1     11f4490/2f39
.cnet.com       TRUE    /       FALSE   2051222400      SITESERVER      ID=£
.salon.com      TRUE    /       FALSE   1293840107      RMID      cea8c36e3a2c
www.salon.com   FALSE   /       FALSE   1070597334      SalonID 206.168.195.
.excite.com     TRUE    /       FALSE   1293796903      registered      no
.excite.com     TRUE    /       FALSE   1293796903      UID       6664697A3A39
openacs.org     FALSE   /       FALSE   1262307600      ad_browser_id    2632
openacs.org     FALSE   /       FALSE   1262307600      last_visit       977£
.advertising.com        TRUE    /       FALSE   1146491100      ACID      ee23
nav4.itworld.com:8080   FALSE   /       FALSE   1103991298      agent_it
.howstuffworks.com      TRUE    /       FALSE   1293840128      RMID      3f5C
.hitbox.com     TRUE    /       FALSE   1009503682      WQ590820M3FV     V1Q£
.metroactive.com        TRUE    /       FALSE   1293840044      RMID      3f5C
ads.enliven.com FALSE   /       FALSE   1893456131      euid      0
www.uconnhuskies.com    FALSE   /       FALSE   1293570861      qid       63.£
www.utladyvols.com      FALSE   /       FALSE   1293571050      qid       63.£
www.businessweek.com    FALSE   /       FALSE   2145801715      NGUserID
data.coremetrics.com    FALSE   /       FALSE   1452129594      CoreID6 100C
.yahoo.com      TRUE    /       FALSE   1271361640      Y       v=1&n=46k9uv
```

Basic cookie operations

Like almost everything else in JavaScript, cookies are accessible through an object, document.cookie. Note that document.cookie does not connect you directly to the user's hard drive; it merely reflects all the cookies stored there. While you can work directly with the document.cookie object, I've written three commonly used functions to save you the trouble: setCookie(), getCookie(), and deleteCookie().

Saving a cookie

The setCookie() function, shown in Example 8-1, can be used to create a cookie and then save a value to that cookie. This is the function you'll use when you need to store the user's name in a cookie, for example.

Example 8-1: The setCookie() function

```
function setCookie(name, value, expires) {
    document.cookie = escape(name) + "=" + escape(value) + "; path=/" +
        ((expires == null) ? "" : "; expires=" + expires.toGMTString());
}
```

Don't worry about understanding how setCookie() works; the whole point of the function is to hide the details of document.cookie and just let you set cookies.

To use this function properly, you need to pass it three things: a name for the cookie, a value to store in the cookie, and an expiration date. The name and the value are easy; just pass in the appropriate strings. The

NOTE

Where do you keep your cookies?

The location of cookies on your hard drive depends on your platform and browser. If you are running Netscape Navigator on a Windows machine, look for a file called *cookies.txt* in Navigator's program directory. If you're running Navigator on a Mac, you'll find a file called *MagicCookie* in Navigator's program folder. If you are running Microsoft Internet Explorer on a Windows machine, you will find all your cookies stored in separate files in the *Windows\Cookies* directory. With IE 5 on a Mac, in the Internet Explorer 5 Folder, look for a *Cookies* file under Preference Panels.

expiration date takes a little more work, because it needs to be specified as a Date object. Example 8-2 shows the code for setting a cookie with an expiration date that is 31 days in the future.

Example 8-2: Setting the expiration date 31 days in the future

```
var exp = new Date( );
exp.setTime(exp.getTime( ) + (1000 * 60 * 60 * 24 * 31));
setCookie("myname", "Bill", exp);
```

First, we create a new Date object, called exp. Then we take the current time in milliseconds, found with exp.getTime( ), and add the equivalent of 31 more days. Once you have the expiration date, you can create the cookie by running setCookie( ) and passing it three things: a name ("myname"), a value ("Bill"), and the expiration date (exp).

Retrieving a cookie

Once you have a cookie saved, you need a way to retrieve it. The getCookie( ) function, shown in Example 8-3, scans through the document.cookie object until it finds the cookie in question and then returns that cookie's value.

Example 8-3: The getCookie( ) function

```
function getCookie(name) {
    var cookiename = name + "=";
    var dc = document.cookie;
    var begin, end;

    if (dc.length > 0) {
        begin = dc.indexOf(cookiename);
        if (begin != -1) {
            begin += cookiename.length;
            end = dc.indexOf(";", begin);
            if (end == -1) {
                end = dc.length;
            }
            return unescape(dc.substring(begin, end));
        }
    }
    return null;
}
```

Though getCookie( ) is clearly more complex than setCookie( ), it's easier to use. To retrieve the value of the cookie named "myname", just pass the name to getCookie( ):

```
getCookie("myname");
```

If the cookie exists, its value is returned; otherwise, null is returned. You can treat getCookie( ) like a variable; passing it, displaying it, and so on. To display the value of the cookie on the page, for example, combine it with document.write( ):

```
document.write(getCookie("myname"));
```

> **NOTE**
>
> ## Days of milliseconds
>
> 31 days in milliseconds is found by multiplying 1000 milliseconds by 60 seconds by 60 minutes by 24 hours by 31 days. To set your cookie to expire in a year, for example, change the 31 to 365.

Customizing a Site with Cookies

Get out of the cookie jar!

How is an individual cookie retrieved? It all happens within the getCookie( ) function. Although it looks complex, the logic is quite simple. For easy reference, here's the function again:

```
function getCookie(name) {
    var cookiename = name + "=";
    var dc = document.cookie;
    var begin, end;

    if (dc.length > 0) {
        begin = dc.indexOf(cookiename);
        if (begin != -1) {
            begin += cookiename.length;
            end = dc.indexOf(";", begin);
            if (end == -1) {
                end = dc.length;
            }
            return unescape(dc.substring(begin, end));
        }
    }
    return null;
}
```

First, you need to understand that the document.cookie object is just a string of text reflecting the names and values of the cookies stored on the user's hard drive. Here is a sample document.cookie object showing what we're really dealing with:

```
dummycookie=dummyvalue; myname=myvalue;
anotherdummy=anothervalue;
```

(We'll use this dummy document.cookie information for the rest of this example.) As you can see, document.cookie contains a long string of names and values. The name and value of each cookie are separated by an equal sign, and the individual cookies are separated by semicolons. This is a reflection of the cookies on the hard drive, filtered through the document.cookie object.

Only cookies created by your web server (or more precisely, your domain, such as *whatever.com*) will appear in document.cookie; all the rest are hidden to prevent you from stealing other domains' cookies. The getCookie( ) function searches through this string of text, finds the correct cookie name ("myname"), and retrieves the cookie's value ("myvalue").

To begin with, the function adds an equal sign to the name of the cookie you are trying to retrieve. If you are looking for "myname", the name becomes "myname=". This new name is assigned to the variable cookiename.

Next, document.cookie (the long string of cookie names and values created by your domain) is assigned to the variable dc (from now on, document.cookie will be referred to as dc). This is to keep us from repeatedly accessing document.cookie, which can be slow, and to cut down on the typing needed to write the function.

An if statement then determines if anything exists in dc, by verifying that the length (in characters of text) is greater than 0. If the length of dc is 0, there are no cookies, and the function skips everything else and returns null. If the length is greater than 0, the function continues.

Next, the indexOf( ) method is used on dc to find the location of the cookie's name. (indexOf( ) is discussed in the "That's not an email address!" section of Chapter 4.) If the cookie name is found using indexOf( ), the location of the start of the name in characters is given to the variable begin. This is very important: begin is being used to mark the location of the cookie's name, and ultimately the cookie's value, inside the string of cookie names and values. Think back to our dc object. If it looks like this:

```
dummycookie=dummyvalue; myname=myvalue;
anotherdummy=anothervalue;
```

and if cookiename (the cookie's name) is "myname=", begin equals 24 (remember, counting starts with 0). If you count the number of characters from the beginning of dc to the first character in "myname=", you will come up with 24, the exact location of the cookie's name in dc.

If indexOf( ) does not find the cookie name in dc, it gives begin a value of -1. If begin is -1, the function returns null.

If the name is found, begin is increased by the length of the cookie name, cookiename. For your cookie, whose name is "myname=" and is seven characters long, begin is now 31. If you count 31 characters from the beginning of dc, you will find that you end up right on the value of your cookie.

Now that the function knows where the value of the cookie begins, it needs to figure out where it ends. Since all cookies in dc are separated by semicolons, the cookie—and therefore its value—must end at a semicolon. indexOf( ) performs a search on dc again, but this time it's searching for a semicolon. Another difference is that the search starts at begin, the beginning of the cookie's value. The placement of the semicolon (the end of the cookie's value) is assigned to the variable end. In our example, end is 38, the location of the semicolon following "myvalue".

Both the beginning and the end of the cookie's value have been determined, so it's a simple task to grab the value in between. Using the substring( ) method on dc, the value of the cookie is finally extracted and returned.

This displays the value of the "myname" cookie: "Bill". As you will see later in this chapter, you can do much more than simply display a cookie's value on the page.

Deleting a cookie

The deleteCookie() function, shown in Example 8-4, deletes a cookie from the cookie file.

Example 8-4: The deleteCookie() function

```
function deleteCookie(name) {
    document.cookie = name + "=; expires=Thu, 01-Jan-70 00:00:01 GMT" +
        "; path=/";
}
```

Just pass deleteCookie() the name of the cookie you want deleted, and the function does the rest. It sets your doomed cookie's value to nothing and its expiration date to a past date, thus deleting the cookie. Use it like this:

```
deleteCookie("myname");
```

Now that you know how to set, get, and delete cookies, what do you do with these new abilities? The scripts in the rest of this chapter provide you with some useful examples of cookies in action. Before you jump into those scripts, though, experiment with the cookies template document, shown in Example 8-5. Remember, to access cookies through JavaScript, you need to use a combination of these three functions in your documents.

Example 8-5: Template for saving, retrieving, and deleting cookies

```
<html>
<head>
<title>The Cookie Jar</title>
<script language="JavaScript">
// Function to create a cookie and set its value
function setCookie(name, value, expires) {
    document.cookie = escape(name) + "=" + escape(value) + "; path=/" +
        ((expires == null) ? "" : "; expires=" + expires.toGMTString());
}

// Function to retrieve a cookie's value
function getCookie(name) {
    var cookiename = name + "=";
    var dc = document.cookie;
    var begin, end;

    if (dc.length > 0) {
        begin = dc.indexOf(cookiename);
        if (begin != -1) {
            begin += cookiename.length;
            end = dc.indexOf(";", begin);
            if (end == -1) {
                end = dc.length;
            }
            return unescape(dc.substring(begin, end));
```

Example 8-5: Template for saving, retrieving, and deleting cookies (continued)

```
        }
    }
    return null;
}

// Function to delete a cookie
function deleteCookie(name) {
    document.cookie = name + "=; expires=Thu, 01-Jan-70 00:00:01 GMT" +
        "; path=/";
}
</script>
</head>

<body bgcolor="#FFFFFF">
<script language= "JavaScript">
var exp = new Date( );
exp.setTime(exp.getTime( ) + (1000 * 60 * 60 * 24 * 31));
setCookie("myname", "Bill Gates", exp);
document.write(getCookie("myname"));
deleteCookie("myname");
</script>
</body>
</html>
```

A welcome for new visitors

Distinguishing between new visitors and long-time regulars is a perfect job for cookies.

Most sites make no distinction between new visitors and longtime regulars. But wouldn't it be nice to take new visitors by the hand, show them around your site, and get them oriented? That's a perfect job for cookies. In this script, we're going to determine automatically whether someone has visited the site before and create a special welcome message for new visitors. A good example of this is My Yahoo!, which identifies new users and gives them guidance about viewing the site. Figure 8-2 shows My Yahoo!'s welcome screen.

Do I know you?

Let's create a script that presents a welcome message to new users. Our script makes use of only one cookie, which we'll call the "welcome" cookie. There are three possible values for this cookie:

- The value "welcome" means the visitor has been to the site before but still wants to be welcomed.

- The value "nowelcome" means the visitor has been to the site before and does not want to be welcomed again.

- A null value means the welcome cookie does not exist and, therefore, that the visitor has never been to the site (or, to be more precise, that the browser has not been to the site, since it's the browser that stores cookies). Or it could mean that the browser has not been to the site since the last cookie expired, or that the user has deleted her cookies, or that the user is running the browser with cookies disabled. In any event, the cookie doesn't exist.

Figure 8-2

My Yahoo! welcome screen for new users

Let's begin by defining some variables for the cookie, as shown in Example 8-6. The first task is to set the expiration date of the welcome cookie and assign it to exp. In this example, the welcome cookie's expiration date is one year. We've also stored the cookie's name in the variable cookieName; it doesn't need to be changed. The most important variable is theMessage, which contains the HTML that first-time visitors will see.

Example 8-6: Defining the name, value, and expiration date for a cookie

```
var exp = new Date();
exp.setTime(exp.getTime() + (24 * 60 * 60 * 1000 * 365));
var cookieName = "welcome";
var theMessage = "Since this is your first time here...";
```

Displaying the welcome message

Now we need to create a function that determines whether the visitor is new and, if so, displays the welcome message. This function, called showWelcome( ), is shown in Example 8-7.

Example 8-7: The showWelcome() function

```
function showWelcome() {
    if (getCookie(cookieName) == null ||
      getCookie(cookieName) == "welcome") {
        setCookie(cookieName, "welcome", exp);
        document.write(theMessage);
    }
    else {
        setCookie(cookieName, "nowelcome", exp);
    }
}
```

If a visitor has never been to your site before, the welcome cookie will be null because it doesn't exist. Thus, if the cookie value is null or "welcome", the welcome message is displayed using document.write( ), and the welcome cookie is reset to "welcome" so it doesn't expire (at least not for 365 more days). If the welcome cookie is set to "nowelcome", the cookie is reset to that same value to keep it fresh.

Toggling the welcome display

So how do we allow the user to turn the welcome cookie off (e.g., set its value to "nowelcome")? We need to create a function to change the value of the welcome cookie. This function, toggleWelcome( ), is shown in Example 8-8. Whenever this function runs, it uses an if statement to toggle the value of the welcome cookie between "welcome" and "nowelcome". In other words, it toggles the display of the welcome message.

Example 8-8: The toggleWelcome( ) function

```
function toggleWelcome( ) {
    if (getCookie(cookieName) == "welcome") {
        setCookie(cookieName, "nowelcome", exp);
    }
    else {
        setCookie(cookieName, "welcome", exp);
    }
}
```

Figure 8-3

Checkbox allowing users to disable the welcome message on future visits

toggleWelcome( ) works in conjunction with the showForm( ) function, shown in Example 8-9. This function displays a small form that allows visitors to disable the welcome message, as shown in Figure 8-3. If the welcome cookie is null or "welcome", the form and its accompanying text (which you can modify) are displayed. The form is simply a single checkbox that runs toggleWelcome( ) via the onClick event handler each time the box is clicked.

Example 8-9: The showForm( ) function

```
function showForm( ) {
    if (getCookie(cookieName) == null ||
      getCookie(cookieName) == "welcome") {
        document.write('<form><input type="checkbox"');
        document.write('onClick="toggleWelcome( );">');
        document.write('Don\'t show this welcome message again.</form>');
    }
}
```

The whole welcome script is put together in Example 8-10. Notice that there's an extra script tag at the beginning of the code. This script tag uses the src attribute to include the file *cookies.js*, which contains the setCookie( ), getCookie( ), and deleteCookie( ) functions. We've put these functions in a separate file so that we can include them in other scripts that need to use them. Then we don't have to include the code itself in every script that needs to use cookies; we can just use a `script` tag with a `src` attribute instead.

Also note that the welcome message and toggle form are displayed where you run showWelcome( ) and showForm( ). This puts most of your code in the head of your document, out of the way of your HTML.

Example 8-10: Source code for the welcome application

```html
<html>
<head>
<title>Welcome!</title>
<!-- Include cookies functions -->
<script language="JavaScript" src="cookies.js"></script>

<script language="JavaScript">
// Function to display welcome message if the visitor is new
function showWelcome( ) {
    if (getCookie(cookieName) == null ||
      getCookie(cookieName) == "welcome") {
        setCookie(cookieName, "welcome", exp);
        document.write(theMessage);
    }
    else {
        setCookie(cookieName, "nowelcome", exp);
    }
}

// Function to toggle the welcome message
function toggleWelcome( ) {
    if (getCookie(cookieName) == "welcome") {
        setCookie(cookieName, "nowelcome", exp);
    }
    else {
        setCookie(cookieName, "welcome", exp);
    }
}

// Function to display a form that allows welcome message to be toggled
function showForm( ) {
    if (getCookie(cookieName) == null ||
      getCookie(cookieName) == "welcome") {
        document.write('<form><input type="checkbox"');
        document.write('onClick="toggleWelcome( );">');
        document.write('Don\'t show this welcome message again.</form>');
    }
}

var exp = new Date( );
exp.setTime(exp.getTime( ) + (24 * 60 * 60 * 1000 * 365));
var cookieName = "welcome";

// Your welcome message
var theMessage = "Since this is your first time here...";
</script>
</head>

<body bgcolor="#FFFFFF">
<script language="JavaScript">
// Place this where you want the welcome message to be displayed
showWelcome( );
</script>
```

Customizing a Site with Cookies

Example 8-10: Source code for the welcome application (continued)

```
<script language="JavaScript">
// Place this where you want the toggle button to be displayed
showForm( );
</script>
</body>
</html>
```

Forms that remember

Have you ever been in the process of filling out a lengthy form, with only a few more elements to complete, when your laptop shuts down suddenly due to a low battery? Or perhaps you've joined a new web community that requires you to enter your user ID and password every time you want to access members-only chat areas. How frustrating!

These scenarios and many others could be handled better with form elements that remember what the user typed. Making form elements remember input is not a complicated process. First, we need to place the following event handlers inside the body of the document that contains the form elements:

```
<body onLoad="getValues( );" onUnload="setValues( );">
```

The onLoad event handler is triggered when the page finishes loading. The onUnload event handler is triggered when the browser unloads the page.

The onLoad and onUnload event handlers are complementary: the onLoad handler is triggered when the browser finishes loading a page, and the onUnload handler is triggered whenever the browser unloads a document (i.e., before it moves to a new page). onUnload runs a function, setValues( ), that stores the user's information in a cookie whenever the user leaves the page. When the user returns to the page, the onLoad event handler calls getValues( ), which retrieves the form data from cookies and inserts it into the appropriate elements.

Place setValues( ) and getValues( ) in the head of the document. Example 8-11 shows these two functions.

Example 8-11: The setValues( ) and getValues( ) functions

```
function setValues( ) {
    // Set cookie values from form data
    setCookie(reg.yourname.name, reg.yourname.value, exp);
    setCookie(reg.yourid.name, reg.yourid.value, exp);
    setCookie(reg.yourpassword.name, reg.yourpassword.value, exp);
}

function getValues( ) {
    // Get cookie values
    var namevalue = getCookie(reg.yourname.name);
    var idvalue = getCookie(reg.yourid.name);
    var passwordvalue = getCookie(reg.yourpassword.name);

    // Display values in form if they exist
    if (namevalue != null) {
        reg.yourname.value = namevalue;
    }
    if (idvalue != null) {
        reg.yourid.value = idvalue;
```

Example 8-11: The setValues( ) and getValues( ) functions (continued)

```
    }
    if (namevalue != null) {
        reg.yourpassword.value = passwordvalue;
    }
}
```

The setValues( ) function creates three cookies, one for each form element, using the form element name as the cookie name (e.g., reg.yourname.name) and the element value as the cookie value (e.g., reg.yourname.value).

The complementary getValues( ) function uses the form element names to retrieve the previously stored values with the getCookie( ) function. Each value is stored in a separate variable (e.g., namevalue), and getValues( ) then checks each variable to see if it has a value. If the value is not null—that is, if there is a cookie with a value for the form element—the value of the form element is set to the stored value, thereby displaying the saved value in the form element.

Figure 8-4 shows the form with text displayed in some of the fields. Example 8-12 lists the code for the entire form. The setValues( ) and getValues( ) functions rely on getCookie( ) and setCookie( ), so we again include those functions with a script tag that uses the src attribute.

Example 8-12: Source code for a form that remembers

```
<html>
<head>
<title>A Form That Remembers</title>
<!-- Include cookies functions -->
<script language="JavaScript" src="cookies.js"></script>

<script language="JavaScript">
// Function to save form's values
function setValues( ) {
    // Set cookie values from form data
    setCookie(reg.yourname.name, reg.yourname.value, exp);
    setCookie(reg.yourid.name, reg.yourid.value, exp);
    setCookie(reg.yourpassword.name, reg.yourpassword.value, exp);
}

// Function to retrieve form's values
function getValues( ) {
    // Get cookie values
    var namevalue = getCookie(reg.yourname.name);
    var idvalue = getCookie(reg.yourid.name);
    var passwordvalue = getCookie(reg.yourpassword.name);

    // Display values in form if they exist
    if (namevalue != null) {
        reg.yourname.value = namevalue;
    }
    if (idvalue != null) {
        reg.yourid.value = idvalue;
    }
    if (passwordvalue != null) {
        reg.yourpassword.value = passwordvalue;
    }
}
```

Figure 8-4

A form that remembers

Customizing a Site with Cookies

Example 8-12: Source code for a form that remembers (continued)

```
var exp = new Date();
exp.setTime(exp.getTime() + (1000 * 60 * 60 * 24 * 31));
</script>
</head>

<body bgcolor="#FFFFFF" onLoad="getValues();" onUnload="setValues();">
<form name="reg">
<p>
Your Name:
<input type="text" name="yourname"></p>
<p>
Your ID:
<input type="text" name="yourid"></p>
<p>
Your Password:
<input type="password" name="yourpassword"></p>
</form>
</body>
</html>
```

Customized pages

So far, you've seen how to customize a message based on whether you recognize a visitor and how to create a form that remembers the text the user has entered. This is just the tip of the iceberg of what's possible with cookies.

Where everybody knows your name

Customized pages, where the user can control appearance, layout, and content, are popular on many sites today, especially portals. Figure 8-5 shows a customized My Yahoo! page, for example.

To customize a My Yahoo! page, users need to fill out forms that specify their preferred content, appearance, and layout. This information is then used to generate the custom view of the site. Figure 8-6 shows My Yahoo!'s Choose Content form.

Cookies can play an integral role in creating customized pages for your visitors. Of course, My Yahoo! almost certainly doesn't use cookies to keep track of all the settings for every visitor; they probably use a single cookie and a very large database. In the one cookie/big database scenario, the cookie likely contains an ID number that is used to reference and retrieve user information in the database. But for a smaller site with fewer visitors, it's certainly feasible to build custom pages with cookies.

Conserving cookies

If you try to implement customized pages using the cookie techniques presented so far, you'll quickly find yourself using up the available cookies. Remember, you're only allowed to use 20 cookies per domain. This is not a problem when you're dealing with a few pieces of information, but

Figure 8-5

A customized My Yahoo! page

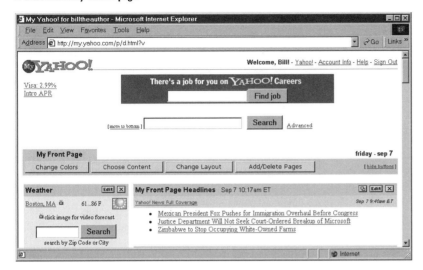

With the crumb technique, we can store several pieces of information within a single cookie.

Figure 8-6

My Yahoo!'s Choose Content form

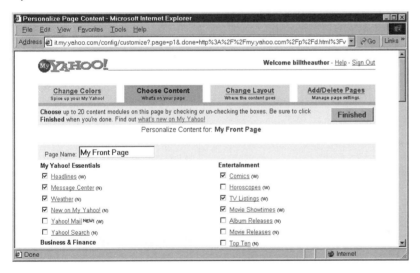

when keeping track of multiple content and layout settings, you have to manage your cookies carefully.

To conserve cookies, we can use a technique I call the crumb. With this technique, we can store several "crumbs" of information within an individual cookie. Example 8-13 shows the setCrumb( ), getCrumb( ), and deleteCrumb( ) functions. These functions rely on the getCookie( ) and setCookie( ) functions, so we have to remember to include those functions when we actually use this code.

Example 8-13: The setCrumb( ), getCrumb( ), and deleteCrumb( ) functions

```javascript
// Function to set crumb value in the cookie
function setCrumb(cookie, name, value) {
    var cookievalue = getCookie(cookie);
    var crumbvalue = getCrumb(name);
    var crumbname = name + '=';

    if (crumbvalue != null) {
        var start = cookievalue.indexOf(crumbname);
        if (start != -1) {
            var end = cookievalue.indexOf('|', start);
            setCookie(cookie,
                        cookievalue.substring(0, start) + crumbname
                        + value + '|'
                        + cookievalue.substring(end + 1, cookievalue.length),
                        exp);
        }
    }
    else {
        if (cookievalue != null) {
            cookievalue += crumbname + value + '|';
        }
        else {
            cookievalue = crumbname + value + '|';
        }
        setCookie(cookie, cookievalue, exp);
    }
}

// Function to get crumb value from the cookie
function getCrumb(cookie, name) {
    var crumbname = name + '=';
    var cookievalue = getCookie(cookie);

    if (cookievalue != null) {
        var start = cookievalue.indexOf(crumbname);
        if (start != -1) {
            start += crumbname.length;
            var end = cookievalue.indexOf('|', start);
            if (end != -1) {
                return unescape(cookievalue.substring(start, end));
            }
        }
    }
    return null;
}

// Function to delete crumb from the cookie
function deleteCrumb(cookie, name) {
    var cookievalue = getCookie(cookie);
    var crumbvalue = getCrumb(name);
    var crumbname = name + '=';

    if (crumbvalue != null) {
        var start = cookievalue.indexOf(crumbname);
        var end = cookievalue.indexOf('|', start);
        setCookie(cookie,
                    cookievalue.substring(0, start) +
                    cookievalue.substring(end + 1, cookievalue.length),
                    exp);
    }
}
```

The setCrumb( ) function takes a cookie name, a crumb name, and a value and stores the crumb name and value as part of the cookie string, using a vertical bar (|) to separate the crumbs stored in the cookie. setCrumb( ) also checks to see whether the crumb name already has a value, and, if so, it overwrites the previous value of that crumb. The getCrumb( ) function retrieves a crumb value, using the specified cookie and crumb names. Finally, deleteCrumb( ) deletes a crumb from a cookie.

The crumb name and value are stored as part of the cookie string, using a vertical bar to separate different crumbs.

Entertainment choices

Now let's put setCrumb( ) and getCrumb( ) to work by creating a page that lets the user choose among various types of entertainment content. Example 8-14 shows an HTML form that does just that.

Example 8-14: Form for selecting entertainment content

```
<script language="JavaScript">
// Set initial cookie value
var exp = new Date( );
exp.setTime(exp.getTime( ) + (1000 * 60 * 60 * 24 * 31));
setCookie("myname", "Bill", exp);

document.write("<h1>Welcome, " + getCookie("myname") + "</h1>")
</script>

<p>Please select the content you'd like on your page:</p>
<form name="choices" onSubmit="processChoices(this);">
<input type="checkbox" name="entertainment" value="comics">Comics<br>
<input type="checkbox" name="entertainment" value="horoscopes">
Horoscopes<br>
<input type="checkbox" name="entertainment" value="tv">TV Listings<br>
<input type="checkbox" name="entertainment" value="showtimes">Movie
Showtimes<br>
<input type="checkbox" name="entertainment" value="albums">Album
Releases<br>
<input type="checkbox" name="entertainment" value="movies">Movie
Releases<br>
<input type="checkbox" name="entertainment" value="topten">Top Ten<br>
<p><input type="submit" value="Finished">
</form>
```

This page first sets an initial value and expiration date for the "myname" cookie and then uses the value of the cookie to present a customized welcome message to the user. Obviously, in a real application, the value of this cookie would be set elsewhere (e.g., in a "Please enter your name" form), but we're going to cheat a little here for demonstration purposes.

The form is just a collection of checkboxes followed by a submit button. When the button is pressed, the form calls the processChoices( ) function, as specified by the onSubmit event handler. As shown in Example 8-15, processChoices( ) sets a crumb for each checkbox so we can keep track of which content options the user selected.

Example 8-15: The processChoices( ) function

```
function processChoices(form) {
    var choices = "";

    // Set "yes" or "no" crumb values for checkboxes
    for (i = 0; i < form.entertainment.length; i++) {
        if (form.entertainment[i].checked) {
            setCrumb("myname", form.entertainment[i].value, "yes");
        }
        else {
            setCrumb("myname", form.entertainment[i].value, "no");
        }
    }

    // Get crumb values to tell the user what was selected
    for (i = 0; i < form.entertainment.length; i++) {
        if (getCrumb("myname", form.entertainment[i].value) == "yes") {
            choices += form.entertainment[i].value + ", ";
        }
    }
    alert("You selected: " + choices.substring(0, choices.length - 2));
}
```

The processChoices( ) function takes a single argument: the form that is being submitted. The function loops through the checkboxes in the form, checking to see whether each one is checked. If the box is checked, processChoices( ) sets a crumb, using the value of the checkbox as the crumb's name and "yes" as the value. If the box isn't checked, the value is set to "no" instead.

processChoices( ) also displays the user's choices in an alert box, using getCrumb( ) to check for crumbs with the value "yes". Obviously, in a real application, you'd want to display customized content based on the user's choices, not just output them. But this code is helpful in showing how to use getCrumb( ) to access that information. You might also consider combining the techniques from this example with the form that remembers input, so the checkboxes are filled in appropriately whenever the user comes back to the form.

Figure 8-7 shows the form and alert box for our application. The whole script is put together in Example 8-16.

Figure 8-7

Entertainment choices

Example 8-16: Source code for the entertainment choices page

```html
<html>
<head>
<title>Entertainment Choices</title>
<!-- Include cookie functions -->
<script language="JavaScript" src="cookies.js"></script>

<script language="JavaScript">
// Function to set crumb value in the cookie
function setCrumb(cookie, name, value) {
    var cookievalue = getCookie(cookie);
    var crumbvalue = getCrumb(name);
    var crumbname = name + '=';

    if (crumbvalue != null) {
        var start = cookievalue.indexOf(crumbname);
        if (start != -1) {
            var end = cookievalue.indexOf('|', start);
            setCookie(cookie,
                    cookievalue.substring(0, start) + crumbname
                    + value + '|'
                    + cookievalue.substring(end + 1, cookievalue.length),
                    exp);
        }
    }
    else {
        if (cookievalue != null) {
            cookievalue += crumbname + value + '|';
        }
        else {
            cookievalue = crumbname + value + '|';
        }
        setCookie(cookie, cookievalue, exp);
```

Example 8-16: Source code for the entertainment choices page (continued)

```
        }
    }

    // Function to get crumb value from the cookie
    function getCrumb(cookie, name) {
        var crumbname = name + '=';
        var cookievalue = getCookie(cookie);

        if (cookievalue != null) {
            var start = cookievalue.indexOf(crumbname);
            if (start != -1) {
                start += crumbname.length;
                var end = cookievalue.indexOf('|', start);
                if (end != -1) {
                    return unescape(cookievalue.substring(start, end));
                }
            }
        }
        return null;
    }

    // Function to delete crumb from the cookie
    function deleteCrumb(cookie, name) {
        var cookievalue = getCookie(cookie);
        var crumbvalue = getCrumb(name);
        var crumbname = name + '=';

        if (crumbvalue != null) {
            var start = cookievalue.indexOf(crumbname);
            var end = cookievalue.indexOf('|', start);
            setCookie(cookie,
                    cookievalue.substring(0, start) +
                    cookievalue.substring(end + 1, cookievalue.length),
                    exp);
        }
    }

    // Function to set crumbs based on form choices
    function processChoices(form) {
        var choices = "";

        // Set "yes" or "no" crumb values for checkboxes
        for (i = 0; i < form.entertainment.length; i++) {
            if (form.entertainment[i].checked) {
                setCrumb("myname", form.entertainment[i].value, "yes");
            }
            else {
                setCrumb("myname", form.entertainment[i].value, "no");
            }
        }

        // Get crumb values to tell the user what was selected
        for (i = 0; i < form.entertainment.length; i++) {
            if (getCrumb("myname", form.entertainment[i].value) == "yes") {
                choices += form.entertainment[i].value + ", ";
            }
        }
        alert("You selected: " + choices.substring(0, choices.length - 2));
    }
</script>
</head>
```

Example 8-16: Source code for the entertainment choices page (continued)

```
<body>
<script language="JavaScript">
// Set initial cookie value
var exp = new Date( );
exp.setTime(exp.getTime( ) + (1000 * 60 * 60 * 24 * 31));
setCookie("myname", "Bill", exp);

document.write("<h1>Welcome, " + getCookie("myname") + "</h1>")
</script>

<p>Please select the content you'd like on your page:</p>
<form name="choices" onSubmit="processChoices(this);">
<input type="checkbox" name="entertainment" value="comics">Comics<br>
<input type="checkbox" name="entertainment" value="horoscopes">
Horoscopes<br>
<input type="checkbox" name="entertainment" value="tv">TV Listings<br>
<input type="checkbox" name="entertainment" value="showtimes">Movie
Showtimes<br>
<input type="checkbox" name="entertainment" value="albums">Album
Releases<br>
<input type="checkbox" name="entertainment" value="movies">Movie
Releases<br>
<input type="checkbox" name="entertainment" value="topten">Top Ten<br>
<p><input type="submit" value="Finished">
</form>
</body>
</html>
```

Chapter 9

Dynamic HTML

Take JavaScript's power over the page and square it: that's what you get with the capabilities of Dynamic HTML (DHTML). As we've seen with the examples in Chapter 7, being able to change an HTML element after the page has loaded can have a powerful visual impact. With DHTML, you can change almost any element on the page. This means you can make elements move, appear and disappear, overlap, change styles, and interact with the user. With DHTML, you can offer your visitors a more engaging and interactive web experience, without constant calls to the web server or the overhead of loading new pages, plugins, or Java applets.

In this chapter, we'll explore the basics of DHTML and use it to implement an interactive navigation toolbar and a tabbed folder interface. In Chapter 10, we'll move on to more advanced, interactive techniques and create drop-down menus, sliding navigation tabs, and scrolling headline tickers.

IN THIS CHAPTER

Understanding DHTML, the Document Object Model, and dynamic Cascading Style Sheets

Creating a dynamic toolbar

Understanding layers

Implementing tabbed folders with DHTML

Detecting browser versions for DHTML

What is DHTML?

DHTML is not actually a separate entity, but rather a combination of the following web technologies:

* HTML 4.0 (or XHTML 1.0)

* JavaScript

* The Document Object Model (DOM), a means of accessing a document's individual elements

* Cascading Style Sheets (CSS), styles dictated outside a document's content

As we've learned throughout this book, there is an object model in Java-Script—the JavaScript tree—that reflects the content of an HTML document and allows us to modify that content to a certain extent. Essentially, the Document Object Model is the evolution of the JavaScript tree, codified in a standard by the World Wide Web Consortium (W3C). The DOM

DHTML is a combination of HTML, JavaScript, the DOM, and CSS.

has greatly expanded the object model, encompassing almost every aspect of the page. With JavaScript, we can use the DOM to manipulate elements on the page. We'll talk more about the DOM in the next section.

Cascading Style Sheets is another W3C standard, used to specify the visual presentation of HTML (or XML) documents. With CSS, the goal is to separate the content of a web page, specified in HTML, from its appearance, which can be defined in a separate style sheet document. From a JavaScript perspective, what's interesting about CSS is that we can write scripts that change the appearance of the HTML elements on a page after the page has already been displayed. As you'll see shortly, this gives us dynamic control over fonts, colors, and more.

Netscape 6, IE 5.5, and IE 6 support the DOM and CSS standards quite well.

In the days before the W3C created the DOM, DHTML was a nebulous concept whose definition depended on your browser. Navigator 4 and IE 4 both introduced their own versions of DHTML and submitted their own proprietary DOMs to the W3C. As a result, creating DHTML was an arduous task that required making two versions of any dynamic content— one for each browser's DOM—doubling production time and making maintenance almost impossible.

At the time of this writing, Netscape 6, IE 5.5, and IE 6 support the DOM and CSS standards quite well, though not perfectly. Fortunately, both major browsers and others, such as Opera and Mozilla, have pledged continued support for W3C standards in all future browsers. That's not to say that different vendors won't add other proprietary extensions, but at least the techniques you'll learn here won't be obsolete next year. If you tried to use DHTML in its earlier incarnations, you know this is a great leap forward.

The Document Object Model

Until now, we've had access to only some of the objects on a web page, such as forms, form elements, and images. For example, in Chapter 7, we used the document.images[] array to manipulate the images on a page, creating rollover effects. What if we had the same kind of access to other items on the page, such as headings, paragraphs, and even individual words within a paragraph, and could manipulate those items in the same way? That's exactly what the DOM provides.

The W3C DOM exposes every element of an HTML page to a scripting language, such as JavaScript. The DOM begins with a base object called the document object, which refers to the HTML page itself and everything in it. All the elements contained within the HTML page, such as headings, paragraphs, images, forms, and links, are represented by separate objects. These objects branch off from the document object, like branches from a tree trunk, to form a hierarchy of elements.

If this description of the DOM sounds a lot like the JavaScript tree, that's because it is. The objects in what we've been calling the JavaScript tree are also informally referred to as DOM Level 0. These objects are still available in the W3C DOM for backward compatibility. In other words, all the techniques that we've used to manipulate images and form elements work in browsers that support the W3C DOM, so you don't have to worry about any of your scripts breaking, and you can keep using these techniques in your pages. What the W3C DOM offers is access to all the elements on a page, not just forms and images. It's as if someone added many more branches to the JavaScript tree.

To change the appearance of a particular element in an HTML document, for example, we first have to reference the object that corresponds to that element. Consider the following HTML document:

```html
<html>
<head>
<title>Sample Document</title>
</head>
<body>
<h1>An HTML Document</h1>
<p id="simple">This is a simple paragraph.</p>
</body>
</html>
```

To refer to the paragraph element in this document, we can use the following JavaScript:

```javascript
var para = document.getElementById("simple");
```

getElementById() is a method of the document object; it returns the HTML element with the specified id attribute in the document. In this case, the element returned is the paragraph in which we are interested. As we get into some DHTML examples, you'll see this technique on a regular basis. We'll assign IDs to the HTML elements that we want to control with DHTML, then use getElementById() to access and manipulate those elements.

Dynamic Cascading Style Sheets

Now that you understand the basics of the DOM, let's take a closer look at how CSS plays a role in DHTML. In web design, CSS is typically used to create style sheets that govern the overall appearance of a web site. With DHTML, we're not concerned with controlling the overall appearance of a page, but rather with making style changes to individual elements to create different effects. In other words, all this talk about manipulating an element is really about changing its appearance or location by modifying its styles.

With the DOM, every HTML element has a style property that provides access to all the CSS attributes that apply to that particular element. We can use this property to change things like the color, font family, and font size of an element. For example, we could change the color of our simple paragraph (as represented by the para variable we created earlier) to green:

```javascript
para.style.color = "#00FF00";
```

getElementById() is a method of the document object that returns the HTML element with the specified ID.

Calling all headings!

The document object also has a getElementsByTagName() method for accessing HTML elements, but this method is much less useful for DHTML. getElementsByTagName() returns an array of objects that represents all the elements of a particular type in the document. For example, you can use getElementsByTagName() to get an array of all the h1 elements on a page:

```javascript
var headings = document.
  getElementsByTagName("h1");
```

Then, if you want to manipulate the third heading, you can access that element through the array as headings[2].

The main problem with getElementsByTagName() is that it requires detailed knowledge of the document's structure. If you rearrange the content of your page and the third heading becomes the fourth heading, you have to remember to change the array access, or you'll be manipulating the wrong element.

Dynamic HTML

Table 9-1 lists some common styles that we can modify with DHTML; it shows both the JavaScript property name and the equivalent CSS attribute name.

Table 9-1: Common style properties

Style property	CSS equivalent	What it controls
fontSize	font-size	The point size of the text's font (e.g., "12px" or "10pt")
fontWeight	font-weight	The weight of the text's font (e.g., "bold")
fontFamily	font-family	The family of the text's font (e.g., "Times" or "serif")
fontStyle	font-style	The slant of the text (e.g., "italic", "oblique", or "normal")
textDecoration	text-decoration	The special effect applied to the text (e.g., "underline", "overline", "strikethrough", or "blinking")
color	color	The color of the element's foreground (e.g., "red" or "#990000")
backgroundColor	background-color	The color of the element's background
backgroundImage	background-image	The image in the element's background

Rollover style changes

Let's take a look at a simple example that demonstrates how HTML, CSS, the DOM, and JavaScript work together. Example 9-1 shows the code for a web page that uses DHTML to change the style of links to red and underlined when the user rolls the mouse over them. This script works similarly to image rollovers, but without the need for images.

Example 9-1: Rollover style changes

```
<html>
<head>
<title>Rollover Style Changes</title>
<style>
a { text-decoration: none; color: #0000FF; }
</style>

<script language="JavaScript">
function turnOn(currentLink) {
    currentLink.style.color = "#990000";
    currentLink.style.textDecoration = "underline";
}

function turnOff(currentLink) {
    currentLink.style.color = "#0000FF";
    currentLink.style.textDecoration = "none";
}
</script>

</head>
<body bgcolor="#FFFFFF">
  <a href="home.html"
    onMouseOver="turnOn(this);" onMouseOut="turnOff(this);">Home</a>
```

Example 9-1: Rollover style changes (continued)

```
<a href="contact.html"
   onMouseOver="turnOn(this);" onMouseOut="turnOff(this);">Contact</a>
<a href="links.html"
   onMouseOver="turnOn(this);" onMouseOut="turnOff(this);">Links</a>
</body>
</html>
```

When the user's mouse goes over a link, the onMouseOver event handler for the link is triggered. The link passes itself as an object, using this, to the turnOn() function, which takes this object as an argument, calling it currentLink. The function then accesses the style property of currentLink and modifies the color and textDecoration styles to turn the link red and underline it. (Notice that we don't have to use getElementById() to access the links in this example, because each link can pass itself as an object using this.)

When the mouse moves back out of the link, the onMouseOut event handler works exactly the same way, but it calls the turnOff() function, which restores the link to its original color and removes the underline.

Note that when you set style properties via the DOM and JavaScript, you have to specify the values as strings, as we did in our rollover script:

```
currentLink.style.color = "#990000";
currentLink.style.textDecoration = "underline";
```

Compare this with the style sheet settings for these same attributes:

```
a { text-decoration: none; color: #0000FF; }
```

If you are having problems with a DHTML script, you should check that all your JavaScript style settings use strings, because this is a common source of errors.

Example 9-1 demonstrates the simple process of handling an event, calling a function, and using the function to modify styles. As we create more elaborate scripts, you'll see that this same process is used over and over to create interactivity and animation in DHTML.

A dynamic CSS toolbar

Now that you have a basic understanding of how the DOM and CSS interact, let's create a navigation toolbar that's dynamic, completely text-based, and can rival any image-based toolbar.

Our toolbar consists of a table row with five cells, each containing a link. Each link uses JavaScript rollover code like that shown in Example 9-1, but rather than just changing the appearance of the links, it also changes the background color of the table cell, highlighting that cell like a button, as shown in Figure 9-1.

When the user moves the mouse over one of the links on the toolbar, the script changes the styles of two different elements: the link and the table cell that contains it. As before, this is done with the onMouseOver event

---

Where did the underlines go?

By default, links on an HTML page are underlined. But in Example 9-1, we only want the links to be underlined while the mouse is over them. To achieve this, we include a style sheet in the document using the style tag. The style sheet simply removes any text decorations (i.e., underlines) from all links and sets the link color to blue. This example shows how we can use a CSS style sheet to set the default styles for a page, then override those defaults dynamically in response to user activity. As you'll see in the rest of the examples in this chapter, this is a common technique in DHTML scripts.

Figure 9-1

A dynamic CSS toolbar

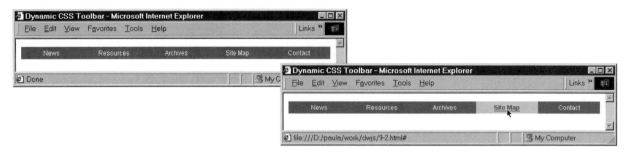

handler, which calls the linkOn() function; linkOff() is the corresponding function for onMouseOut events. Example 9-2 shows the HTML for a single table cell.

Example 9-2: HTML for a single cell of the toolbar

```
<td class="toolbar" id="news" width="120">
  <a href="#"
     onMouseOver="linkOn(this, 'news');"
     onMouseOut="linkOff(this, 'news');">News</a>
</td>
```

Note that we've set the id attribute for the table cell so that we can access this element using the DOM. The linkOn() and linkOff() functions in this script each take two arguments: the link itself and the id of the table cell that contains it.

As shown in Example 9-3, linkOn() accesses the style property of currentLink to change the color, fontWeight, and textDecoration styles. Then linkOn() uses its second argument, cell, to get the object for the specified table cell using getElementById(). Once we have the current cell, we can use the style property to change its backgroundColor style.

Example 9-3: The linkOn() function

```
function linkOn(currentLink, cell) {
    currentLink.style.color = "#990000";
    currentLink.style.fontWeight = "bold";
    currentLink.style.textDecoration = "underline";

    var currentCell = document.getElementById(cell);
    currentCell.style.backgroundColor = "#CCCCCC";
}
```

Again, note that all the style values in linkOn() are specified as strings.

The linkOff() function uses the same techniques to reset the link and table cell to their original appearance when the mouse moves out of the link.

Example 9-4 shows the complete script for the dynamic toolbar. The techniques used in this script are extremely useful and can be applied in a variety of different ways to breathe life into your web pages.

Example 9-4: Source code for the dynamic CSS toolbar

```
<html>
<head>
<title>Dynamic CSS Toolbar</title>
<style type="text/css">
a { font-family: Arial, Helvetica, sans-serif; font-size: 12px;
    color: #FFFFFF; text-decoration: none;}
.toolbar { background-color: #666666; }
</style>

<script language="JavaScript">
// Function to activate a link in the toolbar
function linkOn(currentLink, cell) {
    currentLink.style.color = "#990000";
    currentLink.style.fontWeight = "bold";
    currentLink.style.textDecoration = "underline";

    var currentCell = document.getElementById(cell);
    currentCell.style.backgroundColor = "#CCCCCC";
}

// Function to deactivate a link in the toolbar
function linkOff(currentLink, cell) {
    currentLink.style.color = "#FFFFFF";
    currentLink.style.fontWeight = "normal";
    currentLink.style.textDecoration = "none";

    var currentCell = document.getElementById(cell);
    currentCell.style.backgroundColor = "#666666";
}
</script>
</head>

<body bgcolor="#FFFFFF" text="#000000">
<table width="600" border="0" cellspacing="0" cellpadding="3">
  <tr align="center">
    <td class="toolbar" id="news" width="120">
      <a href="#"
        onMouseOver="linkOn(this, 'news');"
        onMouseOut="linkOff(this, 'news');">News</a>
    </td>
    <td class="toolbar" id="resources" width="120">
      <a href="#"
        onMouseOver="linkOn(this, 'resources');"
        onMouseOut="linkOff(this, 'resources');">Resources</a>
    </td>
    <td class="toolbar" id="archives" width="120">
      <a href="#"
        onMouseOver="linkOn(this, 'archives');"
        onMouseOut="linkOff(this, 'archives');">Archives</a>
    </td>
    <td class="toolbar" id="sitemap" width="120">
      <a href="#"
        onMouseOver="linkOn(this, 'sitemap');"
        onMouseOut="linkOff(this, 'sitemap');">Site Map</a>
    </td>
```

Example 9-4: Source code for the dynamic CSS toolbar (continued)

```
      <td class="toolbar" id="contact" width="120">
        <a href="#"
           onMouseOver="linkOn(this, 'contact');"
           onMouseOut="linkOff(this, 'contact');">Contact</a>
      </td>
    </tr>
  </table>
</body>
</html>
```

Getting acquainted with layers

A layer is a rectangular content container that can be positioned in the x, y, and z dimensions.

So far, our DHTML examples have been limited to changing the appearance of static elements on the page. To produce more sophisticated, dynamic effects, such as moveable elements and items that appear and disappear, you need to understand the concept of a positionable layer. In DHTML, a layer is a rectangular container that can be positioned in the x (horizontal), y (vertical), and z (stacking order) dimensions.* You can think of the z dimension as a third axis pointing out of the screen toward the user. DHTML layers work much like the layers in many graphics programs, such as Adobe Photoshop and Macromedia Fireworks.

Creating a new layer

A layer consists of a div tag that surrounds other HTML elements. The div tag uses special style attributes to define the behavior of the layer. A typical layer has the following style attributes defined:

position
> This attribute is what makes the layer positionable. Possible values for position are absolute and relative. If position is set to relative, the layer is positioned in relation to any containing element, like a table cell or another layer. If the value is absolute, the layer is always positioned in relation to the entire document, rather than any containing element.

left
> Specifies the distance (in pixels) from the left edge of the document (or containing element) to the left edge of the layer.

top
> Specifies the distance (in pixels) from the top edge of the document (or containing element) to the top edge of the layer.

Think of the z-index as a third axis pointing out of the screen toward the user.

z-index
> Defines the stacking order of the layer, which governs how layers are displayed if they overlap each other. z-index simply assigns a number

---

* Don't confuse the general concept of a DHTML layer with the layer tag, a proprietary tag in Navigator 4 that supported limited DHTML functionality. With the advent of the DOM and CSS, the layer tag is no longer needed, and Netscape 6 doesn't even support it.

to a layer. If two layers overlap, the layer with the higher z-index is placed on top, so that layers are stacked on top of each other in ascending order. For example, a layer with a z-index of 2 appears over a layer with a z-index of 1. In addition, layers are positioned on top of any elements without z-index defined, which means that they appear over the main content of an HTML document.

height
   Specifies the height of the layer, in pixels.

width
   Specifies the width of the layer, in pixels.

Example 9-5 presents a simple HTML document that takes a chunk of text—"Welcome to Bill's World!"—and turns it into a visually distinctive header by containing it in a layer, as shown in Figure 9-2. Note that this example simply demonstrates creating a layer, not manipulating it in any way.

Example 9-5: Defining a simple layer

```
<html>
<head>
<title>Welcome to Bill's World!</title>
<style type="text/css">
.welcome { font-family: Arial, Helvetica, san-serif; font-size: 24px;
        font-weight:bold; text-align: center; vertical-align: middle}
</style>
</head>

<body bgcolor="#FFFFFF" text="#000000">
<div id="MyLayer"
     style="position:absolute;
            z-index:1;
            left:100px; top:10px;
            width:300px; height:30px;
            background-color: #FFCC00;">

  <p class="welcome">Welcome to Bill's World!</p>
</div>
</body>
</html>
```

| Figure 9-2 |

A simple layer

WARNING

Mind your units

The values for top, left, width, and height must be written as standard CSS length values, with units (e.g., 100px), not as numbers (e.g., 100). This is different from how the Version 4.0 browsers handled CSS sizes in their proprietary DOMs. If you're accustomed to creating DHTML for these browsers, you should pay special attention when setting up your layers; this is a common mistake for those transitioning to standards-based DHTML.

Dynamic HTML

In this document, the div tag starts by specifying an id attribute, which gives the layer a unique name. We don't use the id in this page, but when we start using the DOM to manipulate layers, the layers will need unique names, so this is a good habit to develop.

In the style attribute, we set position to absolute. Most layers use absolute positioning because it applies the left and top properties literally, not relative to another document element. By setting z-index to 1, we place this layer above all other HTML elements on the page. The left and top attributes define where the layer is placed on the page, relative to the entire document (since position is absolute). Finally, the height and width attributes specify the size of the layer.

Now that we have created a positionable layer, we can modify its style attributes to achieve various effects. Just as with any other HTML element, we can change styles like color and fontWeight to modify the appearance of the layer. But, more importantly, we can use JavaScript to modify the key attributes of a positionable layer. For example, changing the left and top attributes moves the layer, and modifying z-index can change the position of the layer in the stacking order, moving it above or below other layers.

Tabbed folders

File folders, a staple of the office paper trail, are also a key part of the desktop computer interface. It's no surprise, then, that they've also become a common interface metaphor on the Web. For example, Hotmail (*http://www.hotmail.com*), MSN's web-based email service, uses tabs across the site to help users understand where they are in the site's architecture (see Figure 9-3). Each time the user clicks on one of the tabs—Home, Inbox, Compose, or Address Book—he is taken to the appropriate page.

The visibility attribute controls whether a layer is visible or hidden, which allows us to display and hide layers in response to user actions.

Using layers, we can create a tabbed interface that doesn't require loading new pages. Instead, the individual pages are created as layers that are stacked on top of one another, with only the topmost layer visible. CSS supports a visibility attribute that controls whether a layer is visible or hidden. We can change this attribute in response to the user clicking on the different tabs, making the content of the newly selected tab visible and hiding the content of the previous tab. Because all the content is loaded when the page is first viewed, users don't have to wait for the new content to download when they switch tabs.

Figure 9-4 shows our DHTML tabbed folder interface, which is implemented with six different layers. The three tabs are layers positioned side by side, while the three content areas (or folders) are layers stacked on top of one another. At any given time, the selected folder has its visibility set to visible, while the other layers are set to hidden. Each time a tab is clicked, we make style changes to four different layers, highlighting the clicked tab, turning the previously highlighted tab gray,

Figure 9-3

Tabs as a site-navigation metaphor

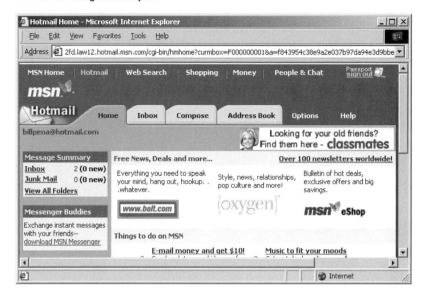

making the folder corresponding to the clicked tab visible, and hiding the previously visible folder. This sequence of changes in response to a single mouse click creates the illusion of switching between folders.

Figure 9-4

Tabbed folders with DHTML

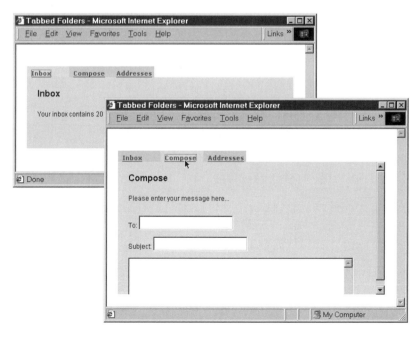

Dynamic HTML

The layers

The layer for each tab has a unique id, but the class attribute for all the tabs is set to tab, so that we can apply some styles to all of them. Each tab layer contains a link that uses a JavaScript URL to run the turnOn( ) function, which is responsible for switching the content when a tab is clicked. Example 9-6 shows the code for the tab layers.

Example 9-6: The tab layers

```
<div id="Tab1" class="tab"
     style="position:absolute; left:20px; top:40px; width:80px;
            height:20px; z-index:1;">
  <a href="javascript:turnOn('Tab1', 'Folder1');">Inbox</a>
</div>
<div id="Tab2" class="tab"
     style="position:absolute; left:100px; top:40px; width:80px;
            height:20px; z-index:1">
  <a href="javascript:turnOn('Tab2', 'Folder2');">Compose</a>
</div>
<div id="Tab3" class="tab"
     style="position:absolute; left:180px; top:40px; width:80px;
            height:20px; z-index:1">
  <a href="javascript:turnOn('Tab3', 'Folder3');">Addresses</a>
</div>
```

Similarly, the layer for each folder has a unique id and a class attribute set to folder. The first folder, Folder1, has its visibility attribute set to visible, because this is the layer that is displayed when the page is first viewed. For the other two layers, visibility is set to hidden. Example 9-7 lists the code for the folder layers.

Example 9-7: The folder layers

```
<div id="Folder1" class="folder"
     style="position:absolute; left:20px; top:60px; width:500px;
            height:300px; z-index:1; visibility:visible; overflow:auto">
  <h1>Inbox</h1>
  <p>Your inbox contains 20 new messages...</p>
</div>
<div id="Folder2" class="folder"
     style="position:absolute; left:20px; top:60px; width:500px;
            height:300px; z-index:2; visibility:hidden; overflow:auto">
  <h1>Compose</h1>
  <p>Please enter your message here...</p>
  <form>
    <p>To: <input type="text">
    <p>Subject: <input type="text">
    <p><textarea rows="10" cols="40"></textarea>
  </form>
</div>
<div id="Folder3" class="folder"
     style="position:absolute; left:20px; top:60px; width:500px;
            height:300px; z-index:3; visibility:hidden; overflow:auto">
  <h1>Address Book</h1>
  <p>Select an address...</p>
</div>
```

Automatic Scrollbars

If you look at Figure 9-3, you'll notice that the Compose folder has an internal scrollbar, while the Inbox folder does not. The display of scrollbars inside each of the folders is controlled by the overflow attribute, which allows us to define what happens when the content of a layer is larger than the layer itself. In this example, we've set overflow to auto, which, as rendered in modern web browsers, creates horizontal or vertical scrollbars when needed. That's why there is a vertical scrollbar in the Compose folder but not in the others.

The style sheet

Our tabbed folder example uses a style sheet to ensure a consistent appearance among all the tabs and folders, as shown in Example 9-8.

Example 9-8: The tabbed folder style sheet

```
<style type="text/css">
.tab { background-color: #CCCCCC; }
.tab a { font-family: Verdana, sans-serif; font-size: 11px;
        font-weight: bold; position: relative; left: 8px; top: 4px;
        color: #663333}
.tab a:visited { color: #663333;}
#Tab1 { background-color: #FFCC99; }

.folder { background-color: #CCCCCC; }
.folder p { font-family: Arial, san-serif; font-size: 12px;
          margin-top: 10px; margin-right: 25px; margin-bottom: 10px;
          margin-left: 20px}
.folder h1 { font-family: Arial, san-serif; font-size: 16px;
           margin-top: 20px; margin-right: 20px; margin-bottom: 20px;
           margin-left: 20px}
#Folder1 { background-color: #FFCC99; }
</style>
```

Since the three tab layers all specify a `class` of `tab`, we can write specific CSS rules to apply to just those layers. The first rule, `.tab`, sets the background color for all the elements in the tabs. The next two rules, `.tab a` and `.tab a:visited`, apply just to the links within the tabs. Notice that the `.tab a` rule applies the `position` attribute to links within the tabs, as you might expect in a layer. In this case, `position` is set to `relative`, so the `left` and `top` attributes define where links are positioned within the containing layer, not within the entire document. The final rule, `#Tab1`, adjusts the background color of the initial tab so that it appears selected.

We use similar style rules for the folder layers, with a rule that applies to all the elements in the folders, a rule that applies to `p` tags within the folders, a rule that applies to `h1` tags, and a rule for the initially selected folder (`#Folder1`).

The techniques we've used here to specify styles—by class name, by tag, and by ID—give us the flexibility to style layers with precision, without the burden of adding `style` attributes to every HTML tag. These few lines of code illustrate the richness of CSS styles and, as part of DHTML, how CSS styles offer new, powerful web design capabilities.

Specifying styles by class name, by tag, and by ID allows us to style layers with precision.

Switching tabs

Now that we've examined the HTML and CSS for this example, let's take on the JavaScript that makes these folders work, as shown in Example 9-9. When the page first loads, we set two variables, `currentTab` and `currentFolder`, to store the IDs of the currently selected tab and the visible folder. These variables allow the `turnOn()` function to hide the previously selected folder and switch focus to the newly selected folder. As we showed back in Example 9-6, each tab contains a link to a JavaScript function named `turnOn()`. This function takes two arguments: the `id` of the clicked tab and the `id` of the corresponding folder.

Example 9-9: The state variables and turnOn() function

```
var currentTab = "Tab1";
var currentFolder = "Folder1";

function turnOn(newTab, newFolder) {
    if (currentTab != newTab) {
        // Adjust the background colors for the tabs
        var thisTab = document.getElementById(newTab);
        thisTab.style.backgroundColor = "#FFCC99";
        var oldTab = document.getElementById(currentTab);
        oldTab.style.backgroundColor = "#CCCCCC";

        // Make the new tab the current tab
        currentTab = newTab;

        // Adjust the visibility and background color for the folders
        var thisFolder = document.getElementById(newFolder);
        thisFolder.style.visibility = "visible";
        thisFolder.style.backgroundColor = "#FFCC99";
        var oldFolder = document.getElementById(currentFolder);
        oldFolder.style.visibility = "hidden";

        // Make the new folder the current folder
        currentFolder = newFolder;
    }
}
```

The `turnOn()` function first checks to see if the newly selected tab is different from the current tab. If they are the same, we don't need to do anything. If they are different, `turnOn()` adjusts the background colors for the two tabs, making the newly selected tab orange and reverting the current tab to gray. (Note the use of `getElementById()` to access the appropriate layers.) Once the style changes for the tabs are complete, `currentTab` is set to `newTab`, so that we can keep track of the current state of the page.

Now `turnOn()` adjusts the `visibility` attributes of the folders, setting the newly selected folder to `visible` and the current folder to `hidden`. Again, after this is done, `currentFolder` is set to `newFolder`, to keep everything in sync.

Example 9-10 shows the complete page for this example. You can easily customize this page by changing any `style` attributes, except for `position`, to suit your tastes. You must leave the `position` values set to `absolute` or `relative`, to place the layers correctly on the page.

Example 9-10: Source code for the tabbed folder interface

```
<html>
<head>
<title>Tabbed Folders</title>
<style type="text/css">
.tab { background-color: #CCCCCC; }
.tab a { font-family: Verdana, sans-serif; font-size: 11px;
    font-weight: bold; position: relative; left: 8px;
    top: 4px; color: #663333}
```

Example 9-10: Source code for the tabbed folder interface (continued)

```
.tab a:visited { color: #663333;}
#Tab1 { background-color: #FFCC99; }

.folder { background-color: #CCCCCC; }
.folder p { font-family: Arial, san-serif; font-size: 12px;
            margin-top: 10px; margin-right: 25px; margin-bottom: 10px;
            margin-left: 20px}
.folder h1 { font-family: Arial, san-serif; font-size: 16px;
            margin-top: 20px; margin-right: 20px; margin-bottom: 20px;
            margin-left: 20px}
#Folder1 { background-color: #FFCC99; }
</style>

<script language="JavaScript">
// State variables to keep track of current tab and folder
var currentTab = "Tab1";
var currentFolder = "Folder1";

// Function to switch tabs and folders
function turnOn(newTab, newFolder) {
    if (currentTab != newTab) {
        // Adjust the background colors for the tabs
        var thisTab = document.getElementById(newTab);
        thisTab.style.backgroundColor = "#FFCC99";
        var oldTab = document.getElementById(currentTab);
        oldTab.style.backgroundColor = "#CCCCCC";

        // Make the new tab the current tab
        currentTab = newTab;

        // Adjust the visibility and background color for the folders
        var thisFolder = document.getElementById(newFolder);
        thisFolder.style.visibility = "visible";
        thisFolder.style.backgroundColor = "#FFCC99";
        var oldFolder = document.getElementById(currentFolder);
        oldFolder.style.visibility = "hidden";

        // Make the new folder the current folder
        currentFolder = newFolder;
    }
}
</script>
</head>

<body bgcolor="#FFFFFF" text="#000000">

<!-- Create Tabs -->
<div id="Tab1" class="tab"
    style="position:absolute; left:20px; top:40px; width:80px;
           height:20px; z-index:1;">
  <a href="javascript:turnOn('Tab1', 'Folder1');">Inbox</a>
</div>
<div id="Tab2" class="tab"
    style="position:absolute; left:100px; top:40px; width:80px;
           height:20px; z-index:1">
  <a href="javascript:turnOn('Tab2', 'Folder2');">Compose</a>
</div>
<div id="Tab3" class="tab"
    style="position:absolute; left:180px; top:40px; width:80px;
           height:20px; z-index:1">
  <a href="javascript:turnOn('Tab3', 'Folder3');">Addresses</a>
</div>
```

Example 9-10: Source code for the tabbed folder interface (continued)

```html
<!-- Create Folders -->
<div id="Folder1" class="folder"
    style="position:absolute; left:20px; top:60px; width:500px;
        height:300px; z-index:1; visibility:visible; overflow:auto">
  <h1>Inbox</h1>
  <p>Your inbox contains 20 new messages...</p>
</div>
<div id="Folder2" class="folder"
    style="position:absolute; left:20px; top:60px; width:500px;
        height:300px; z-index:2; visibility:hidden; overflow:auto">
  <h1>Compose</h1>
  <p>Please enter your message here...</p>
  <form>
    <p>To: <input type="text"></p>
    <p>Subject: <input type="text"></p>
    <p><textarea rows="10" cols="40"></textarea></p>
  </form>
</div>
<div id="Folder3" class="folder"
    style="position:absolute; left:20px; top:60px; width:500px;
        height:300px; z-index:3; visibility:hidden; overflow:auto">
  <h1>Address Book</h1>
  <p>Select an address...</p>
</div>
</body>
</html>
```

Browser detection

Only the latest versions of Netscape Navigator and IE support the DOM and CSS standards used here, so you must use browser detection in DHTML scripts.

As I mentioned at the beginning of this chapter, only the latest versions of Netscape Navigator and IE support the DOM and CSS standards used by our DHTML examples. Therefore, if you want to use one of these examples, you must first check the user's browser type and version to make sure that the browser supports the script. (For more information on browser detection, see Chapter 6.) Each of the DHTML scripts should begin as shown in Example 9-11.

Example 9-11: Browser detection for standard DHTML

```javascript
<script language="JavaScript">
var isNN4, isIE4, isDOM;

if (document.getElementById) {
    isDOM = true;
}
else if (parseInt(navigator.appVersion) >= 4) {
    if (navigator.appName == "Netscape") {
        isNN4 = true;
    }
    if (navigator.appName == "Microsoft Internet Explorer") {
        isIE4 = true;
    }
}
</script>
```

This code checks the identity and version of the browser and sets the appropriate variable to true: isDOM for a standards-compliant version of

Navigator or IE, isNN4 for Netscape Navigator 4, or isIE4 for IE 4. Note the use of object detection (using document.getElementById) to determine whether the browser supports the DOM.

Once we have tested the user's browser and set the appropriate variable, we can test those variables to run the right browser-specific code:

```
if (isDOM) {
    // Insert W3C DOM-based DHTML here
}
else if (isIE4) {
    // Insert IE 4 DHTML here
}
else if (isNN4) {
    // Insert Navigator 4 DHTML here
}
```

Of course, this code assumes that you want to support DHTML specific to IE 4 and Navigator 4, in addition to the DOM-standard DHTML. If you don't want to hassle with the older, proprietary versions of DHTML, you can just support the DOM-standard version for the latest browsers and provide a DHTML-free version of your page for all other browsers.

Dynamic HTML

Chapter 10

Interactive DHTML Techniques

There's a lot more to JavaScript and DHTML than what we've seen so far. Now that we've covered the `style` property and the basics of positioning and switching between layers, we can get to the really fun stuff. In this chapter, we'll add interactivity to your DHTML bag of tricks, creating drop-down menus that open when clicked and close when double-clicked, headline tickers that scroll news items on the screen, and navigation tabs that slide in and out when needed. In short, you'll learn how to animate and manipulate your web pages in new ways, using JavaScript and DHTML to extend beyond the page metaphor.

Drop-down menus

One of the most common interface elements in desktop applications is the menu bar with drop-down menus. We can make the same kind of menus with DHTML by showing and hiding positioned layers, as shown in Figure 10-1. When the user clicks on Resources or Links, a layer with links is displayed below it, just like with a normal menu. When the user double-clicks on the link, the layer is hidden again.

This example creates the layers for the drop-down menus within the context of an HTML table, to keep everything lined up nicely. Example 10-1 shows the HTML for the table cell and the layer within the cell for the Links menu.

Example 10-1: HTML for the Links menu

```
<td width="100">
  <div id="LinksLayer"
      style="position:absolute; left:211px; top:23px;
            width:100px; height:85px; z-index:2;
            background-color:#CCCCCC; layer-background-color:#CCCCCC;
            visibility:hidden">
    <a href="#">DHTML</a><br>
    <a href="#">CSS</a><br>
    <a href="#">HTML</a><br>
    <a href="#">JavaScript</a>
  </div>
```

The onDblClick event handler is triggered when the user double-clicks on a link.

Example 10-1: HTML for the Links menu (continued)

```
<a href="#" onClick="showLayer('LinksLayer');"
   onDblClick="hideLayer('LinksLayer');">Links</a>
</td>
```

Figure 10-1

A drop-down menu with DHTML

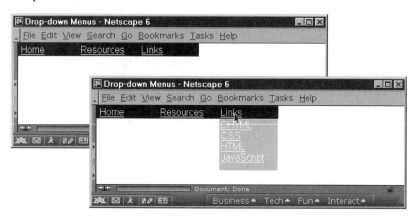

The `div` tag inside the `td` table cell tag creates the layer for the Links menu. As with any DHTML script, the layer is given a specific `id` so we can refer to it later. Various CSS properties are set using the `style` attribute. These properties set the size and position of the layer precisely, so that it appears at the appropriate location for a drop-down menu. The `visibility` attribute is set to `hidden` so that the menu is invisible until the user clicks on Links to activate it.

The table cell also contains a link that controls the menu. The `onClick` event handler calls `showLayer()` to display the menu, and the `onDblClick` event handler calls `hideLayer()` to remove it. Each function is passed the argument `'LinksLayer'`, which tells the function which layer to display and hide. Example 10-2 lists the code for the `showLayer()` and `hideLayer()` functions.

Example 10-2: The showLayer( ) and hideLayer( ) functions

```
function showLayer(layerid) {
    var layer = document.getElementById(layerid);
    layer.style.visibility = "visible";
}

function hideLayer(layerid) {
    var layer = document.getElementById(layerid);
    layer.style.visibility = "hidden";
}
```

In terms of DHTML, there's actually nothing new in these functions. The `showLayer()` function gets the layer for the appropriate menu with `document.getElementById()` and assigns it to the variable `layer`. The ID for the correct layer is passed into the function as an argument, `layerid`. The function then sets the `visibility` attribute for the layer to `visible` to make the menu appear. The `hideLayer()` function works just like the `showLayer()` function, except that it hides the menu by setting `visibility` to `hidden`.

Example 10-3 shows the complete script for the drop-down menus. It is pretty easy to adapt this script for your own site; most of the work is in figuring out the layout for your menu links and then determining the exact size and location for each menu layer. In other words, you'll need to adjust the `top`, `left`, `width`, and `height` attributes for the actual content and layout of your page. You can also adjust the various color styles to suit your purposes. The two attributes you need to leave as is are `position` and `visibility`.

Of course, you can always add menus by adding more table cells following the pattern set in Example 10-3. Just give each menu layer a unique `id` attribute, and then pass that ID to the `showLayer()` and `hideLayer()` functions via the `onClick` and `onDblClick` event handlers for your menu link. You don't need to change the `showLayer()` and `hideLayer()` functions at all.

Example 10-3: Source code for the DHTML drop-down menus

```
<html>
<head>
<title>Drop-down Menus</title>
<script language="JavaScript">
// Function to show a menu
function showLayer(layerid) {
    var layer = document.getElementById(layerid);
    layer.style.visibility = "visible";
}

// Function to hide a menu
function hideLayer(layerid) {
    var layer = document.getElementById(layerid);
    layer.style.visibility = "hidden";
}
</script>

<style type="text/css">
a { font-family: Arial, Helvetica, sans-serif;
    color: #FFFFFF; margin-left: 3px}
</style>
</head>

<body bgcolor="#FFFFFF" text="#000000" topmargin="0" leftmargin="0"
    marginwidth="0" marginheight="0">
<table border="0" bgcolor="#000000" cellspacing="0" cellpadding="2">
  <tr>
    <td width="100"><a href="#">Home</a></td>

    <td width="100">
      <div id="ResLayer"
          style="position:absolute; left:110px; top:23px;
              width:100px; height:62px; z-index:1;
              background-color:#CCCCCC; layer-background-color:#CCCCCC;
              visibility:hidden">
```

> **WARNING**
>
> **User expectations**
>
> Be careful when relying on events that users normally wouldn't expect. For example, this drop-down menu depends on the user double-clicking on a link in order to hide the menu. Users won't expect that a link can be clicked twice, and they probably won't realize it unless they're told. A better drop-down menu example would use single clicks both to display and hide the menu, but we'll leave that as an exercise. In your own pages, be sure to label all navigation clearly and consider your users' expectations. That way, all your hard work won't go ignored!

Example 10-3: Source code for the DHTML drop-down menus (continued)

```
        <a href="#">Scripts</a><br>
        <a href="#">Reference</a><br>
        <a href="#">Weblog</a>
    </div>

    <a href="#" onClick="showLayer('ResLayer');"
        onDblClick="hideLayer('ResLayer');">Resources</a>
  </td>

  <td width="100">
    <div id="LinksLayer"
        style="position:absolute; left:211px; top:23px;
              width:100px; height:85px; z-index:2;
              background-color:#CCCCCC; layer-background-color:#CCCCCC;
              visibility:hidden">
    <a href="#">DHTML</a><br>
    <a href="#">CSS</a><br>
    <a href="#">HTML</a><br>
    <a href="#">JavaScript</a>
    </div>

    <a href="#" onClick="showLayer('LinksLayer');"
        onDblClick="hideLayer('LinksLayer');">Links</a>
  </td>
 </tr>
</table>
</body>
</html>
```

Sliding tabs

Moving an object in DHTML is just a matter of changing the left and top style attributes.

Making an object move in DHTML is like making any other style change. All you are doing is changing one of two style attributes—left or top—to move an object from one place to another. The illusion of motion happens when you change the object's position incrementally and quickly.

In this example, we'll create a tab on the lefthand side of the browser window that is 75 pixels off the left edge of the screen, so the main content of the tab is not visible. When the user clicks on "show>>", the tab moves 5 pixels right every 20 milliseconds until it is completely onscreen, as shown in Figure 10-2. Clicking on "<<hide" returns the tab to its original position. As with the drop-down menu, we are creating a positionable layer and manipulating it with the DOM. What's new is the code for moving the layer. Example 10-4 shows the HTML for the sliding tab layer.

Example 10-4: HTML for the sliding tab

```
<div id="TabLayer"
    style="position:absolute; left:-75px; top:50px;
          width:115px; height:200px; z-index:1;
          background-color: #CCCCCC; layer-background-color: #CCCCCC;">

  <p align="right" class="hideshow">
    <a href="javascript:hideLayer();" class="hideshow">&lt;&lt;hide</a> |
    <a href="javascript:showLayer();" class="hideshow">show&gt;&gt;</a>
  </p>
```

Example 10-4: HTML for the sliding tab (continued)

```
<p align="left" style="margin-left: 5px;">
  <a href="#">Scripts</a><br>
  <a href="#">Weblog</a><br>
  <a href="#">Projects</a><br>
  <a href="#">Contact</a>
</p>
</div>
```

Figure 10-2

A sliding tab with DHTML

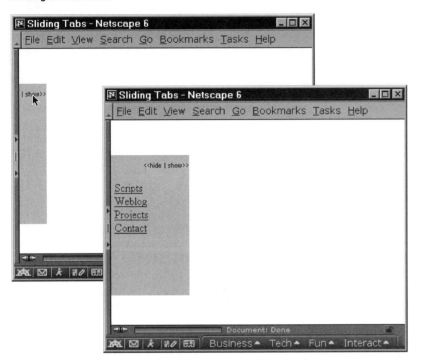

This div tag creates the layer for the sliding tab, TabLayer. Note that left is set to –75 pixels, which is what pushes the content of the tab out of the visible region of the browser window. Because the layer is in fact visible, just off the screen, we don't need to set the visibility attribute. The "<<hide" link uses a JavaScript URL to call the hideLayer() function, while the "show>>" link calls showLayer(). (Note the use of the < and > entities to display actual < and > characters in the web page.) Example 10-5 shows the code for the showLayer() and hideLayer() functions.

Example 10-5: The showLayer() and hideLayer() functions

```
function showLayer() {
    var hiddenLayer = document.getElementById("TabLayer");
    var layerPosition = parseInt(hiddenLayer.style.left);
```

Example 10-5: The showLayer() and hideLayer() functions (continued)

```
        if (layerPosition < 0) {
            hiddenLayer.style.left = (layerPosition + 5) + "px";
            setTimeout("showLayer()", 20);
        }
    }
}

function hideLayer() {
    var hiddenLayer = document.getElementById("TabLayer");
    hiddenLayer.style.left = "-75px";
}
```

WARNING

Of strings and units

Note the inclusion of the "px" here:

```
hiddenLayer.style.left =
    (layerPosition + 5) + "px";
```

This specifies the units (pixels) and converts the whole thing to a string. Whenever you set a location attribute, such as left, top, width, or height, with JavaScript, you need to make sure you use a string value and that you specify the units.

The showLayer() function uses the setTimeout() method we've seen in earlier examples in this book (like the panoramic image viewer and the rotating billboard) to call itself repeatedly and move the tab across the screen, 5 pixels at a time. By now, it should be clear that any time you want to simulate animation in JavaScript, you need to use setTimeout().

showLayer() starts by referencing the layer for our tab and storing it in the variable named hiddenLayer. Since showLayer() needs to work on only one layer, we don't get the layer ID as an argument, but instead refer specifically to TabLayer in the call to getElementById(). Next we use the built-in parseInt() function to get the current position of the layer from the value of the left attribute. Remember that left is set to a string value, such as "-75px". We need to extract a numeric value, so we do that with parseInt() and assign the value to layerPosition.

Once we know the position of the layer, we can test whether it is fully visible yet. If layerPosition is less than 0, the layer isn't fully visible, so we want to move it a bit further to the right. Thus, we increase the value of the layerPosition by 5 and set the left attribute to the new value. If you want to change the distance the layer travels each frame, you can tweak this value. A larger value results in faster movement, whereas a smaller value results in slower movement.

Any time you want to simulate animation in JavaScript, use the setTimeout() method.

After moving the tab layer, showLayer() calls setTimeout() to schedule the next movement of the tab. Each repetition of the function is equivalent to one frame of animation, so the amount of time setTimeout() waits before executing showLayer() is, in effect, our frame rate. The second argument to setTimeout() controls how often showLayer() is called. We're using a value of 20, which refers to 20 milliseconds. To make the animation go more slowly, increase this value.

The hideLayer() function simply moves the tab layer back to its original position so the content of the tab is not visible. In other words, we set left back to "-75px". Example 10-6 shows the complete script for the sliding tab.

Example 10-6: Source code for the DHTML sliding tab

```
<html>
<head>
<title>Sliding Tabs</title>
<style>
```

Example 10-6: Source code for the DHTML sliding tab (continued)

```
.hideshow { color: #333333; font-size: 9px; font-family: sans-serif;
            text-decoration: none; }
</style>

<script language="JavaScript">
// Function to slide the tab into the visible portion of the browser window
function showLayer() {
    var hiddenLayer = document.getElementById("TabLayer");
    var layerPosition = parseInt(hiddenLayer.style.left);
    if (layerPosition < 0) {
        hiddenLayer.style.left = (layerPosition + 5) + "px";
        setTimeout("showLayer()", 20);
    }
}

// Function to hide the tab again
function hideLayer() {
    var hiddenLayer = document.getElementById("TabLayer");
    hiddenLayer.style.left = "-75px";
}
</script>
</head>

<body>
<div id="TabLayer"
     style="position:absolute; left:-75px; top:50px;
            width:115px; height:200px; z-index:1;
            background-color: #CCCCCC; layer-background-color: #CCCCCC;">

  <p align="right" class="hideshow">
    <a href="javascript:hideLayer();" class="hideshow">&lt;&lt;hide</a> |
    <a href="javascript:showLayer();" class="hideshow">show&gt;&gt;</a>
  </p>

  <p align="left" style="margin-left: 5px;">
    <a href="#">Scripts</a><br>
    <a href="#">Weblog</a><br>
    <a href="#">Projects</a><br>
    <a href="#">Contact</a>
  </p>
</div>
</body>
</html>
```

Scrolling layers with clipping

There's one more interesting layer attribute we've yet to discuss: the clip attribute. This attribute defines the rectangular area of the layer that is visible, thereby hiding any part of the layer outside that region. This is just like a browser window with scrollbars, where you can see only a portion of the entire document.

The clip attribute defines the rectangular area of the layer that is visible, thereby hiding any part of the layer outside of that region.

Figure 10-3 illustrates the effect of the clip attribute. The clipping window, represented by the white area in the diagram, is visible to the user, while the rest of the layer, shown here in gray, is hidden. To use the clip attribute, we must define the four sides of the rectangle that constitutes our clipping window. Figure 10-3 also shows how the four values

Figure 10-3

The clipping window

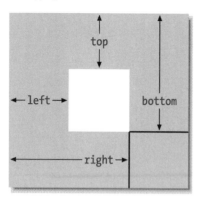

required by `clip` define the distance of each side of the clipping window from the layer's upper left corner.

Here's the syntax to define a clipping window in JavaScript:

```
style.clip = "rect(top right bottom left)";
```

The four edges of the clipping window are specified by defining a rectangle using the `rect()` construct. Note that the values are specified in clockwise order, starting with the top edge. Also note that the entire value is specified as a string and that there are no commas between the different edge values.

Here's the syntax for setting `clip` as a CSS style:

```
style="clip:rect(top right bottom left)"
```

Let's look at an example and see how we can have some fun with clipping. Since we can hide part of a layer with clipping, it makes sense that we can also reveal the hidden portion later. If we reveal the hidden portion over time, as we did with the sliding tab, we can create a scrolling area for headlines and news stories. This example does just that, mimicking a newspaper column that scrolls the latest news for you automatically. It is also possible to create this effect with a Java applet or a Flash movie, but why bother with that when we can do it with DHTML?

This effect is created by moving the news layer up at the same rate that we move the clipping window down, so that what appears on the screen is a "static" clipping window with a layer of text moving behind it. Since clipping is always relative to the layer, moving the clipping window is necessary only because the layer is moving. In other words, we are moving the clipping window to compensate for the layer's movement. As shown in Figure 10-4, both the layer and the clipping window are moving, yet the clipping window appears static.

The layers

This example creates two positionable layers: one for a column title that reads Breaking News and another for the layer that contains the news stories. Example 10-7 shows portions of the HTML for these layers.

Example 10-7: Partial HTML for the layers

```
<div id="NewsLayer"
    style="position:absolute; left:100px; top:40px; width:200px;
        height:900px; z-index:1; clip:rect(0 200 200 0);">
  <div style="margin-top:200px; margin-bottom:200px">
  ...
</div>

<div id="HeadlineLayer"
    style="position:absolute; left:100px; top:15px; width:200px;
        height:25px; z-index:2; background-color:#CCCCCC;">
  <h1>Breaking News</h1>
</div>
```

Figure 10-4

Relative movement of the layer and the clipping window

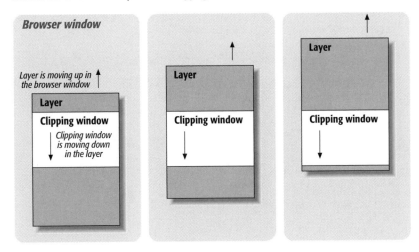

The layer for the news stories, NewsLayer, sets the usual attributes for a positionable layer. The only new attribute is clip, which we've set so that nothing in the layer is visible initially. Note that this layer actually contains a nested div tag that sets top and bottom margins for the content in the news layer. These margins are an essential part of the script, because they force the content to the middle of the news layer.

Scrolling

The body tag for the HTML document uses the onLoad event handler to start the scrolling by calling the startScrolling() function:

```
<body bgcolor="#666666" text="#000000" onLoad="startScrolling();">
```

As shown in Example 10-8, startScrolling() simply calls setTimeout() to schedule the scrollDown() function, which is what handles the actual scrolling.

Example 10-8: The startScrolling() function

```
function startScrolling() {
    setTimeout("scrollDown()", 500);
}
```

When the timeout triggers the first call to scrollDown(), scrollDown() takes over, calling setTimeout() to call itself repeatedly, as we've done in earlier examples. The scrollDown() function is shown in Example 10-9, along with the clipTop, clipRight, clipBotton, and clipLeft variables it uses to keep track of the clipping window.

Example 10-9: State variables and the scrollDown() function

```
var clipTop = 0;
var clipRight = 200;
var clipBottom = 200;
var clipLeft = 0;

function scrollDown() {
    var scrollWindow = document.getElementById('NewsLayer');

    // Check to see if we're at the bottom
    if (clipBottom != 900) {
        // If not, adjust variables for tracking the clipping window
        clipTop = clipTop + 10;
        clipBottom = clipBottom + 10;

        // Move the clipping window down and the layer up
        scrollWindow.style.clip = "rect(" + clipTop + " " + clipRight +
                                  " " + clipBottom + " " + clipLeft + ")";
        var currentTop = parseInt(scrollWindow.style.top);
        scrollWindow.style.top = (currentTop - 10) + "px";

        // Schedule next call to scrollDown
        setTimeout("scrollDown()", 500);
    }
    else {
        // We're at the bottom, so reset the variables
        clipTop = 0;
        clipBottom = 200;

        // Move the clipping window and layers back to their
        // original locations
        scrollWindow.style.clip = "rect(" + clipTop + " " + clipRight +
                                  " " + clipBottom + " " + clipLeft + ")";
        scrollWindow.style.top = "40px";

        // Start the scrolling over again
        setTimeout("scrollDown()", 500);
    }
}
```

The scrollDown() function starts by using getElementById() to get the layer object we're going to be manipulating and assigning it to a variable, scrollWindow. Next, scrollDown() checks to see if it has scrolled to the bottom of the news layer by checking whether clipBottom is 900, the height of the new layer. If it hasn't, the function increments the values of clipTop and clipBottom by 10 to move the clipping window downward, and then it uses these values to set a new value for the clip attribute. Note how we're using string concatenation to specify this value in the appropriate format. We also have to adjust the top attribute of the layer to move it up by 10 pixels. After adjusting the position of the clipping window and the layer, scrollDown() schedules itself to run again using setTimeout().

If scrollDown() determines that is has reached the bottom of the news layer, it resets the values of the clipTop and clipBottom variables to their original values, moves both the clipping window and the layer back to their original locations, and calls setTimeout() to start the scrolling all over again.

Figure 10-5 shows three images of our scrolling layer, so you can get a feel for what it looks like in action. Example 10-10 shows the complete script for the scrolling news example.

Figure 10-5

Scrolling news headlines with DHTML

Example 10-10: Source code for the scrolling news example

```html
<html>
<head>
<title>Clip Scrolling</title>
<script language="JavaScript">
// Variables for keeping track of the clipping window
var clipTop = 0;
var clipRight = 200;
var clipBottom = 200;
var clipLeft = 0;

// Function to start the scrolling
function startScrolling() {
    setTimeout("scrollDown()", 500);
}

// Function to simulate scrolling by moving the layer and the
// clipping window
function scrollDown() {
    var scrollWindow = document.getElementById('NewsLayer');

    // Check to see if we're at the bottom
    if (clipBottom != 900) {
        // If not, adjust variables for tracking the clipping window
        clipTop = clipTop + 10;
        clipBottom = clipBottom + 10;

        // Move the clipping window down and the layer up
        scrollWindow.style.clip = "rect(" + clipTop + " " + clipRight +
                            " " + clipBottom + " " + clipLeft + ")";
        var currentTop = parseInt(scrollWindow.style.top);
        scrollWindow.style.top = (currentTop - 10) + "px";

        // Schedule next call to scrollDown
        setTimeout("scrollDown()", 500);
    }
    else {
        // We're at the bottom, so reset the variables
        clipTop = 0;
        clipBottom = 200;
```

Example 10-10: Source code for the scrolling news example (continued)

```
            // Move the clipping window and layers back to their
            // original locations
            scrollWindow.style.clip = "rect(" + clipTop + " " + clipRight +
                              " " + clipBottom + " " + clipLeft + ")";
            scrollWindow.style.top = "40px";

            // Start the scrolling over again
            setTimeout("scrollDown()", 500);
        }
    }
    </script>

    <style type="text/css">
    #NewsLayer h1 { font-family: Arial, Helvetica, sans-serif;
                    font-size: 14px; margin-left: 8px; margin-right: 5px;
                    font-style: normal; color: #FFFFFF; font-weight: bold; }
    #NewsLayer p { font-family: Arial, Helvetica, sans-serif;
                   font-size: 12px; margin-left: 8px; margin-right: 10px;
                   color: #FFFFFF; }
    #NewsLayer a { font-family: Arial, Helvetica, sans-serif;
                   font-size: 12px; margin-left: 8px; margin-right: 10px;
                   color: #FFFFFF; }

    #HeadlineLayer h1 { font-family: "Times New Roman", Times, serif;
                        font-size: 18px; margin-left: 5px; margin-top: 3px;
                        margin-right: 5px; color: #000000;
                        font-weight: normal; }
    </style>
    </head>

    <body bgcolor="#666666" text="#000000" onLoad="startScrolling();">
    <div id="NewsLayer"
         style="position:absolute; left:100px; top:40px; width:200px;
                height:500px; z-index:1; clip:rect(0 200 200 0);">
      <div style="margin-top:200px; margin-bottom:200px;">
      <h1>First Story</h1>
      <p>Layers got you down? Does document.all give you indigestion? Then
         read this article to learn how to upgrade Navigator 4 and Internet
         Explorer 4 DHTML web pages to support Netscape 6, Mozilla, and the
         W3C Standards!<br>
      </p>
      <h1>Second Story</h1>
      <p>How to spot and diagnose (most) common web page problems for
         Netscape 6/Mozilla.<br>
      </p>
      <h1>Third Story</h1>
      <p>Updated to support Netscape 6, Mozilla, and Internet Explorer 6,
         as well as Netscape Navigator 4 and Internet Explorer 4.<br>
      </p>
      <h1>Fourth Story</h1>
      <p>Create a tab for My Sidebar and submit it today. Learn more about
         the promotion!</p>
         </div>
    </div>

    <div id="HeadlineLayer"
         style="position:absolute; left:100px; top:15px; width:200px;
                height:25px; z-index:2; background-color: #CCCCCC;">
      <h1>Breaking News</h1>
    </div>
    </body>
    </html>
```

Chapter 11

Advanced Applications

This chapter deals with some advanced scripting concepts that may challenge your budding programming skills. It provides a primer on object-oriented scripting, followed by some hard-hitting examples of object-oriented thinking and coding in action. We'll conclude with an example that uses an object-oriented approach to handle the complexity of providing cross-browser DHTML for the W3C DOM (IE 5.5 and later and Netscape 6), Internet Explorer 4, and Navigator 4.

Object-oriented scripting

We deal with objects all the time in JavaScript: the document object, the window object, the navigator object, and many others that let us access the properties we need from the browser while leaving the work to built-in browser magic. The next step in your evolution as a JavaScript programmer is to create your own objects, referred to as user-defined objects. With JavaScript's built-in objects (such as the document and navigator objects), the properties and methods are defined for you. With user-defined objects, you define the objects' properties and methods to suit the needs of your web site.

A good object-oriented script is easier to understand, more adaptable, and more efficient than a script that is not object-oriented. Up to this point, our creations have been relatively small, so they didn't need to be object-oriented. This is not to say that object-oriented means large—object-oriented really means easier to manage. The concepts of object-oriented programming require a different kind of thinking than you've had to do so far with JavaScript. If you don't master them the first time around, feel free to come back to this chapter after you've gained some real-world experience with JavaScript.

Object-oriented scripting is a process for writing JavaScript that focuses on carrying out all actions through objects. You design an object-oriented script by defining all functions relative to the object that they affect. This way, you can define self-contained "black boxes" that can reliably

IN THIS CHAPTER

Creating user-defined objects

Understanding object constructors

Designing a multiple-choice quiz

Creating a relational menu

Using a cross-browser style object

With user-defined objects, you define the properties and methods of an object to suit the needs of your web site.

handle specific tasks, and then you script the interaction between these objects. For example, rather than creating a variable called color, variables for properties like color and brand, and a variety of functions to manipulate that car, such as accelerate() and brake(), you can define a Car object and create methods for each of the functions that interact with a car. Now, anytime you need to use a car, you can create a new Car object that can perform all the same actions, rather than rewriting all the functions and variables for every appearance of a car.

Object-oriented scripting is a process for writing JavaScript that focuses on carrying out all actions through objects.

Let's make this a little more concrete by thinking about an example. Say you need to create a web page that will recommend a car—from a list of some 250 entries—based on four properties: color, brand, horsepower, and price. The user specifies a range for each of these properties and then receives a list of cars that fit those specifications. For example, a user might ask for a blue Ford with at least 180 horsepower and priced between $17,000 and $20,000.

The non-object way

There are two ways to do this task: the object way and the non-object way. We'll begin with the latter. Since there are 250 cars in the list, it makes sense to put them in an array. Because there are four properties, however, we will need four arrays, one for each property. The first element in the color array, color[0], contains the color of the first car. The first element in the brand array, brand[0], contains the brand name of the first car. And so on. A car, in this sense, is made up of specific elements from each of the arrays. If you were to represent cars in these terms, you might organize it as shown in Example 11-1.

Example 11-1: Coding the non-object way

```
// First car
color[0] = "red";
brand[0] = "Ford";
horsepower[0] = 160;
price[0] = 15000;

// Second car
color[1] = "pink";
brand[1] = "Cadillac";
horsepower[1] = 300;
price[1] = 40000;
```

As you can see, the first car's properties are all in the first element of each array, the second car's properties are all in the second element of each array, etc. Although this makes sense conceptually, especially when you organize it like this, if you were actually to try to implement the site using these arrays, you'd quickly find yourself lost in a maze of multiple array accesses.

The object way

Now let's analyze the task in the object-oriented way: instead of having four different arrays, one for each property, why not have one array that contains all four properties within it?

Essentially, each element of the array constitutes one whole car (object), as shown in Example 11-2. The first car is the first element in the cars array, cars[0], and color, brand, horsepower, and price are properties of that element.

Example 11-2: Coding the object way

```
// First car
cars[0].color = "red";
cars[0].brand = "Ford";
cars[0].horsepower = 160;
cars[0].price = 15000;

// Second car
cars[1].color = "pink";
cars[1].brand = "Cadillac";
cars[1].horsepower = 300;
cars[1].price = 40000;
```

Abstraction

One of the key concepts in object-oriented programming is abstraction. Objects abstract, or generalize, similar properties and functions that occur multiple times. For example, the document.images object provides a general way to reference all the images in an HTML document, even though they have different names and property values. Look for places where you often branch your script with if statements and for functions that all manipulate the same element over and over. These are common places where abstraction, in the form of object-oriented scripting, can make the script cleaner and easier to write.

Creating user-defined objects

As you can see from this example, the object-oriented way simply makes more sense. To make it work, however, you have to know how to create your own objects, using something called constructor functions. A constructor function defines an object's properties and methods. Example 11-3 shows a constructor function for the Car object.

Example 11-3: The Car( ) constructor function

```
function Car() {
    this.color;
    this.brand;
    this.horsepower;
    this.price;
}
```

The syntax of the constructor function may seem odd at first glance, but you'll quickly get used to it.

A constructor function defines an object's properties and methods.

Properties

This constructor function creates four properties: color, brand, horsepower, and price. To create a Car object using this function, use the new operator followed by the name of the function:

```
mycar = new Car();
```

This creates a new Car object named mycar with the four properties color, brand, horsepower, and price. These properties are represented in code as mycar.color, mycar.brand, mycar.horsepower, and mycar.price.

Inside an object constructor, the this keyword refers to the object currently being created.

Let's take a closer look at Car(): it's clearly not a conventional function. The Car() function uses the keyword this to define the Car object's properties. We know from earlier chapters that this refers to the current object, so when the Car() function says this.color, it is actually saying "the color of the object that is currently being created using new Car()" which, in this case, is saying mycar. Thus, by saying this.color, the Car() function defines a new property, color, for mycar that you can access like this:

```
mycar.color = "red";
document.write(mycar.color);
```

Since Car() is a function, we can assign the Car object's properties all at once by adding arguments for each of the properties, as shown in Example 11-4.

Example 11-4: The Car() constructor with arguments for each property

```
function Car(color, brand, horsepower, price) {
    this.color = color;
    this.brand = brand;
    this.horsepower = horsepower;
    this.price = price;
}
```

In this scenario, Car() takes four arguments: color, brand, horsepower, and price. The values of each of these arguments are then given to this.color, this.brand, this.horsepower, and this.price, respectively. Thus, as the properties of the new Car object are created, they are given values as well. (Note that the argument names here are the same as the property names, but they don't have to be; it just makes more sense.) Here is the object for a car whose color is red, brand is Ford, horsepower is 160, and price is $15,000:

```
mycar = new Car("red", "Ford", 160, 15000);
```

When you create a new Car object in this way, keep in mind the order of the arguments. You must pass properties in the order defined in the function—color, brand, horsepower, and price.

We can also create new Car objects and assign them to elements of an array. This is especially useful when you have a large number of objects, as in our example scenario. Here is an array with the first two elements defined:

```
cars = new Array();
cars[0] = new Car("red", 'Ford", 160, 15000);
cars[1] = new Car("pink", "Cadillac", 300, 40000);
```

Methods

User-defined objects can have methods as well as properties. A method, as you'll recall, is a function that operates on a specific object. For instance, with the Car object, we can easily add a showBrand() method to display the brand name of the car. First, we create a showBrand() function that uses `document.write()` to display the brand, as shown in Example 11-5.

Example 11-5: Function to display the brand of a car

```
function showBrand() {
    document.write(this.brand);
}
```

Notice the use of `this.brand`: since the `showBrand()` function is (going to be) a method of the `Car` object, it refers to the current object as `this`, so that it can access the object's property value. To turn this function into a method of the `Car` object, we just need to modify the constructor function, as shown in Example 11-6.

Example 11-6: The Car() constructor with showBrand() as a method

```
function Car(color, brand, horsepower, price) {
    this.color = color;
    this.brand = brand;
    this.horsepower = horsepower;
    this.price = price;
    this.showBrand = showBrand;
}
```

Despite the fact that all five lines in this function look similar, they are quite different. The first four lines assign properties to variables, but the last line links the function, `showBrand()`, to the object, thereby creating a method. Notice that there are no double parentheses when you refer to `showBrand` in the constructor; the parentheses are needed when calling a function (or method), but here we are just assigning the function to the object.

Creating a method involves defining a function and then assigning the function to the object in the constructor.

Now that we have created the `showBrand()` function and modified the `Car()` constructor, we can create a new `Car` object and run its `showBrand()` method like this:

```
var mycar = new Car("red", "Ford", 160, 15000);
mycar.showBrand();
```

This simply displays the word "Ford", the `Car` object's brand. Example 11-7 uses the final `Car` constructor and the `showBrand()` method to create a simple page that uses `Car` objects.

Example 11-7: A page that uses Car objects

```
<html>
<head>
<title>Fun with Objects</title>
<script language="JavaScript">
// The Car constructor
function Car(color, brand, horsepower, price) {
    this.color = color;
    this.brand = brand;
    this.horsepower = horsepower;
    this.price = price;
    this.showBrand = showBrand;
}
```

Example 11-7: A page that uses Car objects (continued)

```
// The showBrand() method of the Car object
function showBrand() {
    document.write(this.brand);
}

// Create two Car objects
realcar = new Car("red", "Ford", 160, 15000);
dreamcar = new Car("pink", "Cadillac", 300, 40000);
</script>
</head>

<body bgcolor = "#FFFFFF">
<script language="JavaScript">
document.write("<p>Your dream car is a: ");
dreamcar.showBrand();
document.write("<p>Your real car is a: ");
realcar.showBrand();
</script>
</body>
</html>
```

I hope this section has given you a better understanding of how to create and work with user-defined objects. Although most of this discussion has been heavy on programmer talk, you will find that the next two examples, which rely on user-defined objects, are more practical and applicable to your site.

The quiz: testing your readers

Looking for a way to get your users to interact more with your content? Why not use the old teachers' trick and pop a quiz? Besides providing you with some interesting feedback, it's often entertaining for your visitors. This script creates a simple multiple-choice quiz using form radio buttons, as shown in Figure 11-1. But, unlike school, when you had to wait a day or two to receive your graded quiz, the quiz script gives instant feedback when the user clicks the "Correct Quiz" link. Figure 11-2 shows the correction message, which appears in a separate window.

Understanding the Question object

The Question object represents each question in our quiz.

Since we're learning how to create user-defined objects, we'll create this quiz in an object-oriented way. We'll create one Question object for each question in the quiz.

Example 11-8 shows the constructor function for Question objects. Although it looks daunting at first, you'll soon see that it's not.

Figure 11-1

An interactive multiple-choice quiz

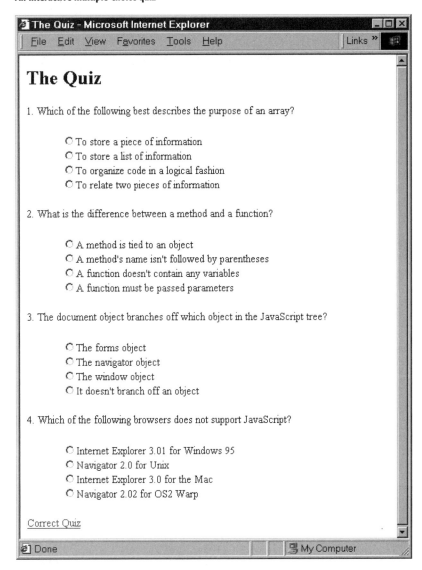

Figure 11-2

Correction box reporting the user's score

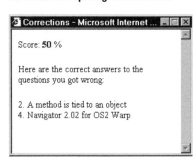

Example 11-8: The Question() constructor

```
function Question(question, correctAnswer) {
    var args = Question.arguments;
    this.question = question;
    this.correctAnswer = correctAnswer;
    this.userAnswer = null;
    this.isCorrect = isCorrect;
    this.showForm = showForm;
    this.userChoices = new Array();
    for (var i = 0; i < args.length - 2; i++) {
        this.userChoices[i] = args[i + 2];
    }
}
```

Let's begin by describing the four properties of the Question object:

- The question property contains the actual content of the question.

- The correctAnswer property contains the number of the correct answer.

- The userAnswer property contains the number the user picks as the answer. If userAnswer matches up with correctAnswer, the question has been answered correctly.

- The userChoices property is an array. That's right, properties can be arrays. The userChoices array contains several possible answers to the question, one of which is correct.

Properties of an object can be arrays.

The args variable defined by the Question() constructor provides a bit of magic that allows us to pass any number of arguments to the constructor, as you'll see shortly. Two of the arguments, question and correctAnswer, have names, while the rest do not. But we can still get to those arguments using the args variable, as you can see in the for loop at the end of the constructor.

In addition to these properties, there are two methods—isCorrect() and showForm()—to this object. The isCorrect() method determines if the question is answered correctly. Example 11-9 shows the isCorrect() method.

Example 11-9: The isCorrect() method

```
function isCorrect() {
    if (this.correctAnswer == this.userAnswer) {
        return true;
    }
    else {
        return false;
    }
}
```

The isCorrect() method simply determines if the user's answer choice, userAnswer, is the same as the correct answer choice, correctAnswer. If they match up, the question was answered correctly and the method returns true. Otherwise, it returns false.

The second method, showForm(), displays the number of the question, the content of the question, and the possible answer choices. It also creates a radio button for each of the choices. Example 11-10 shows the showForm() method.

Example 11-10: The showForm() method

```
function showForm(n) {
    document.write((n + 1) + '. ' + this.question + '<blockquote><form>');
    for (var i = 0; i < this.userChoices.length; i++) {
        document.write('<input type="radio" name="q' + n +
                       '" onClick = "quiz[' + n + '].userAnswer = ' +
                       i + '">');
```

Example 11-10: The showForm() method (continued)

```
        document.write(this.userChoices[i] + '<br>');
    }
    document.write('</form></blockquote>');
}
```

Let's take a closer look at the showForm() method to get a better understanding of how it works. It begins by displaying the number of the question (the value argument n plus one, since array elements start with 0), followed by the question's text, this.question. A blockquote tag is used to set off the answer choices, and a form is started.

Each element in the userChoices array contains one of the answer choices. For example, userChoices[0] contains the first answer choice. A for loop is used to cycle through the array. Inside the for loop, code is run once for each of the answer choices. This code creates a radio button followed by the answer choice's text. If you look closely, you'll see that each radio button contains an onClick event handler. When the radio button is clicked, onClick sets the userAnswer property equal to the number of the choice. Finally, the form and the blockquote are closed off, ending the question.

Making a Question object

Here's how to create a Question object using the Question() constructor function (shown in Example 11-8):

```
var why = new Question(
    "Which of the following best describes the purpose of an array?",
    2,
    "To store a piece of information",
    "To store a list of information",
    "To organize code in a logical fashion",
    "To relate two pieces of information");
```

The first argument is the content of the question. This value is given to the question property of the why Question object.

The second argument is the number of the correct answer. Here the correct answer is 2, which corresponds to "To store a list of information." (Note that the first choice is referred to as 0, the second as 1, etc.) This number is given to the correctAnswer property of the Question object. (Refer back to Example 11-8 if you're unclear about the properties of the Question object.)

A Question should have at least two possible answers, but there is no limit on the maximum number of possible answers.

The remaining arguments are the answer choices. A question should have at least two possible answers, but there is no limit on the maximum number of possible answers. All of these choices are given to the userChoices property of the Question object. Remember that the userChoices property is an array, so choice 0 is assigned to userChoices[0], choice 1 is assigned to userChoices[1], and so on.

After creating the Question object, you can display it and correct it easily using its two methods. For example, to display the why Question object on the page, run its showForm() method:

```
why.showForm(0);
```

Creating the quiz

Now that we know how to make a Question object, we need a way to tie together multiple Question objects into a fully functioning quiz. First, we create an array, quiz, to hold all the Question objects. Next, we create the Question objects. We have four questions, so we'll use elements 0 through 3 of the quiz array, making each element a Question object. Remember the order in which you pass the contents of each Question object to Question(): question, correct answer, answer choices. The quiz array is shown in Example 11-11.

Example 11-11: The quiz array

```
var quiz = new Array();
quiz[0] = new Question(
    "Which of the following best describes the purpose of an array?",
    2,                                              // Correct answer
    "To store a piece of information",              // Choice 0
    "To store a list of information",               // Choice 1
    "To organize code in a logical fashion",        // Choice 2
    "To relate two pieces of information");         // Choice 3
quiz[1] = new Question(
    "What is the difference between a method and a function?",
    0,
    "A method is tied to an object",
    "A method\'s name isn't followed by parentheses",
    "A function doesn't contain any variables",
    "A function must be passed parameters");
quiz[2] = new Question(
    "The document object branches off which object in the JavaScript tree?",
    2,
    "The forms object",
    "The navigator object",
    "The window object",
    "It doesn\'t branch off an object");
quiz[3] = new Question(
    "Which of the following browsers does not support JavaScript?",
    3,
    "Internet Explorer 3.01 for Windows 95",
    "Navigator 2.0 for Unix",
    "Internet Explorer 3.0 for the Mac",
    "Navigator 2.02 for OS2 Warp");
```

Now we have four Question objects, each stored in an element of the quiz array. To display the contents of the first Question object, quiz[0], we can run its showForm() method:

```
quiz[0].showForm(0);
```

Instead of doing this manually for each Question object, let's create a for loop to automatically run each Question object's showForm() method:

```
for (var i = 0; i < quiz.length; i++) {
    quiz[i].showForm(i);
}
```

This loop goes through each element of the quiz array (each Question object) and runs its showForm() method. Essentially, this loop displays the entire quiz on the page.

Correcting the quiz

At this point, we've created the questions and displayed them on the page, but we haven't corrected them. That's what the correctQuiz() function is for: it goes through all the questions, corrects them, opens a new window, and displays the percent correctly answered and the answers to any questions that were done incorrectly (as previously shown in Figure 11-2). Example 11-12 shows the correctQuiz() function.

Example 11-12: The correctQuiz() function

```
function correctQuiz() {
    // Initialize correct and start correctPage string
    var correct = 0;
    var correctPage = '<html><head><title>Corrections</title></head>' +
                      '<body bgcolor="#FFFFFF">';

    // Loop through Question objects, call isCorrect(), and count
    // correct answers
    for (var i = 0; i < quiz.length; i++) {
        if (quiz[i].isCorrect()) {
            correct++;
        }
    }

    // Compute the score and add it to the correctPage string
    var score = Math.round((correct / quiz.length) * 100);
    correctPage += 'Score: <strong>' + score + '</strong> %';

    // If there are incorrect answers, list the correct ones
    if (correct < quiz.length) {
        correctPage += "<p>Here are the correct answers to the ";
        correctPage += "questions you got wrong:<p>";
        for (var i = 0; i < quiz.length; i++) {
            if (!quiz[i].isCorrect()) {
                correctPage += (i + 1) + '. ' +
                    quiz[i].userChoices[quiz[i].correctAnswer] + '<br>';
            }
        }
    }
    else {
        // Otherwise, offer congratulations
        correctPage += "<p>Well done, you aced it.<p>";
    }

    // Finish correctPage, create a new window, and display correctPage
    correctPage += '</body></html>';
    var correctWin = window.open('', '',
                            'height=200,width=300,scrollbars=yes');
    correctWin.document.write(correctPage);
    correctWin.document.close();
}
```

The correctQuiz() function uses the variable correctPage to accumulate the HTML that should be displayed in the correction window. Since we are building an HTML document for the corrections, you can customize it to fit your needs. Just change the attributes in the body tag; it won't mess up the code. If you want a background image or a picture of a graduation hat, just add the appropriate HTML (use absolute URLs for any images).

With a bit of tweaking, you can have your own quiz up and running in no time.

The last thing that our quiz needs is a button to run the correctQuiz() function after the quiz has been finished. We can do this with a simple link:

```
<a href="javascript:correctQuiz();">Correct Quiz</a>
```

Example 11-13 shows how these pieces work together in our complete quiz script. With a bit of tweaking, you can have your own quiz up and running in no time.

Example 11-13: Source code for the quiz script

```
<html>
<head>
<title>The Quiz</title>
<script language="JavaScript">
// The Question constructor function
function Question(question, correctAnswer) {
    var args = Question.arguments;
    this.question = question;
    this.correctAnswer = correctAnswer;
    this.userAnswer = null;
    this.isCorrect = isCorrect;
    this.showForm = showForm;
    this.userChoices = new Array();
    for (var i = 0; i < args.length - 2; i++) {
        this.userChoices[i] = args[i + 2];
    }
}

// Method to determine if question is answered correctly
function isCorrect() {
    if (this.correctAnswer == this.userAnswer) {
        return true;
    }
    else {
        return false;
    }
}

// Method to display contents of Question object
function showForm(n) {
    document.write((n + 1) + '. ' + this.question + '<blockquote><form>');
    for (var i = 0; i < this.userChoices.length; i++) {
        document.write('<input type="radio" name="q' + n +
                       '" onClick = "quiz[' + n + '].userAnswer = ' +
                       i + '">');
        document.write(this.userChoices[i] + '<br>');
    }
    document.write('</form></blockquote>');
}
```

Example 11-13: Source code for the quiz script (continued)

```
// Function to correct the quiz and display score and correct answers
function correctQuiz() {
    // Initialize correct and start correctPage string
    var correct = 0;
    var correctPage = '<html><head><title>Corrections</title></head>' +
                      '<body bgcolor="#FFFFFF">';

    // Loop through Question objects, call isCorrect(), and count
    // correct answers
    for (var i = 0; i < quiz.length; i++) {
        if (quiz[i].isCorrect()) {
            correct++;
        }
    }

    // Compute the score and add it to the correctPage string
    var score = Math.round((correct / quiz.length) * 100);
    correctPage += 'Score: <strong>' + score + '</strong> %';

    // If there are incorrect answers, list the correct ones
    if (correct < quiz.length) {
        correctPage += "<p>Here are the correct answers to the ";
        correctPage += "questions you got wrong:<p>";
        for (var i = 0; i < quiz.length; i++) {
            if (!quiz[i].isCorrect()) {
                correctPage += (i + 1) + '. ' +
                    quiz[i].userChoices[quiz[i].correctAnswer] + '<br>';
            }
        }
    }
    else {
        // Otherwise, offer congratulations
        correctPage += "<p>Well done, you aced it.<p>";
    }

    // Finish correctPage, create a new window, and display correctPage
    correctPage += '</body></html>';
    var correctWin = window.open('', '',
                                'height=200,width=300,scrollbars=yes');
    correctWin.document.write(correctPage);
    correctWin.document.close();
}

// Create four Question objects
var quiz = new Array();
quiz[0] = new Question(
    "Which of the following best describes the purpose of an array?",
    2,                                          // Correct answer
    "To store a piece of information",          // Choice 0
    "To store a list of information",           // Choice 1
    "To organize code in a logical fashion",    // Choice 2
    "To relate two pieces of information");     // Choice 3
quiz[1] = new Question(
    "What is the difference between a method and a function?",
    0,
    "A method is tied to an object",
    "A method\'s name isn't followed by parentheses",
    "A function doesn't contain any variables",
    "A function must be passed parameters");
quiz[2] = new Question(
    "The document object branches off which object in the JavaScript tree?",
    2,
    "The forms object",
```

Example 11-13: Source code for the quiz script (continued)

```
        "The navigator object",
        "The window object",
        "It doesn\'t branch off an object");
quiz[3] = new Question(
        "Which of the following browsers does not support JavaScript?",
        3,
        "Internet Explorer 3.01 for Windows 95",
        "Navigator 2.0 for Unix",
        "Internet Explorer 3.0 for the Mac",
        "Navigator 2.02 for OS2 Warp");
</script>
</head>

<body bgcolor="#FFFFFF">
<h1>The Quiz</h1>
<p>
<script language="JavaScript">
// Place this for loop where you want the quiz to be displayed
for (var i = 0; i < quiz.length; i++) {
        quiz[i].showForm(i);
}
</script>
<!-- This link runs the correctQuiz() function when clicked -->
<a href="javascript:correctQuiz();">Correct Quiz</a>
</body>
</html>
```

Relational menus

Nowhere in the world is it tougher to find your way from point A to point B than on the Web. The Web is a semi-organized, interconnected group of documents, which is both good and bad—good if you're just browsing whimsically, bad if you're rushed and looking for specific information. There are, however, many ways to make the Web—and, more specifically, a web site—more orderly and efficient. One of these ways is the relational menu, a device that organizes all of your site's information in a compact and easy-to-navigate manner.

A relational menu consists of two related menus filled with information from which to choose, as shown in Figure 11-3. These two menus, which I like to call the category menu (the left menu) and the pages menu (the right menu), work in tandem. When the user selects an item from the category menu, a related list of items, most likely web pages, is displayed in the pages menu. In Figure 11-3, for example, relational menus have been used to organize a larger list of cars into smaller, more specialized categories. At first, the pages menu is blank. When the user chooses a category, such as "Sports Cars," the contents of that category are displayed in the pages menu.

Creating your menus

The relational menu system relies on two objects: Category and Page. Example 11-14 shows the constructor functions for these objects.

Figure 11-3

Making a selection in one menu brings up a related list in the accompanying menu

Example 11-14: The Category() and Page() constructors

```
function Category(name) {
    this.name = name;
    this.length = 0;
}

function Page(name, url) {
    this.name = name;
    this.url = url;
}
```

These constructor functions should be fairly self-explanatory by now. To create a Category object, you just pass a name to the Category() constructor. For Page objects, you pass a name and a URL to Page().

The actual work of creating relational menus is handled by two helper functions, newCategory() and newPage(), as shown in Example 11-15.

The Category and Page objects represent the items in the category and pages menus, respectively.

Example 11-15: The newCategory() and newPage() functions

```
// Variables to keep track of Category objects
var categories = new Array();
var categoriesIndex = -1;
var pagesIndex = -1;

// Helper function to create Category objects
function newCategory(name) {
    categoriesIndex++
    pagesIndex = -1;
    categories[categoriesIndex] = new Category(name);
}

// Helper function to create Page objects
function newPage(name, url) {
    pagesIndex++;
    categories[categoriesIndex][pagesIndex] = new Page(name, url);
    categories[categoriesIndex].length++;
}
```

Both newCategory() and newPage() rely on three variables that are used to keep track of the categories and pages in the menus: categories, categoriesIndex, and pagesIndex. Before we look at the specifics of how newCategory() and newPage() work, let's see how to use them. Example 11-16 shows the code used to create the categories and pages for our car menus.

Example 11-16: Creating the categories and corresponding pages

```
newCategory('Luxury Cars');                         // New category
newPage('Euro', 'euro.html');                       // Pages in category
newPage('Alvan', 'alvan.html');
newPage('Gates', 'gates.html');

newCategory('Off Road');                            // New category
newPage('Mountaineer', 'mountaineer.html');         // Pages in category
newPage('Buck', 'buck.html');

newCategory('Sports Cars');                         // New category
newPage('Zippo', 'zippo.html');                     // Pages in category
```

Example 11-16: Creating the categories and corresponding pages (continued)

```
newPage('Flier', 'flier.html');
newPage('Maven', 'maven.html');
newPage('Zoom', 'zoom.html');
```

Because of how they are designed, the newCategory() and newPage() functions must be called as you see here, with the pages for a particular category created right after that category.

How relational menus work

While relational menus are easy to understand on a conceptual level (i.e., the pages menu changes when the user makes a selection from the category menu), they are more complex on a code level. Let's begin by looking at the categories and pages as they are arranged in the code. All of the categories and their respective pages are kept in an array named categories. Each time we call newCategory(), a Category object is added to this array.

The first element of the array, categories[0], contains a user-defined Category object for the first category in the relational menu. So in our demo, categories[0] contains all of the items that fall under the "Luxury Cars" category. To get the name of the category stored in categories[0], use its name property:

```
categories[0].name;
```

This supplies you with the category's name, "Luxury Cars". Here's the fun part: within this array, there is yet another array (this is referred to as a nested or two-dimensional array), as created by the newPage() function. Within the nested array is a user-defined Page object for the pages in the category. This user-defined object has two properties: name and url. The name property contains the name (or description) of the page, and the url property contains the URL of that page. So we can access the name and URL of the first page in the "Luxury Cars" category as follows:

```
categories[0][0].name;
categories[0][0].url;
```

The categoriesIndex and pagesIndex variables, as used in newCategory() and newPage(), take care of managing the nested array elements.

Knowing this, how would you access the name of the second page in the third category ("Sports Cars")? First you'd ask for the third element of the categories array, categories[2], then you'd ask for the second element of the array contained within that array, categories[2][1], and finally you'd ask for the name property, ending up with this:

```
categories[2][1].name;
```

The purpose of all this object-orientation is to make the relational menu's contents easier to create and manipulate in code. When we finally put together the categories and pages for our menus (Example 11-16), the

An array within an array is called a nested, or two-dimensional, array.

format was very intuitive and easy to work with. All we had to do was be sure to create the categories and pages in the right order.

Relating the menus

Now that you understand how the Category and Page objects are arranged into JavaScript arrays, we can look at the code that actually makes the relational menus work. First, let's look at the code that creates the menus on the page, as shown in Example 11-17.

Example 11-17: Creating the relational menus in HTML

```
<body bgcolor="#FFFFFF">
<!-- Place the following script where you want the menus to be displayed -->
<script language="JavaScript">
// Variables for the headings used in the menus
var categoryHeading = 'Choose A Vehicle Type';
var pageHeading = 'Choose A Model';
var betweenHeading = ' then ';

// Output the form and the categories select menu
document.write('<form name="menus">');
document.write('<select name="menu1" ');
document.write('onChange="relatePages(this.selectedIndex);">');
document.write('<option>' + categoryHeading + '</option>');

// Loop through categories array to display all options
for (var i = 0; i < categories.length; i++) {
    document.write('<option>' + categories[i].name + '</option>');
}

// Output the pages select menu
document.write('</select>' + betweenHeading);
document.write('<select name="menu2" ');
document.write('onChange="gotoPage(this.selectedIndex);">');
document.write('<option>' + pageHeading + '</option>');

// Create ten options for pages menu and set them all to null
for (var i = 0; i < 10; i++) {
    document.write('<option></option>');
}
document.write('</select></form>');
for (var i = document.menus.menu2.options.length; i > 0; i--) {
    document.menus.menu2.options[i] = null;
}
</script>
</body>
```

This script, which you'll note resides in the body of the document, creates two HTML select menus for the relational menu system. The categories menu contains an option for each item in the categories array. This menu uses an onChange event handler to call the relatePages() function when the user selects a category. relatePages() takes care of populating the pages menu with the appropriate options. The second half of the script in Example 11-17 simply creates a second select menu for the pages, but it sets all of the options to null initially. Example 11-18 shows the relatePages() function that populates the second menu.

Example 11-18: The relatePages( ) function

```
function relatePages(category) {
    if (category > 0) {
        categoriesIndex = category - 1;
        var pagesMenu = document.menus.menu2;

        // Clear the old options
        for (var i = pagesMenu.options.length; i > 1; i--) {
            pagesMenu.options[i] = null;
        }

        // Add the new pages
        for (var i = 0; i < categories[categoriesIndex].length; i++) {
            pagesMenu.options[i+1] =
                new Option(categories[categoriesIndex][i].name);
        }
        pagesMenu.options[0].selected = true;
    }
    pagesIndex = 0;
}
```

The Option object is a built-in JavaScript object that creates an item for a select menu.

The relatePages( ) function first clears the old options from the pages menu and then loops through the Page objects for the selected category and inserts the name of each page into the pages menu. The Option object is a built-in JavaScript object that creates an item for a select menu.

If you look back at Example 11-17, you'll see that the pages menu also defines an onChange event handler, for when the user selects a page. This onChange event handler calls gotoPage( ), which takes care of loading the appropriate document for the selected page. Example 11-19 shows the gotoPage( ) function.

Example 11-19: The gotoPage( ) function

```
function gotoPage(page) {
    var url = null;
    if (page > 0) {
        url = categories[categoriesIndex][page-1].url;
    }
    if (url != null) {
        window.location = url;
    }
}
```

The gotoPage( ) function accesses the url property for the selected Page object and assigns it to window.location, thereby loading the appropriate document.

Phew! This has been a complicated example. If you understand all of the code shown in Example 11-20, which contains the complete relational menu script, you should have a solid grasp of how user-defined objects work in JavaScript.

Example 11-20: Source code for the relational menu script

```
<html>
<head>
<title>Relational Menus</title>
<script language="JavaScript">
// The Category constructor function
function Category(name) {
    this.name = name;
    this.length = 0;
}

// The Page constructor function
function Page(name, url) {
    this.name = name;
    this.url = url;
}

// Variables to keep track of Category objects
var categories = new Array();
var categoriesIndex = -1;
var pagesIndex = -1;

// Helper function to create Category objects
function newCategory(name) {
    categoriesIndex++
    pagesIndex = -1;
    categories[categoriesIndex] = new Category(name);
}

// Helper function to create Page objects
function newPage(name, url) {
    pagesIndex++;
    categories[categoriesIndex][pagesIndex] = new Page(name, url);
    categories[categoriesIndex].length++;
}

// Function to populate the pages menu based on the selected category
function relatePages(category) {
    if (category > 0) {
        categoriesIndex = category - 1;
        var pagesMenu = document.menus.menu2;

        // Clear the old options
        for (var i = pagesMenu.options.length; i > 1; i--) {
            pagesMenu.options[i] = null;
        }

        // Add the new pages
        for (var i = 0; i < categories[categoriesIndex].length; i++) {
            pagesMenu.options[i+1] =
                new Option(categories[categoriesIndex][i].name);
        }
        pagesMenu.options[0].selected = true;
    }
    pagesIndex = 0;
}

// Function to load the appropriate document based on selected page
function gotoPage(page) {
    var url = null;
    if (page > 0) {
        url = categories[categoriesIndex][page-1].url;
    }
    if (url != null) {
```

Example 11-20: Source code for the relational menu script (continued)

```
        window.location = url;
    }
}

// Create the categories and pages for our cars
newCategory('Luxury Cars');                    // New category
newPage('Euro', 'euro.html');                  // Pages in category
newPage('Alvan', 'alvan.html');
newPage('Gates', 'gates.html');

newCategory('Off Road');                       // New category
newPage('Mountaineer', 'mountaineer.html');    // Pages in category
newPage('Buck', 'buck.html');

newCategory('Sports Cars');                    // New category
newPage('Zippo', 'zippo.html');                // Pages in category
newPage('Flier', 'flier.html');
newPage('Maven', 'maven.html');
newPage('Zoom', 'zoom.html');
</script>
</head>

<body bgcolor="#FFFFFF">
<!-- Place the following script where you want the menus to be displayed -->
<script language="JavaScript">
// Variables for the headings used in the menus
var categoryHeading = 'Choose A Vehicle Type';
var pageHeading = 'Choose A Model';
var betweenHeading = ' then ';

// Output the form and the categories select menu
document.write('<form name="menus">');
document.write('<select name="menu1" ');
document.write('onChange="relatePages(this.selectedIndex);">');
document.write('<option>' + categoryHeading + '</option>');

// Loop through categories array to display all options
for (var i = 0; i < categories.length; i++) {
    document.write('<option>' + categories[i].name + '</option>');
}

// Output the pages select menu
document.write('</select>' + betweenHeading);
document.write('<select name="menu2" ');
document.write('onChange="gotoPage(this.selectedIndex);">');
document.write('<option>' + pageHeading + '</option>');

// Create ten options for pages menu and set them all to null
for (var i = 0; i < 10; i++) {
    document.write('<option></option>');
}
document.write('</select></form>');
for (var i = document.menus.menu2.options.length; i > 0; i--) {
    document.menus.menu2.options[i] = null;
}
</script>
</body>
</html>
```

A cross-browser style object

At this point, you should have a general appreciation for the power of object-oriented scripting. Now let's look at using these techniques with DHTML. As you've seen in Chapter 9 and Chapter 10, writing out DHTML can be quite time-consuming and repetitive. If you throw in support for different versions of the DOM used by older browsers, things get downright scary.

Think about how much easier DHTML would be if you had a cross-browser style object that dealt with all the compatibility headaches for you. Rather than writing out styles for every element and using if statements for every difference in DHTML support, you could just call methods of this object to achieve different effects. Not only would this cross-browser style object save time, but it would also make creating and organizing a large script much easier, by breaking it up into logical chunks.

While we could endeavor to write our own cross-browser style object, fortunately there's no need, because lots of JavaScript programmers have created such tools for their own pages. Instead, we're going to use a cross-browser style object called xbStyle, which was developed by Bob Clary at Netscape. You can find the latest version of xbStyle, as well as more information on cross-browser scripting, at *http://developer.netscape. com/evangelism/docs/api/xbStyle/*. Despite the fact that xbStyle is hosted on a Netscape site, it is truly a cross-browser effort.

xbStyle is a cross-browser style object that greatly simplifies the creation of cross-browser DHTML.

Using xbStyle

To take advantage of the xbStyle object in your own scripts, you need to download the *xbStyle.js* file from the web page listed above. xbStyle also makes use of a browser sniffing script, *ua.js*, which can be downloaded from the same page.

In order to use xbStyle, you must link both the *ua.js* and *xbstyle.js* files to your document, as follows:

```
<script language="JavaScript" src="ua.js"></script>
<script language="JavaScript" src="xbStyle.js"></script>
```

Once that's done, your script can make use of the xbStyle object for creating cross-browser DHTML.

The main difference between using xbStyle and creating DHTML that uses the W3C DOM standard has to do with how you access and manipulate style attributes. With the W3C DOM, once you have a reference to an HTML element, such as a layer, you can use the style property to access and manipulate individual style attributes. With xbStyle, however, once you have an HTML element, you need to create an xbStyle object for that element. You do this with the xbStyle() constructor function, which takes one argument, an element id:

```
var styleObject = new xbStyle("id");
```

Once you've created an xbStyle object, you can use xbStyle's built-in methods, which expand on the W3C and 4.0 DOM methods, to manipulate style attributes, as you'll see in the next section, when we look an a real example.

xbStyle provides methods for manipulating style attributes that expand on the W3C and 4.0 DOM methods. It also implements a document.getElementById() method for 4.0 browsers that don't support the W3C DOM.

xbStyle also implements a document.getElementById() method for 4.0 browsers that don't support the W3C DOM, with the same general functionality as the standard DOM method. If the browser does support the DOM, xbStyle does nothing, and the method works just as expected.

The documentation available at *http://developer.netscape.com/evangelism/docs/api/xbStyle/* contains a full listing of all methods and properties of the xbStyle object.

Cross-browser sliding tabs

To demonstrate xbStyle, we'll take the sliding tab example from Chapter 10 and rewrite it using xbStyle. As you'll recall, the original script uses the W3C DOM to slide a layer across the screen. Example 11-21 shows the showLayer() and hideLayer() functions from the original sliding tab script (Example 10-6).

Example 11-21: The showLayer() and hideLayer() functions

```
function showLayer() {
    var hiddenLayer = document.getElementById("TabLayer");
    var layerPosition = parseInt(hiddenLayer.style.left);
    if (layerPosition < 0) {
        hiddenLayer.style.left = (layerPosition + 5) + "px";
        setTimeout("showLayer()", 20);
    }
}

function hideLayer() {
    var hiddenLayer = document.getElementById("TabLayer");
    hiddenLayer.style.left = "-75px";
}
```

The two functions in our cross-browser sliding menu, xbStyleShowLayer() and xbStyleHideLayer(), mimic the behavior of our original functions, changing only what is necessary to achieve compatibility. In these functions, we'll be using the following methods from xbStyle:

moveBy(*x*, *y*)
    Moves an element the specified number of pixels along the X (horizontal) and Y (vertical) axes, relative to its current position. This method is equivalent to adding to or subtracting from both the top and left style attributes at once

getLeft()
    Returns the value of the left attribute as a number. Note that this is different from the W3C DOM, which returns a string that contains the value plus the units px, for pixels. getLeft() returns a number, which means that we don't have to use parseInt() as we do with the W3C DOM.

setLeft(*n*)

Sets the left attribute to the specified value. Again, there is no need for strings or units here.

Example 11-22 shows the revised xbStyleShowLayer() and xbStyleHide-Layer() functions that implement the sliding tab.

Example 11-22: The xbStyleShowLayer() and xbStyleHideLayer() functions

```javascript
function xbStyleShowLayer() {
    var layer = document.getElementById("TabLayer");
    var styleObject = new xbStyle(layer);
    if (styleObject.getLeft() <= 0) {
        styleObject.moveBy(5, 0);
        setTimeout("showLayer()", 20);
    }
}

function xbStyleHideLayer() {
    var layer = document.getElementById("TabLayer");
    var styleObject = new xbStyle(layer);
    styleObject.setLeft(-75);
}
```

Both functions use document.getElementById() to access the sliding tab layer. For the 4.0 browsers, we get the xbStyle implementation of this method; for the later browsers, we get the W3C standard implementation. Each function then creates a new xbStyle object, which allows cross-browser manipulation of the style attributes of the layer.

In xbStyleShowLayer(), we use the getLeft() method to compare the layer's left style attribute with zero, to see if the tab has been displayed fully. If the tab is still partly offscreen, we use the moveBy() method to move the tab 5 pixels to the right. Compare this with the original version of showLayer(), in which we moved the tab by adding 5 to the current value of left and setting the left attribute to that sum. Now, with xbStyle, we can just use the moveBy() method and save ourselves some math. Example 11-23 shows the full script for the xbStyle version of our sliding tab.

Example 11-23: Source code for xbStyle sliding tab

```html
<html>
<head>
<title>Sliding Tabs with xbStyle</title>
<style>
.hideshow { color: #333333; font-size: 9px; font-family: sans-serif;
            text-decoration: none; }
</style>
<script language="JavaScript" src="ua.js"></script>
<script language="JavaScript" src="xbStyle.js"></script>
<script language="JavaScript">

function xbStyleShowLayer() {
    var layer = document.getElementById("TabLayer");
    var styleObject = new xbStyle(layer);
    var left = styleObj.getLeft();
    if (left <= 0) {
        styleObject.moveBy(5, 0);
```

Example 11-23: Source code for xbStyle sliding tab (continued)

```
            setTimeout("showLayer()", 20);
        }
    }

function xbStyleHideLayer() {
    var layer = document.getElementById("TabLayer");
    var styleObject = new xbStyle(layer);
    styleObject.setLeft(-75);
}
</script>
</head>

<body>
<div id="TabLayer"
     style="position:absolute; left:-75px; top:50px;
            width:115px; height:200px; z-index:1;
            background-color: #CCCCCC; layer-background-color: #CCCCCC;">

  <p align="right" class="hideshow">
    <a href="javascript:xbStyleHideLayer();"
       class="hideshow">&lt;&lt;hide</a> |
    <a href="javascript:xbStyleShowLayer();"
       class="hideshow">show&gt;&gt;</a>
  </p>

  <p align="left" style="margin-left: 5px;">
    <a href="#">Scripts</a><br>
    <a href="#">Weblog</a><br>
    <a href="#">Projects</a><br>
    <a href="#">Contact</a>
  </p>
</div>
</body>
</html>
```

Behind the scenes

Now that you've seen xbStyle in action, let's take a look behind the curtain and see how the magic works. Example 11-24 shows the source code for xbStyle's getElementById() method.

Example 11-24: xbStyle's implementation of getElementById()

```
if (navigator.family == 'ie4' && navigator.version < 5) {
    document.getElementById = new Function("id",
        "return document.all[id];");
}
else if (navigator.family == 'nn4') {
    document.getElementById = nav4GetLayerById;
}

function nav4GetLayerById(id) {
    return nav4FindLayer(this, id);
}

function nav4FindLayer(doc, id) {
    var i;
    var subdoc;
    var obj;

    for (i = 0; i < doc.layers.length; ++i) {
```

Example 11-24: xbStyle's implementation of getElementById( ) (continued)

```
        if (doc.layers[i].id && id == doc.layers[i].id)
            return doc.layers[i];

        subdoc = doc.layers[i].document;
        obj    = nav4FindLayer(subdoc, id);
        if (obj != null)
            return obj;
    }
    return null;
}
```

In IE 4, elements are accessed through the `document.all[]` array. In this case, xbStyle merely takes the id passed to `getElementById()` and redirects it to `document.all[]` instead, which then returns the appropriate element. In Navigator 4, a `div` with an `id` can only be accessed through the `document.layers[]` array. To compensate, xbStyle checks every element in that list against the `id` you're looking for, stops when it finds a match, and returns the correct element.

In IE 4, elements are accessed through the document.all[] array. In Navigator 4, a div tag with an ID can only be accessed through the document.layers[] array.

When you use xbStyle's `getElementById()` method, it doesn't matter whether xbStyle had to pass the `id` to a Navigator- or IE-specific function; all your script sees is the element returned by the function. In other words, all you have to worry about is providing the correct `id`. This is the essence of objects—to hide the hard stuff and let you do real work.

Moving on

JavaScript objects are incredibly powerful. With object-oriented programming techniques, you can reuse code, save time, and avoid compatibility pitfalls. As you continue to learn and work with JavaScript, you'll find that the more complex the script, the more time you'll save by using objects.

You should also look for opportunities to use xbStyle and other user-defined objects that can take the grunt work out of scripting, so you can get back to designing compelling web sites. You can find collections of such objects at a variety of web sites, including:

Netscape's DevEdge site
    http://developer.netscape.com

ZDNet's Net Developer site
    http://www.zdnet.com/devhead/

DynAPI v2, an API for creating cross-browser DHTML
    http://dynapi.sourceforge.net/dynapi/

C|Net's Builder.com
    http://builder.cnet.com

Webmonkey's JavaScript Code Library
    http://hotwired.lycos.com/webmonkey/reference/javascript_code_library/

Doc JavaScript from WebReference.com
    http://www.webreference.com/js/

Common JavaScript Objects

The JavaScript tree is quite complex. This appendix organizes the most commonly used properties and methods into a large reference, grouped by object. Though this covers many of the JavaScript objects supported by Netscape 6 and IE 5.5 and 6, it is not a definitive listing. (For a definitive listing, consult *JavaScript: The Definitive Guide*, by David Flanagan, published by O'Reilly). Many of these objects have been discussed in this book, but there are some methods that I have not discussed.

`window`   The browser window

Properties

`name`	The window's name
`parent`	The parent window (if the window is within a frame)
`top`	The uppermost browser window
`self`	Synonym for the current window
`opener`	The creator of the current window
`status`	The window's status bar
`defaultStatus`	The status bar's default message
`frames[]`	An array of all frames contained within the window

Methods

`open("url","name", "attributes")`	Opens a new window with the specified attributes
`close()`	Closes a window
`focus()`	Focuses a window, placing it front of all other windows
`blur()`	Blurs a window, placing it behind all other windows
`find("text")`	Finds the specified text in the window
`forward()`	Brings the window one level forward in the page history

back()	Brings the window one level back in the page history
scrollTo(*x*, *y*)*	Scrolls the window to the specified pixel coordinates
scrollBy(*x*, *y*)*	Scrolls the window by the specified pixel amounts
moveTo(*x*, *y*)*	Moves the window to the specified pixel coordinates
moveBy(*x*, *y*)*	Moves the window by the specified pixel amounts
resizeTo(*x*, *y*)*	Resizes the window to the specified pixel coordinates
resizeBy(*x*, *y*)*	Resizes the window by the specified pixel amounts
stop()	Stops any downloading in the window
home()	Brings the window to the "home" site
print()	Displays the print dialog box

window.history
The history of the window

Properties

length	The number of pages in the history

Methods

go(*value*)	Travel forward/back a number of pages in the history; a *value* of 0 specifies the current page
back()	Travel one level back in the page history
forward()	Travel one level forward in the page history

window.location
The location of the window

Properties

host	The domain of the current location
href	The full URL of the current location

Methods

replace("*url*")	Replaces the currently displayed page (but does not affect the window's history)
reload()	Performs a soft reload on the current window

window.document
The document displayed in the window

Properties

title	The title of the document
cookie	Your domain's cookies

---

* These methods are supported by both Navigator and IE, but they are not part of the W3C standard DOM.

referrer	The URL that brought the user to the current document (for example, if *a.html* links to *b.html*, *b.html*'s referrer is *a.html*)
bgColor	Background color
fgColor	Foreground color
alinkColor	Active link color
vlinkColor	Visited link color
linkColor	Link color

Methods

write()	Writes text to the current document.
close()	Closes the text stream to a document. When you write to a document after it has been initially created, the write() method should be followed by this method.
getElementById(*id*)	Finds and returns the HTML element with the given *id* attribute.
getElementsByName(*name*)	Finds and returns the HTML element or elements with the given *name* attribute.
getElementsByTagName(*tag*)	Finds and returns the HTML element or elements with the given HTML *tag*.

---

window.document.forms[]   The forms in a document

Example of a form object:

```
<form name="myName" action="/cgi-bin/one.cgi" method="get">
    form elements
</form>
```

Accessing the form object through JavaScript:

```
document.forms["myName"];
```

Properties

action	The action of a form
method	The method of a form (i.e., get or post)
name	The name of a form
target	The target window where the form's output will be displayed

Methods

reset()	Resets a form
submit()	Submits a form, but for security reasons, only when inside an onClick event handler

window.document.images[] The images in a document

Example of an image object:

```
<img name="myName" src="myImageFile.gif">
```

Accessing an image object through JavaScript:

```
document.images.["myName"];
document.myName;
```

Properties

src	The source, or image file, of the image
name	The name of the image

Math An object for performing mathematical operations

Properties

PI	The value of π (i.e., 3.14259...)

Methods

abs(*value*)	Calculates the absolute value of *number*
sin(*value*)	Calculates the sin of *number*
cos(*value*)	Calculates the cosine of *number*
tan(*value*)	Calculates the tangent of *number*
log(*value*)	Calculate the log of *number*
ceil(*value*)	Rounds *value* up to the nearest integer
floor(*value*)	Rounds *value* down to the nearest integer
round(*value*)	Rounds *value* to the nearest integer
random()	Returns a random value from 0 to 1
sqrt(*value*)	Calculates the square root of *number*

string An object for any string of text

Example of a string object:

```
var myString = "This is a string.";
```

Properties

length	Length of the string in characters

Methods

charAt(*string*)	Retrieves character at the location, counted by character, of *string*
indexOf(*string*)	Determines the placement, by character, of *string* within the string (e.g., myString.indexOf("is") returns 2)

substring(*begin*, *end*)	Retrieves the text between the specified beginning and end values
toLowerCase()	Makes all characters in a string of text lowercase
toUpperCase()	Makes all characters in a string of text uppercase

Date

An object that represents the date and time

Example of a Date object:

```
var myDate = new Date();
```

Methods

setDate(), getDate()	Sets/gets the day of the month
setDay(), getDay()	Sets/gets the day of the week (where 0 is Sunday, 6 is Saturday)
setHours(), getHours()	Sets/gets the hour of the day (from 0 to 23)
setMinutes(), getMinutes()	Sets/gets the minute of the hour (from 0 to 59)
setMonth(), getMonth()	Sets/gets the month (where 0 is January and 11 is December)
setSeconds(), getSeconds()	Sets/gets the time in seconds (from 0 to 59)
setTime(), getTime()	Sets/gets the time in milliseconds
setFullYear(), getFullYear()	Sets/gets the year (as its full four digits)
toGMTString()	Gets time in relation to Greenwich Mean Time
toLocaleString()	Gets local time as date and time
toString()	Gets time as date, zone, and time

navigator

Information about the browser

Properties

appCodeName	Browser's code name
appName	Browser's name
appVersion	Browser's version information
userAgent	Browser's user-agent header
cookieEnabled	Indicator of whether cookies are enabled (true or false)
mimeTypes	An array of supported MIME types (IE on Windows systems returns an undefined object)
platform	The browser's platform or operating system

navigator.plugins   Information about plugins available in the browser

Example of a plugins object:

```
navigator.plugins["LiveAudio"];
```

If this plugin is present, this statement returns a plugins object; if it is not present, it returns nothing.

Properties

description	A plugin object's description
filename	A plugin object's primary filename
length	The number of installed plugins
name	A plugin object's name

Methods

refresh()	Refreshes all plugins, which is useful if a plugin has been installed and you don't want to restart the browser

screen   Information about the display

Properties

width	The horizontal dimension, in pixels, of the user's entire screen
height	The vertical dimension, in pixels, of the user's entire screen
pixelDepth	The number of bits per pixel in the display
colorDepth	The number of bits per color, which tells you the number of different allowable colors. 8-bit color supports 256 colors, 16-bit (often called "high color") supports approximately 64,000 colors, and 24-bit color (often called "true color") supports approximately 16 million colors.
availHeight	The vertical dimension, in pixels, of the window's content area
availWidth	The horizontal dimension, in pixels, of the window's content area

Appendix B

Event Handlers

Event handlers allow web pages to interact with the user. Here is a full listing of the JavaScript event handlers supported by both Netscape 6 and IE 5.5 and 6.

Event handler	Occurs when
onAbort	A download is aborted
onBlur	A window or frame loses focus (i.e., it stops being the active window)
onClick	An element is clicked with the mouse
onChange	A form element is changed or modified
onError	An error occurs (e.g., a script syntax error)
onFocus	A window or frame is focused (i.e., it becomes the active window)
onMouseDown	A mouse button is pressed
onMouseOver	The mouse cursor moves over an element
onMouseOut	The mouse cursor moves out of an element
onMouseMove	The mouse moves
onMouseUp	A mouse button is released
onMove	A window is moved
onLoad	The document has finished loading
onReset	A form is reset
onResize	A window is resized
onSubmit	A form is submitted
onSelect	An element is selected
OnScroll	The current document or layer is scrolled
onUnload	The current document is closed (i.e., the user moves on to another page)

Appendix C

Style Properties

Here is a chart of the most common style properties supported in JavaScript by both Netscape 6 and Internet Explorer 5.5 and 6. For complete details on these properties, see *Cascading Style Sheets: The Definitive Guide*, by Eric A. Meyer (O'Reilly).

Property name	Possible values	Description
backgroundAttachment	fixed, scroll	Property that indicates hether background image scrolls with the element
backgroundColor	Hexadecimal value or HTML name	Element's background color
backgroundImage	Filename	Element's background image
backgroundPosition	x,y coordinates in pixels (px) or percentages (%)	Position of the background image
backgroundRepeat	repeat, no-repeat, repeat-x, repeat-y	Property that indicates whether the background image repeats
borderColor	Hexadecimal value or HTML name	Color of element's border
borderWidth	Width in pixels (px)	Width of element's border
bottom	Length in pixels (px) or percentage (%)	Distance of element from bottom edge of window or containing layer
clear	all, none, left, right	Property that keeps other elements from floating around this element
clip	rect(top left bottom right) in pixels	Dimensions of visible layer area
color	Hexadecimal value or HTML name	Color of element
fontFamily	serif, sans-serif, monospace, or a comma-separated list of font families	Specific or generic font family used to render the element
fontSize	Size in em-height (em) or pixels (px)	Size of font used to render the element
fontStyle	normal, italic, oblique	Style of font used to render the element
fontWeight	normal, bold, bolder, lighter	Font weight used to render the element
height	Height in pixels (px)	Height of element
left	Length in pixels (px) or percentage (%)	Distance of element from left edge of window or containing layer

Property name	Possible values	Description
letterSpacing	normal or distance in pixels (px) or em-height (em)	Distance between letters in element
lineHeight	Distance in pixels (px) or em-height (em)	Distance between bottom of line of text and bottom of text or element above it
listStyleImage	Filename of image	Image to use in place of bullets in a list element
listStyleType	disc, circle, square, decimal, lower-roman, upper-roman, lower-alpha, upper-alpha, none	Type of bullets or characters to display beside items in list element
margin	Length in pixels (px)	Distance between element border and other elements
marginBottom, marginLeft, marginRight, marginTop		Same as margin, separated into each side of the element
overflow	scroll, auto, visible, hidden	Indicator of how to handle content larger than the containing layer
padding	Length in pixels (px)	Distance from content of an element to the element's border
paddingBottom, paddingLeft, paddingRight, paddingTop		Same as padding, separated into each side of the element
position	absolute, relative, static	Type of positioning for the element
right	Length in pixels (px) or percentage (%)	Distance of element from right edge of window or containing layer
textAlign	left, right, center, justify	Text alignment in element
textDecoration	none, underline, line-through, overline	Decoration for the text in element; values may be combined
textTransform	uppercase, lowercase, capitalize, none	Case of text in element
top	Length in pixels (px) or percentage (%)	Distance of element from top edge of window or containing layer
verticalAlign	top, bottom, baseline, middle, or relative position as a percentage (%)	Vertical alignment of element
visibility	visible or hidden	Visibility of an elementxs
width	Width in pixels (px) or percentage (%)	Width of element
wordSpacing	Distance in pixels (px) or em-height (em)	Distance between words in text in element

JavaScript Syntax

This appendix lists the syntax for some common JavaScript statements and operators.

Control Flow

Functions

Syntax

```
function function-name (argument1, argument2, ...) {
    statements
}
```

Example

```
function helloFriend(friendName) {
    alert("Hello" + friendName);
}
```

if statements

Syntax

```
if (condition) {
    statements
}
else {
    statements
}
```

Example

```
if (outerEarPressure < innerEarPressure) {
    popEars();
}
else {
    doNothing();
}
```

while loops

Syntax

```
while (condition) {
    statements
}
```

Example

```
while (time < 30) {
    cookRice();
    time++;
}
```

for loops

Syntax

```
for (variable-declaration; condition; variable-operation) {
    statements
}
```

Example

```
for (var rowValue = 0; rowValue < totalRows; rowValue++) {
    document.write(databaseColumn[rowValue]);
}
```

Operators and Conditionals

Testing for conditions

a == b	a equal to b
a != b	a not equal to b
a > b	a greater than b
a < b	a less than b
a >= b	a greater than or equal to b
a <= b	a less than or equal to b
!a	not a (testing for false condition)

Testing for multiple conditions

a && b	condition a and condition b
a || b	condition a or condition b

Operators

a + b	a plus b
a - b	a minus b
a * b	a multiplied by b
a / b	a divided by b
a % b	a modulo (remainder) b
a ++	a increased by one
a --	a decreased by one

Index

Symbols

" (quotes, double)
  code enclosed in, 3
  JavaScript strings, 4
(hashmark), using as
         placeholder, 19, 20
&& (and) operator, 63
  browser version, checking, 87
' (quotes, single), inside double-
         quoted strings, 4
(!) (exclamation point), in
         conditionals, 61
( ) (parentheses)
  functions, assigning to
         objects, 171
  in method names, 14
  statements in, 10
  in function names, 27
. (dot), separating objects from
         properties, 14
/ (forward slash)
  /* */, enclosing multiline
         comments, 9
  //, preceding one-line
         comments, 9
  regular expressions, delimiting, 68
; (semicolon)
  cookie name/values,
         separating, 120
  in program lines, 4
<!-- -->, enclosing HTML
         comments, 9
= (equal sign), 3
  = (assignment) operator, 13
  =, separating name/value pairs, 21

== (equality) operator, 13
  browser versions, checking
         for, 87
>= (greater than or equal to)
         operator, 87
[ ] (brackets)
  accessing array elements, 69
  regular expression character
         classes, 68
^ (caret), negating character class
         elements, 68

A

<a> tags, 20
absolute positioning, 144, 150
abstraction, in object-oriented
         programming, 169
action property (form), 195
<address> element, 11
  validating, 62
alert( ) function, 66
  "Hello" (example), 27
  blank form input dialog, 59
alinkColor property (document), 195
alphabetic characters, checking form
         elements for, 66
and (&&) operator, 63, 87
animation
  frame rate, sliding tab layer, 160
  GIF image rollovers, 105
appCodeName property
         (navigator), 197
application/x-shockwave-flash (MIME
         type), 97
  (see also Flash)

Nick Heinle is the author of Designing with JavaScript, First Edition, an O'Reilly bestseller. When this edition came out, Nick was still a teenager and was profiled in the Boston Globe and Teen People. He currently works as an independent software consultant and studies mathematics.

Bill Peña is a web/information designer who is currently working on the design for Safari, Tech Books Online. He has been using JavaScript since 1996 and learned from studying practical examples he needed as a designer. Bill has a B.A. in digital arts and media from Brown University.

Colophon

Our look is the result of reader comments, our own experimentation, and feedback from distribution channels. Distinctive covers complement our distinctive approach to technical topics, breathing personality and life into potentially dry subjects.

The cover image on *Designing With JavaScript* is a spiral. Spirals have been a part of the human experience as early as ancient Greece, and possibly since pre-history, fascinating the human imagination. In ancient times, spirals were often used to represent what people believed to be portals between the present world and the world of their ancestors. In the Minoan civilization, spirals were commonly used in art and as decoration. In modern times, millions have been entertained by the spiral known as Slinky®.

The spiral shape is found throughout the natural world, most notably in the shell of the nautilus, the design of many spiderwebs, and the blooms of certain flowers. Another form of spiral is the double helix of DNA. In weather patterns, the spiral can be found in hurricanes, tornadoes, and the isobars surrounding high and low pressure centers. Of the known galaxies, the spiral is the most common shape.

The spiral can also be found in architecture. It tops Ionic columns, and from ancient to modern times, the spiral staircase has been a common architectural form. The helical spiral is the central structure of Frank Lloyd Wright's design of the Guggenheim Museum.

Mathematically speaking, spirals are planar curves, circling outward from a central point at a regular ratio. Archimedes discovered the first mathematical representation of a spiral: $r = a^\theta$, where r is the radius, a is any constant, and θ is the angle of rotation from the axis. This spiral is known as the Spiral of Archimedes. Many other, more complex spirals have been found and described by mathematicians since. Spirals can also be nonplanar; these three-dimensional spirals either maintain a constant radius as the central point shifts along the third axis (a helical spiral, as in the thread of a screw), or travel outward from the central point as it moves along the third axis (as in the thread of a cone-shaped drill).

Leanne Soylemez was the production editor and copyeditor for *Designing With JavaScript*. Claire Cloutier proofread the manuscript. Matt Hutchinson, Colleen Gorman, and Mary Anne Weeks Mayo provided quality control. Ellen Troutman-Zaig wrote the index.

Edie Freedman designed the cover of this book, with help from the O'Reilly design team, using Photoshop 5.5 and QuarkXPress 4.1. Emma Colby produced the cover layout with QuarkXPress 4.1, using Adobe's version of Berthold Formata Condensed font.

David Futato designed and implemented the interior layout, using FrameMaker 5.5.6, with help from Mike Sierra; Neil Walls converted the files from Microsoft Word to FrameMaker 5.5.6, using tools created by Mike Sierra. The text and heading fonts are ITC Legacy Sans Book and Formata Condensed; the code font is TheSans Mono Condensed from LucasFont. The illustrations and screenshots that appear in the book were produced by Robert Romano and Jessamyn Read using Macromedia Freehand 9 and Adobe Photoshop 6. This colophon was written by David Futato.

Whenever possible, our books use a durable and flexible lay-flat binding.

the Web Studio series

Learning Web Design: A Beginner's Guide to HTML, Graphics, and Beyond

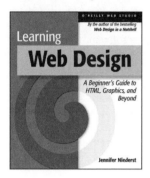

By Jennifer Niederst
March 2001
418 pages, $34.95
ISBN 0-596-00036-7

In *Learning Web Design*, Jennifer Niederst shares the knowledge she's gained from years of experience as both web designer and teacher. She starts from the very beginning—defining the Internet, the Web, browsers, and URLs—assuming no previous knowledge of how the Web works. Jennifer helps you build the solid foundation in HTML, graphics, and design principles that you need for crafting effective web pages.

Designing Web Audio: RealAudio, MP3, Flash, Beatnik

By Josh Beggs & Dylan Thede
January 2001
395 pages, $34.95
ISBN 1-56592-353-7

Designing Web Audio is the most complete Internet audio guide on the market, loaded with informative real-world case studies and interviews with some of the world's leading audio and web producers. Its step-by-step instructions on how to use the most popular web audio formats to stream music make it an invaluable resource for web developers and web music enthusiasts.

Designing with JavaScript, 2nd Edition

By Nick Heinle & Bill Peña
January 2002
230 pages, $34.95
ISBN 1-56592-360-X

Completely rewritten, the second edition of this popular book is a true introduction to JavaScript™ for the designer. By teaching JavaScript in the context of its most powerful capability—document manipulation through the DOM—*Designing with JavaScript*, 2nd Edition, not only teaches the language, object, library, and DOM concepts, it also delivers useful strategies and techniques from the first page to the last.

Web Navigation: Designing the User Experience

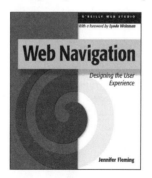

By Jennifer Fleming
September 1998
268 pages, $34.95
ISBN 1-56592-351-0

This book takes the first in-depth look at designing web site navigation using design strategies that help you uncover solutions that work for your site and audience. It focuses on designing by purpose, with chapters on entertainment, shopping, identity, learning, information, and community sites. Comes with a CD-ROM containing software demos and a "netography" of related web resources.

O'REILLY®

To Order: **800-998-9938** • **order@oreilly.com** • **www.oreilly.com**
OUR PRODUCTS ARE AVAILABLE AT A BOOKSTORE OR SOFTWARE STORE NEAR YOU.
For information: **800-998-9938** • **707-829-0515** • **info@oreilly.com**

Web Authoring and Design

Learning WML & WMLScript

By Martin Frost
1st Edition October 2000
208 pages, ISBN 1-56592-947-0

The next generation of mobile communicators is here, and delivering content will mean programming in WML and WMLScript. *Learning WML & WMLScript* gets developers up to speed quickly on these technologies, mapping out in detail the Wireless Application Environment (WAE), and its two major components: Wireless Markup Language (WML), and WMLScript. With these two technologies, developers can format information in almost all applications for display by mobile devices.

ActionScript: The Definitive Guide

By Colin Moock
1st Edition May 2001
720 pages, ISBN 1-56592-852-0

ActionScript: The Definitive Guide is for web developers and web authors who want to go beyond simple Flash animations to create enhanced Flash-driven sites. Regardless of your level of programming expertise, this combination of ActionScript fundamentals, applications, and handy quick-reference will have you scripting like a pro.

Dreamweaver 4: The Missing Manual

By Dave McFarland
1st Edition July 2001
480 pages, ISBN 0-596-00097-9

Dreamweaver 4: The Missing Manual is the ideal companion to this complex software. Following an anatomical tour of a web page to orient new users, author Dave McFarland walks you through the process of creating and designing a complete web site. Armed with this handbook, both first-time and experienced web designers can easily use DreamWeaver to bring stunning, interactive web sites to life.

Web Design in a Nutshell, 2nd Edition

By Jennifer Niederst
2nd Edition September 2001
640 pages, ISBN 0-596-00196-7

Web Design in a Nutshell contains the nitty-gritty on everything you need to know to design Web pages. Written by veteran Web designer Jennifer Niederst, this book provides quick access to the wide range of technologies and techniques from which Web designers and authors must draw. Topics include understanding the Web environment, HTML, graphics, multimedia and interactivity, and emerging technologies.

O'REILLY®

To Order: **800-998-9938** • **order@oreilly.com** • **www.oreilly.com**
OUR PRODUCTS ARE AVAILABLE AT A BOOKSTORE OR SOFTWARE STORE NEAR YOU.
For information: **800-998-9938** • **707-829-0515** • **info@oreilly.com**

Web Authoring and Design

HTML & XHTML: The Definitive Guide, 4th Edition

By Chuck Musciano & Bill Kennedy
4th Edition August 2000
680 pages, ISBN 0-596-00026-X

This complete guide is full of examples, sample code, and practical hands-on advice for creating truly effective web pages and mastering advanced features. Web authors learn how to insert images, create useful links and searchable documents, use Netscape extensions, design great forms, and much more. The fourth edition covers XHTML 1.0, HTML 4.01, Netscape 6.0, and Internet Explorer 5.0, plus all the common extensions.

Cascading Style Sheets: The Definitive Guide

By Eric A. Meyer
1st Edition May 2000
470 pages, ISBN 1-56592-622-6

CSS is the HTML 4.0-approved method for controlling visual presentation on Web pages. *Cascading Style Sheets: The Definitive Guide* offers a complete, detailed review of CSS1 properties and other aspects of CSS1. Each property is explored individually in detail with discussion of how each interacts with other properties. There is also information on how to avoid common mistakes in interpretation. This book is the first major title to cover CSS in a way that acknowledges and describes current browser support, instead of simply describing the way things work in theory. It offers both advanced and novice Web authors a comprehensive guide to implementation of CSS.

Information Architecture for the World Wide Web

By Louis Rosenfeld & Peter Morville
1st Edition February 1998
224 pages, ISBN 1-56592-282-4

Learn how to merge aesthetics and mechanics to design Web sites that "work." This book shows how to apply principles of architecture and library science to design cohesive Web sites and intranets that are easy to use, manage, and expand. Covers building complex sites, hierarchy design and organization, and techniques to make your site easier to search. For Webmasters, designers, and administrators.

Perl for Web Site Management

By John Callender
1st Edition October 2001
528 pages, 1-56592-647-1

Learn to do everyday tasks on your web site using Perl—even if you have no programming background. *Perl for Web Site Management* shows how to write CGI scripts, incorporate search engines, convert multiple text files to HTML, monitor log files, and track visitors to your site. Whether you're a developer, a designer, or simply a dabbler on the Web, this is the hands-on introduction to Perl you've been waiting for.

O'REILLY®

To Order: **800-998-9938** • **order@oreilly.com** • **www.oreilly.com**
OUR PRODUCTS ARE AVAILABLE AT A BOOKSTORE OR SOFTWARE STORE NEAR YOU.
For information: **800-998-9938** • **707-829-0515** • **info@oreilly.com**

How to stay in touch with O'Reilly

1. Visit Our Award-Winning Web Site

http://www.oreilly.com/

★ "Top 100 Sites on the Web" — *PC Magazine*
★ "Top 5% Web sites" — *Point Communications*
★ "3-Star site" — *The McKinley Group*

Our Web site contains a library of comprehensive product information (including book excerpts and tables of contents), downloadable software, background articles, interviews with technology leaders, links to relevant sites, book cover art, and more. File us in your Bookmarks or Hotlist!

2. Join Our Email Mailing Lists

New Product Releases

To receive automatic email with brief descriptions of all new O'Reilly products as they are released, send email to:

ora-news-subscribe@lists.oreilly.com

Put the following information in the first line of your message (*not* in the Subject field):

subscribe ora-news

O'Reilly Events

If you'd also like us to send information about trade show events, special promotions, and other O'Reilly events, send email to:

ora-news-subscribe@lists.oreilly.com

Put the following information in the first line of your message (*not* in the Subject field):

subscribe ora-events

3. Get Examples from Our Books via FTP

There are two ways to access an archive of example files from our books:

Regular FTP

· FTP to:
  ftp.oreilly.com
  (login: anonymous
  password: your email address)
· Point your web browser to:
  ftp://ftp.oreilly.com/

FTPMAIL

· Send an email message to:
  ftpmail@online.oreilly.com
  (Write "help" in the message body)

4. Contact Us via Email

order@oreilly.com
  To place a book or software order online. Good for North American and international customers.

subscriptions@oreilly.com
  To place an order for any of our newsletters or periodicals.

books@oreilly.com
  General questions about any of our books.

cs@oreilly.com
  For answers to problems regarding your order or our products.

booktech@oreilly.com
  For book content technical questions or corrections.

proposals@oreilly.com
  To submit new book or software proposals to our editors and product managers.

international@oreilly.com
  For information about our international distributors or translation queries. For a list of our distributors outside of North America check out:
  http://www.oreilly.com/distributors.html

5. Work with Us

Check out our website for current employment opportuninites:
http://jobs.oreilly.com/

O'Reilly & Associates, Inc.

1005 Gravenstein Highway North
Sebastopol, CA 95472 USA
TEL 707-829-0515 or 800-998-9938
      (6am to 5pm PST)
FAX 707-829-0104

O'REILLY®

To Order: **800-998-9938** · **order@oreilly.com** · **www.oreilly.com**
OUR PRODUCTS ARE AVAILABLE AT A BOOKSTORE OR SOFTWARE STORE NEAR YOU.
For information: **800-998-9938** · **707-829-0515** · **info@oreilly.com**

Titles from O'Reilly

Programming

C++: The Core Language
Practical C++ Programming
Practical C Programming, 3rd Ed.
High Performance Computing, 2nd Ed.
Programming Embedded Systems in C
    and C++
Mastering Algorithms in C
Advanced C++ Techniques
POSIX 4: Programming for the Real World
POSIX Programmer's Guide
Power Programming with RPC
UNIX Systems Programming for SVR4
Pthreads Programming
CVS Pocket Reference
Advanced Oracle PL/SQL
Oracle PL/SQL Guide to Oracle8i
    Features
Oracle PL/SQL Programming, 2nd Ed.
Oracle Built-in Packages
Oracle PL/SQL Developer's Workbook
Oracle Web Applications
Oracle PL/SQL Language Pocket
    Reference
Oracle PL/SQL Built-ins Pocket
    Reference
Oracle SQL*Plus: The Definitive Guide
Oracle SQL*Plus Pocket Reference
Oracle Essentials
Oracle Database Administration
Oracle Internal Services
Oracle SAP
Guide to Writing DCE Applications
Understanding DCE
Visual Basic Shell Programming
VB/VBA in a Nutshell: The Language
Access Database Design &
    Programming, 2nd Ed.
Writing Word Macros
Applying RCS and SCCS
Checking C Programs with Lint
VB Controls in a Nutshell
Developing Asp Components, 2nd Ed.
Learning WML & WMLScript
Writing Excel Macros
Windows 32 API Programming with
    Visual Basic
ADO: The Definitive Guide

Graphics & Multimedia

MP3: The Definitive Guide
Photoshop 6 in a Nutshell, 3rd Ed.
Director in a Nutshell
Lingo in a Nutshell
FrontPage 2000 in a Nutshell

Web

Apache: The Definitive Guide, 2nd Ed.
Apache Pocket Reference
ASP in a Nutshell, 2nd Ed.
Cascading Style Sheets
Designing Web Audio
Designing with JavaScript, 2nd Ed.
DocBook: The Definitive Guide
Dynamic HTML: The Definitive Reference
HTML Pocket Reference
Information Architecture for the WWW
JavaScript: The Definitive Guide, 3rd Ed.
Java and XML
JavaScript Application Cookbook
JavaScript Pocket Reference
Practical Internet Groupware
PHP Pocket Reference
Programming Coldfusion
Photoshop for the Web, 2nd Ed.
Web Design in a Nutshell
Webmaster in a Nutshell, 2nd Ed.
Web Navigation: Designing the
    User Experience
Web Performance Tuning
Web Security & Commerce
Writing Apache Modules with Perl and C

Unix

SCO UNIX in a Nutshell
Tcl/Tk in a Nutshell
The Unix CD Bookshelf, 2nd Ed.
UNIX in a Nutshell, 3rd Ed.
Learning the Unix Operating System,
    4th Ed.
Learning vi, 6th Ed.
Learning the Korn Shell
Learning GNU Emacs, 2nd Ed.
Using csh & tcsh
Learning the bash Shell, 2nd Ed.
GNU Emacs Pocket Reference
Exploring Expect
TCL/TK Tools
TCL/TK in a Nutshell
Python Pocket Reference

Using Windows

Windows Millenium: The Missing
    Manual
PC Hardware in a Nutshell
Optimizing Windows for Games,
    Graphics, and Multimedia
Outlook 2000 in a Nutshell
Word 2000 in a Nutshell
Excel 2000 in a Nutshell
Paint Shop Pro 7 in a Nutshell
Windows 2000 Pro: The Missing
    Manual

Java Series

Developing Java Beans
Creating Effective JavaHelp
Enterprise Java Beans, 2nd Ed.
Java Cryptography
Java Distributed Computing
Java Enterprise in a Nutshell
Java Examples in a Nutshell, 2nd Ed.
Java Foundation Classes in a Nutshell
Java in a Nutshell, 3rd Ed.
Java Internationalization
Java I/O
Java Native Methods
Java Network Programming, 2nd Ed.
Java Performance Tuning
Java Security
Java Servlet Programming
Java ServerPages
Java Threads, 2nd Ed.
Jini in a Nutshell
Learning Java

X Window

Vol. 1: Xlib Programming Manual
Vol. 2: Xlib Reference Manual
Vol. 4M: X Toolkit Intrinsics
    Programming Manual, Motif Ed.
Vol. 5: X Toolkit Intrinsics Reference
    Manual
Vol. 6A: Motif Programming Manual
Vol. 6B: Motif Reference Manual, 2nd Ed.

Perl

Advanced Perl Programming
CGI Programming with Perl, 2nd Ed.
Learning Perl, 2nd Ed.
Learning Perl for Win32 Systems
Learning Perl/Tk
Mastering Algorithms with Perl
Mastering Regular Expressions
Perl Cookbook
Perl in a Nutshell
Programming Perl, 3rd Ed.
Perl CD Bookshelf
Perl Resource Kit – Win32 Ed.
Perl/TK Pocket Reference
Perl 5 Pocket Reference, 3rd Ed.

Mac

AppleScript in a Nutshell
AppleWorks 6: The Missing Manual
Crossing Platforms
iMovie: The Missing Manual
Mac OS in a Nutshell
Mac OS 9: The Missing Manual
REALbasic: The Definitive Guide

Using the Internet

Internet in a Nutshell
Smileys
Managing Mailing Lists

Linux

Building Linux Clusters
Learning Debian GNU/Linux
Learning Red Hat Linux
Linux Device Drivers
Linux Network Administrator's Guide,
    2nd Ed.
Running Linux, 3rd Ed.
Linux in a Nutshell, 3rd Ed.
Linux Multimedia Guide

System Administration

Practical UNIX & Internet Security, 2nd Ed.
Building Internet Firewalls, 2nd Ed.
PGP: Pretty Good Privacy
SSH, The Secure Shell: The Definitive
    Guide
DNS and Bind, 3rd Ed.
The Networking CD Bookshelf
Virtual Private Networks, 2nd Ed.
TCP/IP Network Administration, 2nd Ed.
sendmail Desktop Reference
Managing Usenet
Using & Managing PPP
Managing IP Networks with Cisco
    Routers
Networking Personal Computers with
    TCP/IP
Unix Backup & Recovery
Essential System Administration,
    2nd Ed.
Perl for System Administration
Managing NFS and NIS
Volume 8: X Window System
    Administrator's Guide
Using Samba
Unix Power Tools, 2nd Ed.
DNS on Windows NT
Windows NT TCP/IP Network
    Administration
DHCP for Windows 2000
Essential Windows NT System
    Administration
Managing Windows NT Logons
Managing the Windows 2000 Registry

Other Titles

PalmPilot: The Ultimate Guide, 2nd Ed.
Palm Programming:
    The Developer's Guide

O'REILLY®

To Order: **800-998-9938** • *order@oreilly.com* • *www.oreilly.com*
OUR PRODUCTS ARE AVAILABLE AT A BOOKSTORE OR SOFTWARE STORE NEAR YOU.
For information: **800-998-9938** • **707-829-0515** • *info@oreilly.com*

International Distributors

UK, Europe, Middle East and Africa

(except France, Germany, Austria, Switzerland, Luxembourg, and Liechtenstein)

INQUIRIES

O'Reilly UK Limited
4 Castle Street
Farnham
Surrey, GU9 7HS
United Kingdom
Telephone: 44-1252-711776
Fax: 44-1252-734211
Email: information@oreilly.co.uk

ORDERS

Wiley Distribution Services Ltd.
1 Oldlands Way
Bognor Regis
West Sussex PO22 9SA
United Kingdom
Telephone: 44-1243-843294
UK Freephone: 0800-243207
Fax: 44-1243-843302 (Europe/EU orders)
or 44-1243-843274 (Middle East/Africa)
Email: cs-books@wiley.co.uk

Germany, Switzerland, Austria, Luxembourg, and Liechtenstein

INQUIRIES & ORDERS

O'Reilly Verlag
Balthasarstr. 81
D-50670 Köln
Germany
Telephone: 49-221-973160-91
Fax: 49-221-973160-8
Email: anfragen@oreilly.de (inquiries)
Email: order@oreilly.de (orders)

France

INQUIRIES & ORDERS

Éditions O'Reilly
18 rue Séguier
75006 Paris, France
Tel: 1-40-51-71-89
Fax: 1-40-51-72-26
Email: france@editions-oreilly.fr

Canada (French language books)

Les Éditions Flammarion ltée
375, Avenue Laurier Ouest
Montréal (Québec) H2V 2K3
Tel: 00-1-514-277-8807
Fax: 00-1-514-278-2085
Email: info@flammarion.qc.ca

Hong Kong

City Discount Subscription Service, Ltd.
Unit A, 6th Floor, Yan's Tower
27 Wong Chuk Hang Road
Aberdeen, Hong Kong
Tel: 852-2580-3539
Fax: 852-2580-6463
Email: citydis@ppn.com.hk

Korea

Hanbit Media, Inc.
Chungmu Bldg. 210
Yonnam-dong 568-33
Mapo-gu
Seoul, Korea
Tel: 822-325-0397
Fax: 822-325-9697
Email: hant93@chollian.dacom.co.kr

Philippines

Global Publishing
G/F Benavides Garden
1186 Benavides Street
Manila, Philippines
Tel: 632-254-8949/632-252-2582
Fax: 632-734-5060/632-252-2733
Email: globalp@pacific.net.ph

Taiwan

O'Reilly Taiwan
First Floor, No.21, Lane 295
Section 1, Fu-Shing South Road
Taipei, 106 Taiwan
Tel: 886-2-27099669
Fax: 886-2-27038802
Email: taiwan@oreilly.com

India

Shroff Publishers & Distributors Pvt. Ltd.
12, "Roseland", 2nd Floor
Mumbai 400 050
Tel: 91-22-641-1800/643-9910
Fax: 91-22-643-2422
Email: spd@vsnl.com

China

O'Reilly Beijing
SIGMA Building, Suite B809
No. 49 Zhichun Road
Haidian District
Beijing, China PR 100080
Tel: 86-10-8809-7475
Fax: 86-10-8809-7463
Email: beijing@oreilly.com

Japan

O'Reilly Japan, Inc.
Yotsuya Y's Building
7 Banch 6, Honshio-cho
Shinjuku-ku
Tokyo 160-0003 Japan
Tel: 81-3-3356-5227
Fax: 81-3-3356-5261
Email: japan@oreilly.com

Singapore, Indonesia, Malaysia and Thailand

TransQuest Publishers Pte Ltd
30 Old Toh Tuck Road #05-02
Sembawang Kimtrans Logistics Centre
Singapore 597654
Tel: 65-4623112
Fax: 65-4625761
Email: wendiw@transquest.com.sg

All Other Asian Countries

O'Reilly & Associates, Inc.
101 Morris Street
Sebastopol, CA 95472 USA
Tel: 707-829-0515
Fax: 707-829-0104
Email: order@oreilly.com

Australia

Woodslane Pty., Ltd.
7/5 Vuko Place
Warriewood NSW 2102
Australia
Tel: 61-2-9970-5111
Fax: 61-2-9970-5002
Email: info@woodslane.com.au

New Zealand

Woodslane New Zealand, Ltd.
21 Cooks Street (P.O. Box 575)
Waganui, New Zealand
Tel: 64-6-347-6543
Fax: 64-6-345-4840
Email: info@woodslane.com.au

Argentina

Distribuidora Cuspide
Suipacha 764
1008 Buenos Aires
Argentina
Phone: 5411-4322-8868
Fax: 5411-4322-3456
Email: libros@cuspide.com